CHARTING GLOBAL RESPONSIBILITIES

Legal Philosophy and Human Rights

Kevin T. Jackson, J.D., Ph.D.
Fordham University

UNIVERSITY
PRESS OF
AMERICA

Lanham • New York • London

Copyright © 1994 by
University Press of America®, Inc.
4720 Boston Way
Lanham, Maryland 20706

3 Henrietta Street
London WC2E 8LU England

All rights reserved
Printed in the United States of America
British Cataloging in Publication Information Available

Library of Congress Cataloging-in-Publication Data
Jackson, Kevin T.
Charting global responsibilities : legal philosophy and human rights /
Kevin T. Jackson
p.   cm.
Includes bibliographical references.
1. Human rights.   2. Human rights — Philosophy.
I. Title.
K3240.4.J33   1993   342'.085—dc20   [342.285]   94-5988   CIP

ISBN 0-8191-9478-6 (paper : alk. paper)

 The paper used in this publication meets the minimum requirements of American National Standard for Information Sciences—Permanence of Paper for Printed Library Materials, ANSI Z39.48–1984.

TABLE OF CONTENTS

Preface

Introduction

**Chapter 1 Jurisprudential Paradigms for
International Human Rights**   1
    Introduction
        Justifying Human Rights Doctrine
        Foundations of International Legal Obligation
        What Are International Human Rights?
            The I-I Approach
            The O-I Approach
            The E-C Approach
        The "Generations" of Human Rights

Chapter 2   **Legal Positivism: Human Rights as
"Plain Fact"**   21
    Introduction
    Human Rights and the Concept of
     International Law
    The Concept of Law
    Background Conceptions of Law
    Legal Positivism
        Austin
        Kelsen
        Hart
    Is International Human Rights Law Really Law?
    The Impasses of Human Rights Positivism

> The "Enforceability" Argument
> The "Rule of Recognition" Argument
> Ad Computum
> Summary of Arguments

Chapter 3 **Legal Realism and Critical Theory: Human Rights as the "Fictions" of Factions**   39
> Introduction
> Legal Realism
>> Sociological Jurisprudence
>> American Legal Realism
>> Critical Legal Studies
>
> The Impasses of Realism and Critical Theory
> Critical Theory
> The Public Sphere
> Human Rights Norms as Presuppositions of Ideal Speech for the International Community
> Summary of Arguments

Chapter 4 **Law-as-Integrity: Mediating Law, Morality, and Human Rights in a Global Context**   57
> Introduction
> The "Third Theory" of Law (Early Dworkin)
> Law-as-Integrity (Later Dworkin)
> Integrity Internationalized
> Is Dworkin's Concept of Law Too Narrow?
> Critical Legal Studies Versus Integrity
> The "Patchwork" Hypothesis
> The "Duck-Rabbit" Hypothesis
> A Decisionmaking Schemata for Conflicting Interpretations
> The "Truncation" Hypothesis
> Integrity in the Widening Gyre

Chapter 5 **Interpretive Contexts for Global Responsibilities**   92
> Introduction
> Adjudicative Contexts
> Human Rights Law in United States Courts
> The Evolution of Human Rights as Legal Standards
> Criticism of *Fujii* and Its Progeny

Should *Fujii* Be Overturned?
Customary International Human Rights Law
Filartiga v. Pena-Irala and Its Progeny
  Limitations on *Filartiga*
International Human Rights Standards as a
  Normative Interpretive Chart for Domestic Law
Fundamental Human Rights Obligations of
  Multinational Corporations
Provisional Analysis
Some Skeptical Objections
Replies
Summary
Non-Adjudicative Contexts
  Beyond the Institution of Adjudication:
  Law and the Different Forms of Social
    Ordering
  Law-as-Process
  The Implicit Laws of Law-Making
  The Aspirational Dimension of Law
  Interpreting Global Responsibilities in the
    Absence of Formal Adjudications of Human Rights
    Standards
  Taking International Human Rights
    Codes Seriously
  International Codes of Conduct in General
    Human Rights-Related Provisions in Existing
    Codes
  Freedom from Apartheid and the Comprehensive
    Anti-Apartheid Act
  The Right to Adequate Nutrition and the WHO
    Code of Conduct
  Charting Global Institutional Rights
    Chart 1, 2, 3
  Complexity of Ethical Interpretation
  Enforceability

Chapter 6 Interpreting Human Rights Texts   137
  Human Rights Texts
  Levels of Human Rights Texts
  Juridic Interpretation
  Interpreting "Universality"
  Methods of Legal Interpretation of Texts
  The Received View

v

        Dworkin's "Constructive" Interpretation
        Senses of "Interpretation"
        The Problem of Intent
        Girard's "Structural" Interpretation
        Habermas' "Psychoanalytic" Interpretation
        The Dilthey-Gadamer Debate
        Psychoanalytic Interpretation
        Constructive Interpretation and the Texts
          of Human Rights Law
        How "Constructive" Should a Legal Interpretation
          Be?

Chapter 7 The International Community as the "Audience" of Human Rights   160
        Introduction
        Dworkin's "Community Personified"
        Criticism of the Community Personified
        Construing the Consensus of the International
        Community as an "Interpretive Concept"
        Milne's "Qualified" Realism
        Criticism of Milne
        The "Universal Audience"
        Aarnio's Critique of Perelman
        Consensus as a Multilayered Concept
        First-Level Consensus
        Second-Level Consensus
        Third-Level Consensus
        Summary of Arguments

Chapter 8 Justifying Institutional Theories of Human Rights   177
        Introduction
        Definition of Justifying Theories
        Functions of Justifying Theories
        Weighting
        Scope Delimitation
        "Booting"
        Showing Entailment Relations
        Acceptability of Justifying Theories
        Factual vs. Counterfactual Aspects of Acceptability
        The "One Right Answer" Thesis
        The Audience for Justifying Theories
        Interpretive Convergence

Institutional Manifestations of Convergence
Conclusion

Appendix

PREFACE

This book reflects my desire to respond to what I perceive as an increasing need for multidisciplinary scholarship (canvassing the fields of law and philosophy) focused on controversial moral and jurisprudential issues surrounding the appropriate way to conceptualize and justify interpretations of international human rights standards at domestic, regional, and global levels. In our increasingly competitive world, multinational corporations continue to expand their foreign markets, and governments persist in aggressively asserting their sovereign powers, using methods which not infrequently result directly or indirectly in allegations of human rights deprivations of stakeholders throughout the global community.

The global activities of businesses and governments are becoming increasingly interlaced. Accordingly, our traditional ways of conceptualizing the respective responsibilities of private and public sectors is being challenged in new ways. Recently, harsh criticism has been launched against the use of cheap prison labor of political dissidents to produce goods for export from China.[1] Airline companies in the United States employ their own security guards to detain foreigners seeking asylum pending INS hearings. The refugees, among them infants and children, are held --- at times shackled --- in hotel rooms which some have dubbed "private prisons."[2] And the "Group of 77" developing countries have decried political abuses associated with uninvited interventions of developing nations in humanitarian disaster relief.[3]

At the same time, a parade of jarring world events ranging from the BCCI scandal to the unification of the EC, and the dissolution of the Soviet Union, indicate that we are currently witnessing an unprecedented intertwining of transnational economic, legal, social, and political relations. Meanwhile, significant cultural and ethical diversity exists

---

[1]. *See*, Daniel Southerland, "The Witness Against China," *Washington Post*, September 29, 1991, at H1.

[2]. *See*, Al Kamen, "'Private Prison' Holds Airline Passengers Seeking U.S. Asylum," *Washington Post*, January 19, 1992, at A1. The practice has been condemned as "a human rights outrage" by Arthur Helton from the Lawyers Committee for Human Rights. *Id.* at A16.

[3]. *See*, Paul Lewis, "Disaster Relief Proposal Worries Third World," *New York Times*, November 13, 1991 at 9.

within the ever-tightening world community, posing special problems for making sense of the kind of universal standards human rights embody. The ethical and legal status of many institutional norms seeking to regulate international business and governmental activities in accordance with human rights standards --- such as those contained in the proposed UN Code of Conduct for Transnational Corporations, the ILO Tripartite Declaration of Principles Concerning Multinational Enterprises and Social Policy, and in domestic legislation such as the Foreign Corrupt Practices Act[4] and the Comprehensive Anti-Apartheid Act ---- are deeply puzzling, and invite continuing controversy among business academics, lawyers, philosophers, and the public at large.

It is my belief that the peculiarly global responsibilities incorporated in contemporary human rights standards represents a fertile ground for sustained and rigorous philosophical analysis that is sensitive to both the moral imperatives of those standards as well as the practical realities facing contemporary business enterprises and nation-states.

Within the last decade it has become well established that fundamental human rights institute a variety of international legal obligations --- enforceable in some cases with multimillion dollar court judgments for compensatory and punitive damages --- that are binding both on individuals[5] and on governments.[6] Indeed, as van Boven has observed, especially since the Second World War, "international human rights law has been developing in an unprecedented way and has become a very substantive part of international law as a whole."[7] At the same time, to increased corporate business activities around the globe, the interdependence of business and governmental interests, and the trends towards formalization of basic human rights into global legal rights, it is imperative to inquire into the extent to which international human rights law imposes authoritative legal obligations on multinational corporations,

---

[4]. Although the FCPA is not, strictly speaking, a "human rights document," its prohibition on foreign bribery payments offered to influence decisionmaking of elected officials holding the public trust may be seen as a means of upholding the basic human right to political participation.

[5]. *See, e.g.*, *Filartiga v. Pena-Irala*, 577 F. Supp. 860 (1984).

[6]. *See, e.g.*, *Trajano v. Marcos*, 878 F.2d 1439 (9th Cir., 1989; Unpublished Disposition, Text in Westlaw, No. 86-2448, 86-15039).

[7]. T. C. van Boven, "Survey of the Positive Law of Human Rights," in The International Dimensions of Human Rights (ed. K. Vasak, revised and edited for the English edition by P. Alston (1982) at 87.

as well as on individuals, nation-states, and other organizations.

Recently, great strides have been taken by philosophers and legal scholars in demonstrating the central role of advanced municipal legal systems in protecting individual rights and in illustrating the profound interrelationships between law and morality.[8] And recent work in international ethics has made significant progress in establishing how fundamental human rights --- construed as "base line" moral standards --- may legitimately constrain certain activities of global business[9] and of individuals and national governments.[10] However, such scholarship has yet to tackle the problem of establishing a cogent philosophical basis for corporate and governmental obedience to international human rights standards --- construed as a legitimate form of authority constituted by the world community through a variety of regionally- and globally-based institutions. In this book I will critically assess and offer reflections on theories advanced from various fields of professional expertise --- law, philosophy, and business ethics --- which currently attempt to characterize the nature and limits of international human rights law as it applies to the themes undertaken in this study.

Thus, this book centers around two foundational issues. First, it confronts the general question of to what extent existing philosophies of law adequately explain and justify international law in general, and human rights law in particular. In addressing this first question, I will show how an "integrity" approach as applied to international law --- a perspective which takes seriously the notion of civil and human rights in the international arena and the institutional obligations they impose on individuals, nation-states, and corporations --- provides a *provisional* philosophical paradigm within which to understand the special legal responsibilities facing the global community. One central claim that will emerge from my discussion of this issue is that obligations to respect human rights law, though closely tied to moral obligations, are not completely reducible to the latter.

Second, this study addresses the more specific question of what *form* a philosophy of international human rights law must take when it is

---

[8]. *See, e.g.*, G. Postema, "In Defence of 'French Nonsense:' Fundamental Rights in Constitutional Jurisprudence," in *Enlightenment, Rights, and Revolution: Essays in Legal and Social Philosophy*, (N. MacCormick & A. Bankowski, eds., 1989); G. Haarscher, *Philosophie des Droits de L'Homme* (1987); R. Dworkin, *Law's Empire* (1986).

[9]. *See, e.g.*, T. Donaldson, The Ethics of International Business (1989).

[10]. *See,e.g.*, J. Nickel, Making Sense of Human Rights (1987).

applied to international actors (nation-states, individuals, transnational corporations) *qua* addressees or duty-holders of that law. To focus the discussion of this issue, the book considers concrete cases in which the international responsibilities of multinational corporations and of governments must be interpreted both in "formal" adjudicative contexts involving court opinions, and in "informal" decisionmaking settings, which, though not involving judicial pronouncements, nevertheless involve the legal process at large and (sometimes implicitly) human rights standards in a material way. In particular, the human rights responsibilities of transnational business with respect to such issues as employment discrimination abroad, restraints on international trade with systematic human rights outlaws, and rights to security of the person and autonomy in cases such as the infant formula controversy are examined. The human rights responsibilities of governments, on the other hand, are examined chiefly in connection with basic rights pertaining to torture, genocide, slavery, free speech and expression, and political participation.

Because this is a multidisciplinary work, it places special demands on the reader. To avoid misunderstanding some of the arguments presented in this book, it is important to know both the empirical limitations that currently constrain universal recognition of human rights norms, and the varied and complex mechanisms which afford possibilities for enforcement and implementation of such norms in the international legal order. For this reason, I offer at various points detailed expositions of current municipal and international law relating to the human rights standards under scrutiny therein. My objective in doing so is not to burden the reader with excessive technical legal terminology (whenever possible I attempt to carry on both legal and philosophical discussions in "plain English") but rather to lend authoritativeness, precision, and concrete detail to the discussions.

I do not purport to provide a blueprint for a centralized world order where human rights laws are routinely enforced by global police. While there is perhaps some comfort to be drawn from thinking that the most egregious human rights violations might someday be handled with the same ease with which traffic infractions are in modern municipal legal systems, at the present time, this prospect seems most improbable.

The conceptual core of this book consists of a philosophical inquiry into authoritative interpretations of international human rights law as they are addressed to the tripartite duty-holders which together comprise the international community: nation-states, individuals, and corporations. The study of such sources of human rights law, though independently important for advancing our knowledge about the philosophy of law as applied to the international legal order, has special practical import for business managers, government policy-makers, and citizens of the global community.

Precisely because of the often negligible coercive measures available to back up international norms, the members of the world order will either comply with --- or violate --- international law in ways that do not trigger traditional mechanisms common to municipal legal systems. But saying, as many do today, that law exists only in connection with enforceable sanctions does not do justice to the subtlety and complexity of the concept of law, especially in international settings. Corporations, to give one example, can respect basic human rights in the international order through their participation in initiatives such as codes of conduct and guidelines which need not be backed by centralized coercive governmental sanctions to be efficacious. By complying with standards set out in the World Health Organization (WHO) Code of Marketing Breast Milk Substitutes, a corporation respects the basic rights to nutrition and physical security of infants in less developed countries and the right of autonomy of the mothers of such infants. Saying this raises a number of complex issues concerning the legal status proper (as opposed to the moral status) of such human rights and their corresponding obligations in the international realm. Accordingly, I devote a significant portion of this book to a systematic analysis of such issues.

Perhaps the single most important insight offered in this book is that our conceptions of institutional rights (and associated conceptions of international law and human rights law) and the interpretations we give to law, are often intractably *elliptic* and hence, appropriate subjects for philosophical reflection and analysis. It is my hope that this book engenders such an approach to thinking about the basic responsibilities attending the joint activities of businesses, governments, and citizens in today's interdependent world community.

ACKNOWLEDGMENTS

I am grateful to Conrad Johnson, my dissertation advisor in Philosophy at the University of Maryland at College Park, who provided many constructive criticisms in my preparation of earlier drafts which have been incorporated into the present work. I would also like to thank Alan Mabe, my masters thesis advisor of the Department of Philosophy, Florida State University, who helped kindle my early undergraduate interests in legal philosophy and who assisted me greatly in undertaking pluridisciplinary graduate study while I attended law school. Others who have given me support and encouragement, both personal and professional, deserve mention: Thomas Donaldson and Dennis Quinn were kind and instructive colleagues of mine at Georgetown University; Guy Haarscher of the Centre de Philosophie du Droit in Brussels offered encouragement and inspiration for my study of Chaim Perelman's work. Thanks also go out to the following scholars at the University of Maryland who read and commented on various parts of this study: Richard Harvey Brown (Sociology), Ralph Heyndels (Comparative Literature), Robert Fullinwider (Institute for Philosophy and Public Policy), W. Ernest Schlaretzki and Allen Stairs (Philosophy).

Finally, I would like to express my appreciation to the Department of Philosophy and to the Department of Legal Studies and Ethics, College of Business Administration, at Fordham University for providing a stimulating and supportive atmosphere for my teaching and research activities.

INTRODUCTION

UNDERSTANDING INTERNATIONAL HUMAN RIGHTS THROUGH PARADIGMS OF LEGAL PHILOSOPHY

The general topic of this book concerns the legal and philosophical justifications for emerging international human rights obligations of moral agents comprising the contemporary world community. The strategy I take in this study is to investigate the extent to which current models of legal philosophy (which are chiefly directed towards understanding legal norms in domestic, or national, milieux) can be "refitted" to facilitate our comprehension of human rights norms in the environment of trans- and inter-national institutions). Taken as a whole, the scope of human rights discussed in this book includes within the class of assignable addressees of various combinations of those rights the following three moral agents: (i) nation-states, (ii) individuals, and (iii) multinational corporations.[1]

Today the three dominant philosophical paradigms for legal rights interpretation are legal positivism, legal realism, and law-as-integrity. Each of these approaches may be concisely characterized as follows. Positivism recognizes as valid only those rights which are identifiable as a matter of plain empirical fact based on actual conventions and practices of a determinate community. As such positivism presupposes a "scientific" conception of human rights interpretation. Realism views rights as useful social/political fictions at best. Thus, realism finds judicial interpretations of rights to be ultimately subjective or arbitrary,

---

[1]. As will be seen, I do not maintain that all human rights (even the most fundamental of them) impose obligations on all of these categories of addressees, nor do I assert that the way of respecting the human rights are the same for each category.

relativized to the interpreter's values. This amounts to a radically "creative" or "rhetorical" conception of human rights interpretation. Law-as-integrity, which is advanced as a philosophical alternative to legal positivism and legal realism, mediates these extreme positions by identifying interpretations of rights with normative political theories which seek to take rights seriously through constructing the best possible justifications for settled law. Thus law-as-integrity is committed to a "constructive" conception of legal rights and hence, ultimately human rights as well.

As a backdrop for my analysis, I will discuss cases which pose special problems for the attribution of international human rights obligations. How we view transnational legal responsibilities depends to a significant degree on the legitimacy, or authoritative status, that we ascribe to human rights documents such as the Universal Declaration of Human Rights, the United Nations Charter, the International Covenant on Civil and Political Rights; various codes of ethics and guidelines for transnational business enterprises, such as the Sullivan Principles, the World Health Organization (WHO) Code of Marketing Breast Milk Subsitutes, and the OECD Declaration on Multinational Enterprises; domestic legislation promoting international human rights standards, such as the Comprehensive Anti-Apartheid Act; and judicial interpretations and applications of human rights law by United States courts. I will initially investigate whether traditional models of legal rights interpretation, which have been based primarily on the concept of domestic law, and then typically extended by their originators to international law, are able to explain and justify the "new" law of international human rights as applied to global public and private activity both by domestic courts of the United States and by a variety of international legal tribunals and regulatory institutions.

Summary of Arguments

I will argue, inter alia, that although the background theories of positivism and realism are insightful as "half-truths" they largely misrepresent the enterprise of human rights interpretation in actual cases. Influential positivist thinkers take exaggerated stances on the legal status of the international law which parents human rights. At one extreme positivist "skeptics" such as H.L.A. Hart see international legal norms either as mere "positive morality" or as a kind of "primitive" or "quasi" law. For skeptics human rights law does not satisfy criteria (e.g., a rule of recognition) for valid legal rules, and hence cannot really be law. At the other extreme, antiskeptics such as Anthony D'Amato argue that since international law bears many empirical similarities to municipal law (e.g., existence of enforcement mechanisms) it must be law after all. So positivist skeptics and antiskeptics are polarized in their conceptions of human rights by how they answer the query "is international law really law?" I will contend, however, that this general inquiry is a red herring as regards the legal validity of fundamental human rights such as those which constrain the transnational operations of business and government.

In Chapter One I examine some arguments concerning the nature and extent of human rights obligations as they bear on the three principal agents of international law: nation-states, individuals, and corporations.

A number of different senses of "validity" are involved in my arguments in Chapter Two against the purported facticity of human rights law. First, it is important to distinguish between the question of the existence of a legal system and the validity of particular laws within that system. For positivists, there is an important connection between the existence of a legal system and the existence of valid rules. According to Hart, for example, the existence of a legal system requires a combination of primary and secondary rules, the presence or absence of which is a matter of empirical fact. The dependence of the existence of a system (expressed as $E(S)$) on the existence of a fact of this sort (expressed as $E(F_1)$) may be represented by the following scheme:

(i) $E(F_1) \longrightarrow E(S)$

The validity of particular rules within a system of law is dependent on facts at two stages. In addition to the facts represented by (F_1), the validity of a particular rule is dependent on its being traceable to some procedure specified by a secondary rule (for Hart).[2] The existence of such a valid rule $V(R)$, which is also a matter of fact (F_2), may be represented by the following scheme. (The arrows symbolize that terms to the right of an arrow are dependent on the term to the left of an arrow. The arrows do not express material implication. The dependence of a term on two or more terms to its left is illustrated by brackets and braces.)

(ii) $\{[E(F_1) \longrightarrow E(S)] \longrightarrow E(F_2)\} \longrightarrow V(R)$
    (Existence   (Existence   (Existence   (Validity
    of Fact$_1$)   of System)   of Fact$_2$)   of System)

As figure (ii) illustrates, only those laws (R) in (S) with the appropriate "pedigree" (F_2) are counted as valid.

Finally, the issue of the validity of the application of a particular

---

[2]. A simple example of a secondary rule of recognition might be "whatever Rex I enacts is law." H.L.A. Hart, The Concept of Law at 93.

rule to a set of facts may be distinguished. For positivists, the valid application of a (valid) rule to a set of facts will obtain when the rule "fits the facts" of the case in accordance with the way legal institutions have decided like cases in the past. The existence of such institutional precedents constitutes a third genre of facts (F_3). If the latter are not identifiable as a matter of fact, (i.e., there are no apposite case precedents) then the judicial discretion supplies the basis for decision. The cumulative fact-dependence thus involved in the validity of an application of a rule (V(RA)) may therefore be represented as follows:

(iii) $\{\{[E(F_1) ---> E(S)] ---> E(F_2)\} ---> V(R)\} ---> E(F_3) ---> V(RA)$

The senses of validity which positivists lean on in speaking of valid law (i.e., in the senses represented at V(R) and V(RA)) presuppose that questions of legal validity are resolvable by criteria of empirical fact given at points (F_1)-(F_3). Although I would concede that such factual criteria constitute an integral part of the interpretation of legal validity of human rights, I maintain that the creative or constructive dimension of human rights interpretation (elaborated in Chapter Six) is at least as important as the factual aspects which dominate positivist analyses of legal validity.

A principal virtue of elaborating the "constructive interpretation" dimension of legal validity is that it renders a robust conception of international human rights law consonant with a "realistic" view that human rights, even though "universal" in the abstract and general sense implicated in comprehending their moral content, are nevertheless subject to exceptions and restrictions in scope (i.e., they are qualified by empirical factual conditions) when interpreted and applied in concrete business and political situations by the relevant authoritative decisionmaking institutions.

In Chapter Three I show how legal realism (including its contemporary form as "critical" theory) engenders a different set of human rights skeptics and antiskeptics. Realist skeptics (e.g., MacIntyre) find human rights discourse incoherent due to a purportedly intractable moral disagreement fueled by world-wide (as well as intrasocietal) cultural and ethical relativity. Antiskeptics in the realist camp admit to relativity attending rights-talk but urge that there is at least a fundamental "core" of human rights which must be acknowledged because respect for such rights is a necessary condition for social existence (Milne) or a presupposition of "communicative action" within an "ideal speech situation" (Habermas). Aside from obscuring debate with many overgeneralizations and unproved hypotheses, the realist approach fails to recognize the need for casuistic contextualization of authoritative interpretations of human rights. Thus realism is an implausible theoretical framework for understanding interpretations of human rights.

In Chapter Four I argue that a principal advantage of law-as-integrity over positivism and realism is that it enables disputes surrounding the legality of human rights at general as well as specific levels to remain cogent and fertile. From the perspective of law-as-integrity disagreement about interpretations and applications human rights centers around the competing interpretive claims of justifying theories instead of as exaggerated ideological opposition between broadly "skeptical" and "optimistic" philosophies of international law.

Once we acknowledge that international human rights are increasingly being recognized by United States courts, international legal organizations, and by corporate decisionmakers, the most pressing concern for jurisprudence is how to construct the best interpretations of those rights in particular cases of application. In Chapter Five I exposit interpretive contexts for human rights taken as institutional norms (in Dworkin's sense). The first such interpretive context considers human rights adjudication in the "narrow" sense in which rights and responsibilities are established in response to formal pleadings entertained in court and backed up by relatively elaborate articulated judicial opinions. This particular interpretive context is squarely within the scope of Dworkin's theory since it is restricted to adjudications of human rights by U.S. courts. But this special interpretive context exposes a problem for applying the integrity conception to human rights law. The problem is this: the claimants of human rights law are typically aliens, not United States citizens, and the addressees are typically foreign officials and foreign governments or institutions. Thus, such claimants and addressees are outside the scope of the "true" community as Dworkin defines it. I urge that rather than declaring an entire body of common law illegitimate we see if there is something wrong with Dworkin's imaginary "community personified" (the "community of principle").

The second interpretive context takes an inverse perspective on human rights relative to the adjudicative frame of reference. I attempt to illustrate how legislative initiatives, codes, and guidelines can institute a constellation of international legal obligations correlative to basic human rights outside of court decisionmaking as such. Treating human rights norms as institutional standards interpreted and applied by nonjudicial bodies requires looking at law through a wider lens than the one used by law-as-integrity. I will term this broadened jurisprudential outlook "law-as-process," and highlight its most prominent features as they have been shaped by Lon Fuller.

Law-as-integrity offers a special thesis about the nature of legal interpretations of rights. In Chapter Six I set out that thesis and then show how it is defective. The remedy involves recognizing a peculiar dialogic relationship in legal interpretation which can be most closely assimilated to psychoanalytic interpretation (which is a type of "constructive" interpretation) as studied by Habermas.

Another central tenet of integrity concerns the community and its relationship to legal interpretation. I show in Chapter Seven how Dworkin's notion of the political community is underinclusive *vis a vis* determinations of corporate and governmental human rights obligations by United States courts and international organizations. I contrast Dworkin's thesis about the homogeneity of the community (there is a consensus about the general principles of justice, fairness, and due process) with Milne's thesis about the diversity of the community. Rejecting both of the above theses, I illustrate how, with the appropriate modifications, Perelman's notion of the universal audience may plausibly be seen to offer a better model for the relationship between the global community (including as well the regional communities which comprise subsets of the global community) and justified interpretations of transnational human rights responsibilities.

Thus, the ultimate objective of this book is to demonstrate how abstracting and universalizing central tenets of law-as-integrity's conception of "constructive" rights interpretation from its domestic origins (e.g., Ronald Dworkin's theory of civil rights) to an international context (which is still tied in part to domestic adjudication of rights, however) yields a cogent philosophical basis for holding multinational corporations, nation-states, and individuals accountable to fundamental human rights standards. This foundation is afforded by positing justifying theories as a central mechanism for adjudicating competing construals of, e.g., jurisdiction, international custom and consensus, signatory intent, and the notion of universality which underlies human rights texts as they bear on transnational business practices.

The focus on justifying legal theories that I advocate in detail in Chapter Eight transports questions surrounding the legality of human rights norms (as interpreted and applied by United States courts and international organizations) to a firmer and more fertile ground. Disputes about the validity of human rights law arise as competing interpretive disagreements among justifying theories, instead of as exaggerated polarities between broadly "skeptical" and "optimistic" positivist and realist philosophies of international law. Human rights have increasingly become an integral part of how we conceptualize political, moral, and legal relations between nations. Once we recognize that international human rights must be "taken seriously," one of the most pressing questions concerns how to find the best interpretations of those rights in specific cases of application and implementation by courts and other decisionmaking bodies.

Consequently, the salient features of justifying theories I will analyze are their roles in defining (specifying concrete meanings for canonical language in human rights provisions of treaties, conventions, and declarations); weighting (prioritizing some rights over others in conflicts); delimiting scope (specifying what purported rights are to); and "booting" (giving abstract starting points for fundamental rights). In addition, I will discuss the importance of justifying theories in indicating entailment relations between different levels of abstraction and generality of human rights in adjudication. For instance, a justifying theory might account for how abstract rights like the right to dignity are presupposed by concrete rights like freedom from torture; or, a theory might show how general rights such as the right to due process support arguments for more specific rights such as the right to a fair trial.

Any robust conception of human rights adjudication (including the one I will advance) must accept some basic postulates, for example, the premise that there is objectivity to argumentation about rights. The justification for such an assumption may of course be called into question on its own terms, but the mere possibily of skepticism of this kind is not *per se* a persuasive reason for doubting the legitimacy of judicial recognition of the law of fundamental human rights. Indeed, a "constructive" conception of human rights interpretation provides a powerful theoretical perspective from which many traditional skeptical challenges to the idea of universal fundamental human rights may be defused.

CHAPTER ONE

JURISPRUDENTIAL PARADIGMS FOR INTERNATIONAL HUMAN RIGHTS

Introduction

The subject of this book concerns philosophical justifications for emerging international human rights[1] obligations of the moral agents which comprise the contemporary world community. The strategy I take in this study is to investigate the extent to which current models of legal philosophy (which are chiefly directed towards understanding legal norms in domestic, or national, *milieux*) can be "refitted" to facilitate our comprehension of the complex relationship between law and morality involved with interpretations of international human rights norms.

---

[1]. It is salubrious to distinguish three important senses of human rights at the outset. First, human rights exist as linguistic formulations in texts such as declarations, conventions, and treaties. In this first sense, human rights are conceived of as high-priority normative standards published in international documents with a generalizable and often universalizable legal and moral vocabulary. Second, human rights consist of interpretations of the meaning of such textual formulations by various juridic organs, policymakers, and scholars. Interpretations enable specific judgments to be made about the applicability and scope of rights in relation to specific factual states of affairs. Finally, human rights norms may be identified with abstract justifying theories of institutional (legal and quasi-legal) rights which, ideally, legitimate particular interpretations of human rights by reference to relevant established institutional material as well as political morality.

Today the three dominant philosophical paradigms for legal rights interpretation are legal positivism, legal realism, and law-as-integrity. Each of these approaches may be concisely characterized as follows. Positivism recognizes as valid only those rights which are identifiable as a matter of plain empirical fact based on actual conventions and practices of a determinate community. As such positivism presupposes a "scientific" conception of human rights interpretation. Realism views rights as useful social/political fictions at best. Thus, realism finds judicial interpretations of rights to be ultimately subjective or arbitrary, relativized to the interpreter's values. This amounts to a radically "creative" or "rhetorical" conception of human rights interpretation. Law-as-integrity, which is advanced as a philosophical alternative to legal positivism and legal realism, mediates these extreme positions by identifying interpretations of rights with normative political theories which seek to take rights seriously through constructing the best possible justifications for settled law. Thus law-as-integrity is committed to a "constructive" conception of legal rights and hence, ultimately human rights as well.

As a backdrop for my analysis, I will discuss cases which pose special problems for the attribution of international human rights obligations. How we view transnational legal responsibilities depends to a significant degree on the legitimacy, or authoritative status, that we ascribe to human rights documents such as the Universal Declaration of Human Rights, the United Nations Charter, the International Covenant on Civil and Political Rights; various codes of ethics and guidelines for transnational business enterprises, such as the Sullivan Principles, the World Health Organization (WHO) Code of Marketing Breast Milk Subsitutes, and the OECD Declaration on Multinational Enterprises; domestic legislation promoting international human rights standards, such as the Comprehensive Anti-Apartheid Act; and judicial interpretations and applications of human rights law by United States courts. I will initially investigate whether traditional models of legal rights interpretation, which have been based primarily on the concept of domestic law, and then typically extended by their originators to international law, are able to explain and justify the "new" law of international human rights as applied to global public and private activity both by domestic courts of the United States and by a variety of international legal tribunals and regulatory institutions.

I will argue, *inter alia*, that although the background theories of positivism and realism are insightful as "half-truths" they largely misrepresent the enterprise of human rights interpretation in actual cases. Influential positivist thinkers take exaggerated stances on the legal status of the international law which parents human rights. At one extreme positivist "skeptics" such as H.L.A. Hart see international legal norms either as mere "positive morality" or as a kind of "primitive" or "quasi" law. For skeptics human rights law does not satisfy criteria (e.g., a rule of recognition) for valid legal rules, and hence cannot really be law. At the other extreme, antiskeptics such as Anthony D'Amato argue that since international law bears many empirical similarities to municipal law (e.g., existence of enforcement mechanisms) it must be law after all. So positivist skeptics and antiskeptics are polarized in their conceptions of human rights by how they answer the query "is international law really law?" I will contend, however, that this general inquiry is a red herring as regards the legal validity of fundamental human rights such as those which constrain the transnational operations of business and government.

A number of different senses of "validity" are involved in my arguments in Chapter Two against a positivistic reduction of human rights law to facticity. First, it is important to distinguish between the question of the existence of a legal system and the validity of particular laws within that system. For positivists, there is an important connection between the existence of a legal system and the existence of valid rules. According to Hart, for example, the existence of a legal system requires a combination of primary and secondary rules, the presence or absence of which is a matter of empirical fact. The dependence of the existence of a system (expressed as $E(S)$) on the existence of a fact of this sort (expressed as $E(F_1)$) may be represented by the following scheme:

(i) $E(F_1) \longrightarrow E(S)$

The validity of particular rules within a system of law is dependent on facts at two stages. In addition to the facts represented by (F_1), the validity of a particular rule is dependent on its being traceable to some procedure specified by a secondary rule (for Hart).[2] The existence of such a valid rule $V(R)$, which is also a matter of fact (F_2), may be represented by the following scheme. (The arrows symbolize that terms to the right of an arrow are dependent on the term to the left of an arrow. The arrows do not express material implication. The dependence of a term on two or more terms to its left is illustrated by brackets and braces.)

(ii) $\{[E(F_1) \longrightarrow E(S)] \longrightarrow E(F_2)\} \longrightarrow V(R)$
(Existence (Existence (Existence (Validity
of Fact$_1$) of System) of Fact$_2$) of System)

---

[2]. A simple example of a secondary rule of recognition might be "whatever Rex I enacts is law." H.L.A. Hart, *The Concept of Law* at 93.

As figure (ii) illustrates, only those laws (R) in (S) with the appropriate "pedigree" (F_2) are counted as valid.

Finally, the issue of the validity of the application of a particular rule to a set of facts may be distinguished. For positivists, the valid application of a (valid) rule to a set of facts will obtain when the rule "fits the facts" of the case in accordance with the way legal institutions have decided like cases in the past. The existence of such institutional precedents constitutes a third genre of facts (F_3). If the latter are not identifiable as a matter of fact, (i.e., there are no apposite case precedents) then judicial discretion supplies the basis for decision. The cumulative fact-dependence thus involved in the validity of an application of a rule (V(RA)) may therefore be represented as follows:

(iii) $\{\{[E(F_1) ---> E(S)] ---> E(F_2)\} ---> V(R)\} ---> E(F_3) ---> V(RA)$

The senses of validity which positivists lean on in speaking of valid law (i.e., in the senses represented at V(R) and V(RA)) presuppose that questions of legal validity are resolvable by criteria of empirical fact given at points (F_1)-(F_3). Although I would concede that such factual criteria constitute an integral part of the interpretation of legal validity of human rights, I maintain that the creative or constructive dimension of human rights interpretation (elaborated in Chapter Six) is at least as important as the factual aspects which dominate positivist analyses of legal validity.

A principal virtue of elaborating the "constructive interpretation" dimension of legal validity is that it renders a robust conception of international human rights law consonant with a "realistic" view that human rights, even though "universal" in the abstract and general sense implicated in comprehending their moral content, are nevertheless subject to exceptions and restrictions in scope (i.e., they are qualified by empirical factual conditions) when interpreted and applied in concrete business and political situations by the relevant authoritative decisionmaking institutions.

In Chapter Three I show how legal realism (including its contemporary form as "critical" theory) engenders a different set of human rights skeptics and antiskeptics. Realist skeptics (e.g., MacIntyre) find human rights discourse incoherent due to a purportedly intractable moral disagreement fueled by world-wide (as well as intrasocietal) cultural and ethical relativity. Antiskeptics in the realist camp admit to relativity attending rights-talk but urge that there is at least a fundamental "core" of human rights which must be acknowledged because respect for such rights is a necessary condition for social existence (Milne) or a presupposition of "communicative action" within an "ideal speech situation" (Habermas). Aside from obscuring debate with many overgeneralizations and unproved hypotheses, the realist approach fails to recognize the need for casuistic contextualization of authoritative interpretations of human rights. Thus realism is an implausible theoretical framework for understanding interpretations of human rights.

In Chapter Four I argue that a principal advantage of law-as-integrity over positivism and realism is that it enables disputes surrounding the legality of human rights at general as well as specific levels to remain cogent and fertile. From the perspective of law-as-integrity disagreement about interpretations and applications human rights centers around the competing interpretive claims of justifying theories instead of as exaggerated ideological opposition between broadly "skeptical" and "optimistic" philosophies of international law.

Once we acknowledge that international human rights are increasingly being recognized by United States courts, international legal organizations, and by corporate decisionmakers, the most pressing concern for jurisprudence is how to construct the best interpretations of those rights in particular cases of application. In Chapter Five I exposit interpretive contexts for human rights taken as institutional norms (in Dworkin's sense). The first such interpretive context considers human rights adjudication in the "narrow" sense in which rights and responsibilities are established in response to formal pleadings entertained in court and backed up by relatively elaborate articulated judicial opinions. This particular interpretive context is squarely within the scope of Dworkin's theory since it is restricted to adjudications of human rights by U.S. courts. But this special interpretive context exposes a problem for applying the integrity conception to human rights law. The problem is this: the claimants of human rights law are typically aliens, not United States citizens, and the addressees are typically foreign officials and foreign governments or institutions. Thus, such claimants and addressees are outside the scope of the "true" community as Dworkin defines it. I urge that rather than declaring an entire body of common law illegitimate we see if there is something wrong with Dworkin's imaginary "community personified" (the "community of principle").

The second interpretive context takes an inverse perspective on human rights relative to the adjudicative frame of reference. I attempt to illustrate how legislative initiatives, codes, and guidelines can institute a constellation of international legal obligations correlative to basic human rights outside of court decisionmaking as such. Treating human rights norms as institutional standards interpreted and applied by nonjudicial bodies requires looking at law through a wider lens than the one used by law-as-integrity. I will term this broadened jurisprudential outlook "law-as-process," and highlight its most prominent features as they have been shaped by Lon Fuller.

Law-as-integrity offers a special thesis about the nature of legal interpretations of rights. In Chapter Six I set out that thesis and then show how it is defective. The remedy involves recognizing a peculiar dialogic relationship in legal interpretation which can be most closely assimilated to psychoanalytic interpretation (which is a type of "constructive" interpretation) as studied by Habermas.

Another central tenet of integrity concerns the community and its relationship to legal interpretation. I show in Chapter Seven how Dworkin's notion of the political community is underinclusive *vis a vis* determinations of corporate and governmental human rights obligations by United States courts and international organizations. I contrast Dworkin's thesis about the homogeneity of the community (there is a consensus about the general principles of justice, fairness, and due process) with Milne's thesis about the diversity of the community. Rejecting both of the above theses, I illustrate how, with the appropriate modifications, Perelman's notion of the universal audience may plausibly be seen to offer a better model for the relationship between the global community (including as well the regional communities which comprise subsets of the global community) and justified interpretations of transnational human rights responsibilities.

Thus, the ultimate objective of this book is to demonstrate how abstracting and universalizing central tenets of law-as-integrity's conception of "constructive" rights interpretation from its domestic origins (e.g., Ronald Dworkin's theory of civil rights) to an international context (which is still tied in part to domestic adjudication of rights, however) yields a cogent philosophical basis for holding multinational corporations, nation-states, and individuals accountable to fundamental human rights standards. This foundation is afforded by positing justifying theories as a central mechanism for adjudicating competing construals of, e.g., jurisdiction, international custom and consensus, signatory intent, and the notion of universality which underlies human rights texts.

The focus on justifying legal theories that I advocate in detail in Chapter Eight transports questions surrounding the legality of human rights norms (as interpreted and applied by United States courts and international organizations) to a firmer and more fertile ground. Disputes about the validity of human rights law arise as competing interpretive disagreements among justifying theories, instead of as exaggerated polarities between broadly "skeptical" and "optimistic" positivist and realist philosophies of international law. Human rights have increasingly become an integral part of how we conceptualize political, moral, and legal relations between nations. Once we recognize that international human rights must be "taken seriously," one of the most pressing questions concerns how to find the best interpretations of those rights in specific cases of application and implementation by courts and other decisionmaking bodies.

Consequently, the salient features of justifying theories I will analyze are their roles in defining (specifying concrete meanings for canonical language in human rights provisions of treaties, conventions, and declarations); weighting (prioritizing some rights over others in conflicts); delimiting scope (specifying what purported rights are to); and "booting" (giving abstract starting points for fundamental rights). In addition, I will discuss the importance of justifying theories in indicating entailment relations between different levels of abstraction and generality of human rights in adjudication. For instance, a justifying theory might account for how abstract rights like the right to dignity are presupposed by concrete rights like freedom from torture; or, a theory might show how general rights such as the right to due process support arguments for more specific rights such as the right to a fair trial.

Any robust conception of human rights adjudication (including the one I will advance) must accept some basic postulates, for example, the premise that there is objectivity to argumentation about rights. The justification for such an assumption may of course be called into question on its own terms, but the mere possibily of skepticism of this kind is not *per se* a persuasive reason for doubting the legitimacy of judicial recognition of the law of fundamental human rights. Indeed, a "constructive" conception of human rights interpretation provides a powerful theoretical perspective from which many traditional skeptical challenges to the idea of universal fundamental human rights may be defused.

I will be arguing in the chapters of this book which follow that getting a cogent and full-bodied conception of international legal obligation requires taking an appropriately expanded and nuanced notion of law beyond the narrow coercionist and nationalist portrayals of the positivists, on the one hand, and also beyond the skeptical ethical-relativist portrayals of the realists. The proper way to view international legal obligation for purposes of ascribing human rights duties, I will argue, is as a *cosmopolitan associational obligation* that derives from the character of an agent's membership and participation in the world community. International legal obligation is, moverover, *interpretively complex*. There remains considerable controversy among reasonable and morally sensitive individuals about the nature of international law and the special interpretive demands it places on us if we take seriously the rights and duties it assigns.

Justifying Human Rights Doctrine

There is obviously an identifiable distinction between domestic legal systems and the international legal system. To the extent that human rights have been instantiated into domestic law, they are typically referred to as civil rights or constitutional rights, such as the right to nondiscrimination in employment as protected by Title VII of the Civil Rights act, and the right to due process as protected by the Fourteenth Amendment under United States law. Whereas, when human rights are implemented into international law they continue to be considered as human rights. But sometimes a domestic court must interpret (and possibly also apply) human rights which are accorded under international law. Similarly, an international court may be charged with interpreting the domestic law of the individual nations which are in a dispute over which the international tribunal has jurisdiction. Of course, it is entirely possible for a right to be present in more than one legal system. Moreover, a given legal right can also exist as a moral right, considered quite apart from its recognition and implementation in a system of law. For example, one might plausibly argue that the right not to be tortured is both a moral right and a legal right. As a *legal* right, the right not to be tortured inheres in a variety of different dimensions as a result of the distinct senses of rights mentioned previously in this chapter (textual sources, judicial interpretations, justifying theories) and as a result of the distinct systemic treatments that may be given to the right. Thus, the right may exist as a domestic *civil right* backed up by criminal and civil laws enforceable by municipal courts. On the other hand, the right against torture may also enjoy an existence as an international human right. But in this case, there are two possibilities concerning its interpretation and application that must be distinguished. First, if the right is recognized by an international court (or other international tribunal) then it is clearly an international human right. Second, if the right is recognized by a domestic court on the basis of that court's interpretation of international law (with the assistance of the court's parochial interpretive background understandings) *and* if the proper claimant of that right is not a citizen of the nation in which the court is situated, then such a right is also, properly speaking, an international human right. This latter situation constitutes the special institutional framework for the present study.

It is important to isolate this special sense of international human rights because failing to do so invites a number of criticisms which, though significant in other contexts, are irrelevant to the present study. One such objection would point to the lack of any appreciable international application, by an international court, of the right. Since the judgment is being issued from a domestic tribunal, the objection continues, it remains a purely national norm, so it becomes a procrustean use of terminology to denominate such a right an international human right. This objection overlooks the peculiar normative relation that is established by adjudications of human rights law in domestic courts. Specifically, an authoritative interpretation of a right presupposes the existence of some identifiable claimant (C) who has an entitlement to some object of the right (O), which is assertable against an addressee (A). Now, within this schema, it is evident that there is an international dimension to each of the components of the normative relation constituted by the human right in question. The claimant (C) of the right is not a citizen (a "national") of the country in which the court is situated, but rather an "international." The object (O) of the right (e.g., freedom from acts of torture) is provided for in a variety of international instruments, such as the U.N. Declaration of Human Rights. Finally, the addressee of the right (A) is, like (C), an "international" with respect to the domestic court. A final point to note in this regard is that once justified by its own institutional methods, a domestic court's interpretation of an international human right is "exportable" in the sense that courts of other legal systems as well as international tribunals, may look to the interpretation as a standard for constructing their own interpretation of the same or a similar right. This is especially likely in the case of the opinions of United States courts, which are to be counted among the most sophisticated decision-issuing bodies in the world.

Skeptics may counter that, though conventional institutional foundations for human rights standards may not be gainsaid, what may still be disputed is whether those standards have a "deep" justification.

In rebuttal, a key point worth bearing in mind is that no matter how "constructive" (in Dworkin's sense) the compartments of human rights doctrine may be, and even though in large part they have been "created" to promote human interests, the norms do not for these reasons lack objectivity. Other human "artifacts" such as the stock market, microwave ovens, and condominiums have been designed to facilitate our wants and needs, yet they are objective nevertheless. Whether they are tangible objects is another matter. But our ontological committment to human rights does not and need not involve the claim that they are *concreta*.

Foundations of Human Rights Obligations

What obligations, if any, do contemporary human rights standards impose on the activities of nation-states, individuals, and multinational corporations? How are human rights obligations related to, and how do they differ from, domestic legal obligations and moral obligations? Does the right to be free from discrimination in employment --- now recognized as a basic human right by a number of international documents authored by various nongovernmental organizations as well as numerous intergovernmental treaties and agreements --- apply to transnational employment practices everywhere? Must companies doing business in less developed countries refrain from emploitative employment practices involving child labor, and sweatshop working conditions in *maquiladoras*,[3] even if such practices are permissible under the host country's laws? To what extent may governments properly pass and enforce legislation restricting trade with foreign governments which systematically violate international human rights laws?

Because of the plurality of systems (legal, moral, political, economic) pertaining to such questions, the issues tend to get addressed within the context of narrow specialized intellectual traditions focused on a single system, to the exclusion of the others.

Thus, lawyers, ethicists, political philosophers, and business academics are prone to discuss issues relating to the basic social responsibilities of business at cross purposes, with each discipline offering its own limited perspective corresponding to its traditional concerns and research methods. Thus, when questions of international corporate responsibility arise for business academics, typically the economic justification for corporate activity is paramount, although even the most conservative views often hold that corporations have a general social obligation to obey valid law..[4]

There are at least two embarrassing gaps in jurisprudential scholarship today which become evident when one asks what duties agents in the international community have *vis a vis* human rights law. The first gap stems from uncertainty about the theoretical foundations of the international law of which human rights norms consistitue a special

---

[3]. *See*, J. Russell, "U.S. Sweatshops Across the Rio Grande," *Business and Society Review* (Summer 1987) No. 50, at 17-20.

[4]. *See, e.g.*, M. Friedman, *Capitalism and Freedom* (1962). In what became something of a credo for those opposed to the movement towards social responsibility in business, Friedman proclaims: "[T]here is one and only one social responsibility of business --- to use its resources and engange in activities designed to increase its profits so long as it stays within the rules of the game, which is to say, engages in open and free competition without deception or fraud." *See*, "A Friedman Doctrine: The Social Responsibility of Business is to Increase Its Profits," *The New York Times Magazine*, September 13, 1970 at 126.

subset. Regrettably, our understanding of the theoretical foundations of law and of legal obligation is largely limited to the arena of domestic law. Over the centuries philosophers of law have, for the most part, sought to explain the nature of law and legal obligation by using municipal legal systems as paradigm cases of what we mean by "law." Then, after their theories of domestic law are firmly in place, they apply them, almost as an obligatory afterthought, to try to illuminate our comprehension of the nature of international law.[5] More often than not, international law comes to be portrayed by classical legal philosophy as a "defective" kind of social ordering, relative to the municipal legal systems to which it is compared.

The two leading philosophies of law --- positivism and realism --- give unacceptably exaggerated views of the nature of contemporary international law. As regards positivism, I will argue against its basic assumption that the legal validity of international law depends entirely on empirical facts about textual sources of that law and customary practices of agents in the international community.

Reflecting on what the international legal obligations of multinational agents are in regard to both "formal" and "informal" human rights laws calls into question the nature of international law as such,[6] as well as the relationship between law and morality in international contexts.

A second gap in scholarship today stems from the scant attention philosophers of law have paid to the idea that *corporations* are addressees of international rights. Certainly, at least, more attention is paid to individuals and especially to nation-states on such issues.[7] But the rationale for holding that human rights burdens fall on individuals and nation-states extends to corporations as well. Corporations commonly

---

[5]. Chapter X of H.L.A. Hart, *The Concept of Law* (1961) is a notable illustration of this.

[6]. Regrettably, there is no shorthand recipie we can consult which lists the essential ingredients of the nature of domestic law, much less for international law. The problems associated with this state of affairs will be addressed in detail in Chapter Three.

[7]. In particular, the following works on international normative theory primarily focus on nation-states as moral agents, to the exclusion of corporations. See, C. Beitz, Political Theory and International Relations (1979); H. Shue, *Basic Rights: Subsistence, Affluence, and U.S. Foreign Policy* (1980); J. Fishkin, The Limits of Obligation; T. Nardin, *Law, Morality, and the Relations of States* (1983).

engage in human-rights violating activities. In addition, corporations and governments jointly influence public policy and legislation so that in many respects the obligations of government intersect with the obligations of business. Some of the largest multinational corporations are more powerful than the governments of small countries.[8] The human rights obligations of multinational corporations are becoming increasingly formalized in both domestic and international texts.[9] The peculiarly legal dimension of human rights standards promulgated in such texts is perhaps best apprehended by taking them as ingredients of an authoritative interpretive enterprise of a global community of principle.

In part, the second gap is due to the first gap: because international law is often seen as a kind of defective or quasi-law, the idea that *any* moral agent --- whether it be an individual, nation-state, or a corporation --- has genuine legal rights and responsibilities in the world community is simply not taken very seriously. But there is another independent aspect to the second gap which stems from the fact that traditional analyses of the concept of legal obligation as such have grown up around problems of the *individual* and his or her obligation to the *state*. This is perhaps not so surprising, since the standard concept of domestic law is so firmly anchored to the positivist notion of law as a form of state coercion deployed against individuals living within the jurisdiction of a sovereign to whom habitual obedience is given.

What Are International Human Rights?

It is salubrious to distinguish three important senses of human rights which figure into interpretations of international obligations. First, there is the sense in which human rights exist as often abstract and vague linguistic formulations in texts such as declarations, conventions, and treaties. In this first sense, human rights are conceived of as high-

---

[8]. As of 1975, the ten biggest United States-based multinational enterprises had total revenues in excess of the gross national products of the majority of the countries in which they conducted business. In that year, the top 100 U.S.-based MNCs reported total revenues of $1.3 trillion and foreign revenues of $409 billion. *Forbes*, July 28, 1986.

[9]. The following texts containing human rights provisions which apply specifically to the activities of international corporations are illustrative: Sullivan Principles, World Health Organization Code of Marketing Breast Milk Substitutes, International Labor Organization's Tripartite Declaration of Principles Concerning Multinational Enterprises and Social Policy, the proposed United Nations Code of Conduct for Transnational Enterprises.

priority normative standards published in international documents with a generalizable and often universalizable legal and moral vocabulary. Second, human rights consist of authoritative interpretations of the concrete meanings of such texts by various juridic organs, policymakers, and scholars. Interpretations enable specific judgements to be made about the applicability and scope of rights in relation to specific factual states of affairs. Finally, human rights norms may be identified with justifying theories of institutional (legal and quasi-legal) rights which, ideally, legitimate particular interpretations of human rights by reference to relevant established institutional material as well as political morality. That there may be competing justifying theories relative to human rights means that reasonable disagreement surrounds differing interpretations of human rights by different tribunals which may be situated in separate legal and ethical systems.

A standard conception one finds in the literature on human rights is that human rights are background moral rights (a) which individuals possess in virtue of being a human being, and (b) which exist at all times and in all places. The standard conception is given a rather explicit expression in the text of the Universal Declaration of Human Rights which seeks to establish "a common standard for all peoples and all nations," and which maintains that "all human beings are born free and equal in dignity and rights." This conception is such an overly ambitious one for human rights, however, that it has invited strong opposition in the form of denials (easy to construct) of both theses (a) and (b), and in the claim that the Universal Declaration is merely an expression of empty rhetoric. The interpretive contexts which I propose for human rights in this book avoids entanglement in the "standard" conception by identifying human rights as institutional norms (i) which individuals (referred to herein as "claimants") possess in virtue of justifying theories of rights which affirm those rights in particular cases of interpretation and applications, rather than as "automatic" entitlements for all human beings; and (ii) which exist with a variety of scope restrictions (of which time and place are only two); and (iii) which establish obligations for other individuals, nation-states and corporations (referred to herein as "addressees").

Since the contemporary concept of human rights law that comprises a focal point for my discussion is a subset not only of human rights but also of rights in general, I will give a brief exposition of some of the salient theories of rights as a conceptual backdrop. These theories of rights fall into three main varieties: (1) theories that construe rights as institutionally-implemented norms ("I-I" theories), (2) theories that construe rights as obligation-imposing norms ("O-I" theories), and (3) theories that construe rights as entitlement-conferring norms ("E-C" theories).

The I-I Approach

For some rights theorists, the concept of a right is principally a legal notion and as such, the only full-fledged rights are taken to be those for which legal enforcement and implementation procedures (such as those connected with contract, adjudication and legislation) exists. An especially strident advocate of such a position was the utilitarian philosopher Jeremy Bentham, who maintained that the notion of rights that have not been instituted by positive law was, in a word, nonsensical. In particular, to speak of rights in the absence of a judicial tribunal to ascertain just who may claim the right and what that right means, is, for Bentham, to utter no more than "a sound to dispute about." The notion that claims to normative concepts alone, without institutional legislative and adjudicative procedurees to provide sufficient determinacy, yields mere rhetoric is within the general spirit of the legal positivist challenge to the legal status of purported rights in international law. I will examine and critique such positivist approaches in the next chapter.

As regards Bentham, one renowned objection to his pessimistic construal of rights worth noting is that his own much touted principle of utility (taking right actions and policies as those which lead to the greatest good for the greatest number of those affected) --- which he advocates as the ultimate standard for settling moral and political controversies --- iteslf lacks a formal system of adjudication to give it the kind of determinacy that he demands for meaningful assertions of rights.

The O-I Approach

A somewhat less restrictive view of rights than the I-I perspective construes rights as claims to entitlements which carry with them legal or moral obligations to be respected by some individual or social group to whom they are addressed. For John Stuart Mill, respect for the principle of utility can generate rights and obligations upon which individuals may predicate demands even in the absence of their formal recognition in a legal system. Thus, for Mill, assertions of rights need not be limited to instances in which mechanisms of legal enforcement already exist. Rather, by referring to something that is an individual's right

> we mean that he has a valid claim upon society to protect him in the possession of it, either by the force of law or by that of education and opinion. If he has what we consider a sufficient

claim, on whatever account, to have something guaranteed to him by society, we say that he has a right to it.[10]

A modification of the above approach is provided by Joseph Raz, who maintains that X has a right if and only if X can have rights and, other things being equal, an aspect of X's well-being (his interest)) is a sufficient reason for holding some other person(s) to be under a duty.[11]

There are two primary components comprising the above accounts of rights that must be distinguished. First, there is the supposition of an entitlement to something that possession of the right confers. Second, there is the assertion of the obligation or duty that the right imposes on some individual or group. Concerning the first of these components, although traditional views tend to represent all rights as establishing claims, more recent analyses have shown that what the bearer of a right is entitled to, depending on the circumstances, may be expressed as a claim, liberty, immunity, or a power.[12]

The E-C Approach

An even less restrictive construal of rights than the approach discussed in the previous section considers rights to be assertions of important moral grounds for why individuals ought to have some good or benefit. So construed, the vocabulary of rights can be rather liberally employed to state what entitlements people have without at the same time implying that there is an identifiable addressee of that right with a duty correlative to the right.[13] From this perspective, a statement of purportedly universal human rights such as the following can be deemed

---

[10]. J.S. Mill, *Utilitarianism* (O. Priest, ed., 1977) at 66.

[11]. J. Raz, *The Morality of Freedom* (1986) at 166.

[12]. *See, e.g.*, C. Wellman "Upholding Legal Rights," 86 *Ethics* (1975) at 52; R. Martin and J. Nickel, "Recent Work on the Concept of Rights," 17 *American Philosophical Quarterly* (1980) at 165. *Cf.* W. Hohfeld, *Fundamental Legal Conceptions* (1964). Although Hohfeld classifies rights into claim rights, liberty rights, power rights, and immunity rights, he urges that rights talk be limited to claim rights exclusively.

[13]. *See* the section "Duties Correlative to Human Rights" *infra*.

to be a genuine assertion of rights, without necessarily asserting obligations on behalf of anyone to "make good" on them:

> Everyone has the right to a standard of living adequate for the health and well--being of himself and his family, including food, clothing, housing, and medical care and necessary social services, and the right to security in the event of unemployment, sickness, disability, widowhood, old age or other lack of livelihood in circumstances beyond his control.[14]

The "Generations" of Human Rights

Another conventional way in which human rights have been conceptually categorized is in accordance with their historical evolution. Karel Vasak, a French jurist, groups human rights into first, second, and third "generations," corresponding to: civil and political rights; social, economic, and cultural rights; and collective rights, respectively. Under Vasak's classification, first-generation rights (also sometimes termed "freedoms from") are seen as (predominantly, though not exclusively) negative rights, which limit the extent of legitimate governmental intervention into the realm of human liberty.[15] Such rights, then, have traditionally concerned the relationship between the individual and the state, serving to maintain a juridic security of the person against the political forces of absolutism and arbitrary power, as manifested, for instance, in the *ancien regime*.

Second-generation rights (so-called "freedoms to"), on the other hand, are deemed to be (once again, predominantly, but not exclusively) positive rights which promote the involvement of the government in the interest of securing equality in political participation and in the distribution of social and economic goods.[16]

---

[14]. Article 25(1), Universal Declaration of Human Rights, Dec. 10, 1948, U.N.G.A. Res. 217 A(III), U.N. Doc. A/810, at 71 (1948).

[15]. Typical examples include rights to freedom from: torture, slavery, cruel and unusual punishment; arbitrary arrest, detention, and exile. Historically such rights originated with 17th and 18th Century political reform movements as manifested in the English, French, and American revolutions.

[16]. Standard examples would include rights to education, suffrage, and work. Generally speaking, second-generation rights are connected with the rise of socialist revolutions as a reaction to a number of shortcomings (*i.e.*, economic inequalities) of capitalistic development.

Finally, third-generation rights (alternatively dubbed "solidarity rights") reflect the need for cooperative action (*e.g.*, as between developed and developing nations, and as between business enterprises and governments) in bringing about two chief objectives. First, a redistribution of wealth and power away from developed countries and towards developing countries, in the interest of securing a "new international economic order."[17] Second, such collective rights relate to humanity's aspirations for its preservation and harmonious existence.[18] Thus, broadly speaking, third-generation rights evince the spirit of anti-colonial revolutions following the Second World War.

On a general level, this taxonomy of rights into three "generations" is reminiscent of law-as-integrity's portrayal of legal doctrine in terms of familiar evolved "compartmentalizations," such as tort, contract, and property law.[19] For our purposes, we may note that, just as American constitutional law has evolved through specific historical conditions (civil rights originating with the abolition of slavery, progressing through the "separate but equal" stage, on to *Brown v. Board of Education* desegregation, and then into the development of affirmative actions programs and subsequent challenges thereto) and accordingly given rise to settled doctrines, human rights have developed (and one assumes, will

---

[17]. Included among such rights are: the right to food, the right to social and economic development, the right to self-determination, the right to the "common heritage of humankind."

[18]. Included are: the right to a livable (or decent) environment, the right to peace, and the right to humanitarian aid.

[19]. *See*, R. Dworkin, *Law's Empire* (1986) at 250-54. According to Dworkin, compartmentalizations are a necessary part of rights interpretations, and legal decisions and judicial argument honor traditional divisions, such as torts vs. crimes, intentional vs. unintentional harm, public vs. private law. But the challenge for law-as-integrity is to "find an explanation of the practice of dividing law into departments that shows that practice in its best light. The boundaries between departments usually match popular opinion . . . . Dividing departments of law to match that sort of opinion promotes predicability and guards against sudden official reinterpretations that uproot large areas of law, and it does this in a way that promotes a deeper aim of law as integrity. If legal compartments make sense to people at large, they encourage the protestant attitude integrity favors, because they allow ordinary people as well as hard-pressed judges to interpret law within practical boundaries that seem natural and intuitive." *Id.* at 252.

continue to develop) in connection with distinct historical events. For example, the movement from first-generation rights instituted as checks on absolutism and arbitrariness in domestic governmental regimes towards the establishment of second-generations rights within those regimes; the eventual "internationalization" of such rights against foreign governments as well; the calls for the inclusion of international corporations as duty-holders for human rights standards. The entrenchment of human rights standards in institutional sources thus may be seen as providing a conventional backdrop to interpretations --- and to any proposed reinterpretations --- of those standards. The interpreter of human rights, in other words, may refer to "local priority" of settled precedents in judging contested claims about rights. It is possible for an interpreter to depart from lines of precedent --- in effect, forging new compartments for doctrine as is involved in contemporary debates about the legitimacy of third-generation human rights --- but in this case a suitable "theory of mistakes" is needed to justify departures from conventional interpretations. (This peculiar problem of "rewriting" settled doctrine is addressed in Chapter Six.)

One way of buttressing a more expansive interpretation of rights, whether in domestic or international settings, is to appeal to broader notions, such as justice and fairness, in one's claim that prevailing accounts of rights and responsibilities fall short of protecting what justice and fairness, properly understood demands. For instance, by applying the basic framework of Rawl's theory of justice (imagining oneself situated in an "original position" behind the "veil of ignorance") to the international arena, we might find a perspective from which to legitimate various third-generation rights, say the right to humanitarian assistance on behalf of developing countries, on the grounds that respect for such rights are demanded by considerations of international distributive justice.[20] Taking a Rawlsian point of view in this fashion leads one to query whether any rational, self-interested agent in the "original position" would be willing to concede that the sort of social and economic institutions prevalent in developed countries --- those with transnational reach and vast economic holdings which make substantial profits from the resources of developing countries in which many people struggle simply to reach subsistence --- were free of any obligation to aid those in desperate circumstances?

---

[20]. I apply this notion in Chapter Four to challenge the assertion that multinational corporations do not have duties to render aid except in extraordinary circumstances.

A consideration of the hardships stemming from current world economic inequities underscores the importance of this issue. Thomas Donaldson notes in a recent study on international ethics that:

> Half of the world's population lives in countries where the per capita annual income is less than $400. In those countries, 15 percent of all children die before reaching the age of five, and those who live often suffer the permanent effects of malnutrition. Almost a billion people, about 800 million, are said by respected UN sources to live below standards prescribed by any "rational definition of human decency." Years ago *Fellowship* magazine drew a succinct analogy: "If the world were a global village of 100 people, 70 of them would be unable to read, and only one would have a collge education . . . . Over 50 would be suffering from malnutrition. 6 [villagers] would be Americans. These 6 would have one half the village's entire income.[21]

Indeed, considerations such as those contained in this passage help to remind us that when we are talking about human rights obligations we are dealing with the welfare of actual people --- a sobering point that is all too often lost in the relatively detached way that many philosophers discuss rights theory. Yet difficult questions persist, even if we concede that everyone in an "original position" would find unpersuasive the idea that institutions in the developed world had no obligations to ameliorate the status of developing countries in some fashion. How should individuals, nation-states and multinational corporations discharge the duty to provide humanitarian assistance? Some might argue that a multinational firm should simply give a percentage of its profits directly to a host government, contending that aiding citizens in distress is, after all, a central role of a government. Yet realistically speaking such a suggestion is problematic given the unscrupulousness of many governments. Thus, even in what many would hold as a model case of a national government mindful of human rights and responsive to public need --- the United States --- grave questions can be raised about its ability or commitment to assist those most in need. The years of the Reagan and Bush administrations saw the incomes of the richest 5 percent of the population grow nearly 60 percent while the incomes of the bottom 60 percent of the population decreased roughly 15 percent. During this period, the poverty rate grew to more than 13 percent of the population, yet the richest 1 percent experienced an increase in their incomes of more

---

[21]. T. Donaldson, *The Ethics of International Business* (1989) at 63.

than 100 percent.[22] Surely, the risk is equally as great in a developing country that people in positions of economic and political power would direct the humanitarian contributions of a multinational in ways that fail to advance the interests of relatively powerless individuals most in need. Is the corporation, then, morally obligated to engage directly in activities aimed to reduce the incidence of homelessness, hunger, and disease in countries in which it operates? Should a multinational firm commit itself to build homes, open soup kitchens, and provide health care? And what of the many basic rights that go beyond subsistence? Does a multinational have a responsibility to aid in the protection of fundamental political rights --- such as freedom of expression or freedom from torture for political "crimes"? If so, how does the corporation fulfill its responsibilities?

What my proposed framework for human rights suggests is the need for a continuing inquiry into the many possibilities for contested claims about what responsibilities members of the international community would have if we were to take human rights as seriously as we do the rights afforded by the law of our more immediate national community.

---

[22]Thomas White, *Business Ethics: A Philosophical Reader* (1993)

CHAPTER TWO

LEGAL POSITIVISM: HUMAN RIGHTS AS "PLAIN FACT"

Introduction

In this chapter I will criticize legal positivism --- a predominant philosophical paradigm which, though insightful as an account of the nature of domestic law, distorts our understanding of international human rights law and the responsibilities it entails for the subjects of human rights norms. I will argue against a widespread assumption held by contemporary legal scholars in the positivist camp that the legal validity of fundamental human rights depends entirely on empirical facts[1] about human rights texts and customary practices of the international community.[2] I concede that in a restrictive sense of "validity" the positivist view explains rudimentary or threshold criteria for identifying international human rights law in general. However, positivism fails to satisfactorily account for a more sophisticated sense of legal validity (which is profoundly "theory-laden") that I believe is required for making

---

[1]. As will be seen, however, I do not deny that empirical facts constitute an important ingredient in interpretations of human rights law.

[2]. My analysis on this point is similar to Ronald Dworkin's critique of what he terms the "plain fact" view of law attributable to legal positivism. According to Dworkin, the "plain fact" conception holds that "[t]he law is only a matter of what legal institutions . . . have decided in the past." *Law's Empire* at p.7.

philosophical sense of human rights law.

Human Rights and the Concept of International Law

The predominant postivist portrayals of the interpretation of international law provide poor background for human rights analysis. Influential positivist thinkers in international jurisprudence take exaggerated stances on the legal status of international law. At one extreme, "skeptics" see international law either as "positive morality" or a kind of "primitive law." For positivist skeptics international law does not satisfy criteria for valid legal rules, and hence cannot really be law. At the other extreme, positivist antiskeptics (or "optimists") argue that since international law bears many of the hallmarks of municipal law it must be law after all. So skeptics and antiskeptics within the positivist framework are polarized by how they answer the query "is international law really law?".

Basically, I will be arguing that we should take human rights law seriously (though not quite as seriously as the positivists), and at the same time we should also take moral and cultural diversity seriously (though not quite as seriously as the realists).

The Concept of Law

Theories of international human rights presuppose various background conceptions of the general concept of law itself. (The general concept of law typically is derived from philosopical analysis of domestic law.) As it turns out, these background conceptions of law are fundamentally philosophical and, as a result perhaps, highly controversial among lawyers, legal scholars, and philosophers. To gain some understanding of the different theoretical traditions *vis a vis* the concept of law, the theories of key writers within the principal schools of legal positivism, legal realism, and the "third theory"[3] of law, the "integrity" conception will be scrutinized.

Background Conceptions of Law
Legal Positivism
(i) Austin

John Austin's theory of law is known as the "command theory." It is important in terms of its methodological contributions to analytical

---

[3]. This terminology comes from an article by J.L. Mackie entitled "The Third Theory of Law," 7 *Philosophy and Public Affairs*, No. 1 (Fall 1977).

jurisprudence, or positivism. In his famous tome,[4] Austin states that it is up to jurisprudence to separate "improperly" called laws from "properly" called laws. In the former category, Austin places scientific laws of nature and moral laws. The latter category constitutes the commands of the sovereign.

A "command" for Austin is an intention that a person act or not act in some manner. Moreover, a command entails a threat of harm to the person who declines to obey that intention. Austin states that commands are "orders backed by threats." The sovereign command places a duty to obey upon the greater part of the population which is under the sovereign's authority. This duty to obey does not arise out of the morality or the legitimacy of the command, but rather, out of the source of the command itself.

With regard to judge-made law, Austin argues that a court's authority to issue the sovereign command stems from the jurisdiction given the court by the sovereign.[5] For Austin, law is identified by reference to the obedient acts of the bulk of society carried out in accordance with the dictates of political superiors, who are themselves habitually obeyed and do not habitually obey anyone else. The commands of the sovereign are the laws of the state. Although the question of whether the commands of the sovereign are moral or not remains important for Austin, he does not consider it to be a legal question proper. In Austin's famous dictum: "the existence of law is one thing; its merit or demerit is another."

The command theory is challenged by, *inter alia*, Lon Fuller. Briefly, Fuller's view is that Austinian commands may be inadequate as laws if they are violative of an "inner morality" of law. The "inner morality" exists when the following conditions are met: (1) there are general rules, (2) the rules are known, (3) the rules are not retroactive, (4) the rules are reasonably clear, (5) no laws are contradictory, (6) laws do not require either what is impossible or unreasonable, (7) laws remain constant through time, (8) law does not conflict with the administration of law.[6] Fuller disagrees with Austin's extreme view that any command whatsoever of the sovereign amounts to law. Fuller does not claim, as traditional natural law theory had, that laws whose content violate natural law are not law. Rather, he argues that, although there may be no absolute criteria for the content of law, there are at least certain absolute

---

[4]. J. Austin, *The Province of Jurisprudence Determined* (1954).

[5]. *Id.*, Lecture I.

[6]. L. Fuller, The Morality of Law (1966).

standards with regard to the procedure of making law which, if violated by the "sovereign" when it issues its commands, will not be law.

(ii) Kelsen

According to Kelsen, a legal norm is valid if it can be derived from a valid higher norm which is ultimately derived from the basic norm. The validity of the basic norm cannot be derived from any other norm, rather, its validity is presupposed. Kelsen draws a distinction between validity and effectiveness, or efficacy. Valid norms are not necessarily efficacious because efficacy relates to a quality of behavior whereas normativity relates only to the quality of validity or invalidity. However, efficacy and validity are not necessarily completely independent of each other, for the basic norm must generate on the whole a substantially efficacious order. Kelsen writes, ". . . effectiveness is a condition for the validity, but it is not validity."[7] Without a largely effective legal order, there would be no validity; however, the reason for the validity of legal norms is the basic norm, according to which the validity of all other norms may be tested. Says Kelsen, ". . . the answer to the question why the norms of this legal order ought to be obeyed and applied --- is the presupposed Basic Norm, according to which one ought to comply with an actually established, by and large effective, constitution."[8] The basic norm determines which norms are legally valid and also provides the justification as to why they should be obeyed. Kelsen writes, "by the word, 'validity' we designate the specific 'existence' of a norm."[9] And, in addition:

> To say that a norm is "valid" . . . means something else than that it is actually applied and obeyed; it means that it ought to be obeyed and applied, although it is true that there may be some connection between validity and effectiveness. A general legal norm is regarded as valid only if the human behavior that is regulated by it actually conforms with it, at least to some degree.[10]

---

[7]. H. Kelsen, *The Pure Theory of Law* (1966).

[8]. *Id.* at 212.

[9]. *Id.* at 10.

[10]. *Id.* at 10-11.

For Kelsen, the existence of a valid norm implies that there is a duty to obey that norm. Kelsen argues that the duty to obey may be implied by casting legal norms into the following logical form: if A *is*, then B *ought* to be. This form of rule does not itself create a duty, rather, the duty derives from the negation of a delict.

Thus, Kelsen states that ". . . the statement that somebody is legally obligated (has a legal duty) to behave in a certain way, refers to a behavior which is the opposite of the behavior that is the condition of a coercive act as a sanction."[11] It does not make sense to speak of what someone "ought" to do, for, according to Kelsen's formulation, an official is directed to impose a sanction only when some delict is committed. Says Kelsen, "legal obligation is not, or not immediately, the behavior that ought to be. Only the coercive act, functioning as a sanction, ought to be."[12]

Under Kelsen's theory it is unclear how a citizen can ever be said to have a "duty" since there is apparently no "law" to be violated. Rather, the citizen may simply act in such a way that will direct officials to enforce certain sanctions against him or her. For Hart (whom I discuss separately in section (iii) *infra*) the notion of legal duty is treated in the following way. Hart wants to make a distinction between (1) the situation where "X ought to do A in C," and (2) the situation where "X has a duty to do A in C." Number (1) exists when there is some social rule, that is, a generally-known practice which, if deviated from, will produce a critical response. Although Hart holds that saying one ought to do something implies the existence of a rule, he states that "it is not always the case that where rules exist the standard of behavior required by them is conceived of in terms of obligation."[13] According to Hart, it is only possible to assert (2) if there are three conditions in addition to those which are necessary to utter (1). Those conditions are that there be: (a) an "insistent" demand for conformity and a "severe" degree of social pressure or critical reaction, (b) an individual who does not want to do what the rule requires, and (c) a belief that the rule is needed to maintain social life or a substantially valued aspect of it.[14]

Both Kelsen and Hart accept the positivist notion that rules or norms that are "laws" may be identified through reference to their

---

[11]. *Id.* at 118-19.

[12]. *Id.* at 119.

[13]. H.L.A. Hart, *The Concept of Law* (1961) at 81.

[14]. *Id.* at 84-85.

pedigree rather than their content. Legal validity arises from the conformity of a rule or a norm to a criteria of validity that exists in the basic norm (Kelsen) or the rule of recognition (Hart). Under Kelsen's theory, the validity of a norm comes from some higher norm, not from any empirical fact. Valid norms are traceable back to the basic norm whose validity is presupposed, an assumption which Kelsen is led to by Kantian epistemology. Thus, Kelsen writes:

> Kant asks: "How is it possible to interpret without a metaphysical hypothesis, the facts perceived by our senses, in the laws of nature formulated by natural science?" In the same way, the Pure Theory of Law asks: "How is it possible to interpret without recourse to meta-legal authorities, like God or nature, the subjective meaning of certain facts as a system of objectively valid legal norms describable in rules of law?" The epistemological answer of the Pure Theory of Law is: "By presupposing the basic norm that one ought to behave as the constitution prescribes, that is, one ought to behave in accordance with the subjective meaning of the constitution-creating act of will --- according to the prescriptions of the authority creating the constitution." The function of this basic norm is to found the *objective* validity of a positive legal order, that is, to interpret the *subjective* meaning of the acts of human beings by which the norms of an effective coercive order are created, as their objective meaning.[15]

In order to render the positive legal order meaningful, Kelsen presupposes a basic norm which gives validity to a hierarchy of legal norms, despite the fact that the basic norm is not itself a part of the legal system. Introducing the basic norm into a coercive order brings legitimacy to that order. It thereby becomes a legal order and may be distinguished from, say, the merely coercive order of Austin.

For Kelsen, the legal order becomes comprehensible only when a conceptual framework is brought to it. That is, the conceptual act of presupposing the basic norm enables one to interpret a particular coercive order as being a legal system.

Like Kelsen's basic norm is Hart's "rule of recognition," which establishes criteria of validity for other rules and norms without any reference to their content. Hart's rule of recognition also allows the legal order to be distinguished from the merely coercive order. For Kelsen, the basic norm remains something that must be "brought to" the coercive order to make it a legal order. On the other hand, Hart's rule of

---

[15]. Kelsen at 202.

recognition belongs to the legal system in virtue of brute social fact. Although the validity of a given rule may be determined by the rule of recognition, it does not allow for a determination as to whether the system, conceived as a whole, is valid. A legal system exists for Hart when there is a "union" of "primary and secondary" rules, and a majority of a social group generally obeys "primary" rules while officials take an "internal view" of "secondary" rules.

The rule of recognition is within the legal system, however, it cannot be valid or invalid. It is purely a matter of social fact. Says Hart:

> We only need the word 'validity,' and commonly only use it, to answer questions which arise within a system of rules where the status of a rule as a member of the system depends on its satisfying certain criteria provided by the rule of recognition. No such question can arise as to the validity of the very rule of recognition which provides the criteria; it can neither be valid nor invalid but is simply accepted as appropriate for use in this way.[16]

Hart's emphasis is on the *existence* of the rule of recognition --- either it exists or it does not --- whereas Kelsen stresses the *validity* of the basic norm --- it is either presupposed to be valid or it is not. Hart distinguishes the rule of recognition from the basic norm so that we will be able to speak of whether or not a legal rule "really" exists. A rule will exist when it is "valid given the system's criteria of validity."[17]

Thus, Hart is concerned with what is meant by the claim that some rule is valid within a particular system of law, whereas Kelsen is concerned with how to determine whether some coercive order can be said to be within a system of law. Accordingly, the basic norm is "external" to the legal system, while the rule of recognition is "internal" to the system.

(iii) Hart

Hart seeks to remedy in *The Concept of Law* certain shortcomings that he perceives in Austin's command theory. Thus, Hart points out that legal control via commands must be general[18] and possess the characteristic of being standing orders which are followed consistently by

---

[16]. Hart, *supra*, at 105.

[17]. *Id.* at 107.

[18]. *Id.* at 21.

groups of people.[19] Moreover, commands must be backed by threats[20] and involve a habit of obedience and continuity.[21] The sovereign which issues the commands has legislative powers which are both limited and supreme within the system.[22]

Hart notes that there are situations where legal relations are established, as in the case of contracts and wills, which do not involve or, for that matter, even resemble commands, and therefore must be analyzed in a more sophisticated manner than the one provided by Austin's command paradigm.

Hart also argues that Austin's theory is inadequate in describing the continuity of the sovereign's existence. A system of law does not just fade away when one particular sovereign is replaced by another. On the contrary, contends Hart, the status of the sovereign depends upon a legally established existence wwhich continues even though particular sovereigns may come and go.

Hart also takes issue with Austin's characterization of a legal system in terms of a general habit of obedience of the majority of the members of a society to the sovereign. Hart's view is that to say someone has an obligation implies that some rule exists.[23] Legal obligations cannot be reduced to mere habits. Plus, the fact that the sovereign's existence is due to its legal make-up, rather than to the presence of some particular command given, means that a legal system is better explained in terms of the existence of rules.

As was mentioned in section (ii) *infra*, Hart makes a distinction between "primary rules" and "secondary rules." It is primary rules which set out primary obligations. These rules of obligation impose "restrictions on the free use of violence, theft, and deception to which human beings are tempted but which they must, in general, repress if they are to coexist in close proximity to each other."[24]

Hart points out that if a society had only primary rules with which to live by, several problems would surface. First, there would be

---

[19]. *Id.* at 23.

[20]. *Id.* at 27.

[21]. *Id.* at 50.

[22]. *Id.* at 76.

[23]. *Id.* at 83.

[24]. *Id.* at 89.

uncertainty with regard to the primary rules. Thus, the boundaries of permissible behavior within the society would be unclear. Hart states that "if doubts arise as to what the [primary] rules are or as to the precise scope of some given rule, there will be no procedure for settling this doubt, either by reference to an authoritative text or to an official whose declarations on this point are authoritative."[25] The solution to this problem lies in rules of recognition, which allow a society to move from "the pre-legal into the legal world," assuming that the society is stable and has overcome the problem of uncertainty. Such rules of recognition are secondary rules, and are essential to those societies which, although possessing rules of obligation, are not, on the whole, well ordered.

The second problem that would arise in a society with only primary rules is that only the old rules would exist --- there would be no way for them to ever change, and therefore the system would take on a "static" quality and eventually die. The cure for this problem is found in "rules of change," which permit the introduction of new primary rules or the abolishment of old primary rules.

The third problem is that of the "inefficiency" that would result from trying to maintain compliance on behalf of the population with the primary rules. Some of the rules will be ambiguous, or contradictory, or it may be difficult to apply the rules to particular factual circumstances. This problem is resolved by Hart with the introduction of "rules of adjudication," which set out the kinds of procedures that are necessary for the specific application of the primary rules in various circumstances. With regard to the establishment of law courts as adjudicative tribunals, Hart states that "the rule which confers jurisdiction will also be a rule of recognition, identifying the primary rules through the judgments of the courts and these judgments will become a 'source' of law."[26] The "recognition" thus consists in the identification of the rules that confer authority upon the law court and establish the procedures which the court must follow in performing its adjudicative function.

Is International Human Rights Law Really Law?

Legal philosophers are prone to ponder whether international law

---

[25]. *Id.* at 90.

[26]. *Id.* at 95.

is really law.[27] Several of the classical positivists discussed earlier in this chapter --- Austin, Kelsen, and Hart --- have all attempted, in their own ways, to answer the question. I want to first diagnose the ailments that arise from unprotected exposure to this general inquiry and then prescribe a cure. In testing the soundness of traditional positivist responses to this question, I choose these theories in particular because of the insightfulness of their writings. Progress in jurisprudence seems to demand respect for the "classics" coupled with a keen eye for error. In addressing whether international law is really law, all of these philosophers, albeit in variant ways, give theories of empirical criteria for valid law. The problem with such theories, however, is that they confuse the issue of the appropriate criteria for the existence of law with the question of the empirical conditions for law.

Thus, for Austin, international law is not law but "positive morality," since it lacks a "common and determinate" sovereign issuing "orders backed by threats." Kelsen sees international law as "primitive law" because of its decentralized character. Hart reaches a similar conclusion on the grounds that he finds no rule of recognition for international law. D'Amato, a recent maverick, insists that international law is really law because it is enforceable and has a rule of recognition.

But these positions are confused. First, they wrongly equate features and conditions taken as appropriate for analysis of the validity of domestic (or municipal) law with features and conditions pertaining to the validity of international law. Second, and worse, they are misled at the outset in the way they treat legal validity as such. Whatever the merits of positivist theories in articulating central features of valid law, like enforceability, centrality of enactment, and rule-like character, there is no single core of features constituting what law "really" is. At best, some features of legality are more or less typical of what we deem clear instances of law. So positivist construals of general international law do a disservice by clarifying *obscurum per obscurius*. The complex status international legal validity requires a fundamental test no more than that of legal validity in domestic law.

What is so wrong with simply analogizing international law to modern domestic law and to primitive law? International human rights law as interpreted by domestic courts is *sui generis* --- it lies somewhere

---

[27]. See, e.g., H.L.A. Hart, *The Concept of Law*, Chapter X; Lane, "Mass Killing by Governments: Lawful in the World Legal Order?," 12 *N.Y.U.J. Int'l L. & Pol.* 239 (1979); Watson, "Legal Theory, Efficacy and Validity in the Development of Human Rights Norms in International Law, 1979 *U. Ill. L.F.* 609; D'Amato, "Is International Law Really 'Law'?," 79 *Northwestern University Law Review*, 1293.

between "domestic" law and "international" law. The exaggerated analogies are therefore out of place. Even if positivist characterizations of municipal law as the command of the sovereign, or as relatively centralized systems derivable from a basic norm, are accepted *arguendo* as accurate ones, it simply does not follow that such characterizations are sufficient as definitions for "law" in all of its possible applications. It is one thing to make an adverse comparison between what are taken to be essential characteristics of municpal law on the one hand, and international law on the other. However, it is quite a different assertion to say that municipal law and international law are members of different classes and to conclude that the former is entitled to classification as "law" and the latter not. There may be great differences between two objects of the same general class --- buses and bicycles for instance --- but it does not follow from a description of the vast empirical differences between these objects that they are not both properly referred to as "vehicles."

The Impasses of Human Rights Positivism

How far does Hart's model of law as a union of primary and secondary rules (presented earlier in this chapter) go in providing a framework for human rights in international law? One the virtues of the model lies in its respect for empirical sources of law as providing a relative degree of certainty in the identification of rules of law. This is important given the frequently assumed controversial nature of the legality of human rights in the world order. In addition, Hart's model commendably takes cognizance of the connection between law and social relations. But the critical issue that Hart's analysis poses for international human rights law is this: is there a rule of recognition for such rights?

The question is especially puzzling, in part because of problems in Hart's analysis of international law, and in part because of an ambiguity (elaborated in Chapter Five *infra*) surrounding the status of human rights law as a genre of domestic law, or as a genre of international law, or both. (As I will show, this is an "interpretive" question.) At present, I shall address some special problems with Hart's treatment of the question of whether there exists a rule of recognition for international law.

While Hart devotes the bulk of *The Concept of Law* to the make-up of domestic systems of law, he considers the nature of international law in the last chapter of the book. There he asserts that there is no rule of recognition for international law. However, Hart refrains from completely denying the legality of the rules of international law. That is, he maintains that rules of international law have some sort of binding force, though not in virtue of a rule of recognition. Rules of international law are binding, says Hart, since "they are accepted and function as such."[28]

Unfortunately, Hart does not offer detailed argumentative support the bold claim that international law lacks a rule of recognition. Rather, he advances this view of international law more as a basic postulate, stating that "in this simple form of social structure, we have not something which we do have in municipal law: namely a way of demonstrating the validity of individual rules by reference to some ultimate rule of the system."[29]

So, instead of continuing the inquiry taken in the rest of the book, and investigating if international law has any rule of recognition, Hart changes the focus for his discussion of international law by denying that a rule of recognition is a necessary condition for the existence of rules of obligation or binding rules.[30] According to Hart, a rule of recognition is a luxury, not a necessity, which happens to exist in relatively advanced social orders, though not in the "primitive" international system.

Certainly, given Hart's concern for certainty regarding the legal character of primary rules, the presence of a rule of recognition in an advanced legal order would seem to be much more than a "luxury," and it is surprising that Hart so readily dismisses the idea that there could be a rule of recognition for international law. Rather, he directs his attention toward "two sources of doubt" about the legality of international law. The first of these doubts pertains to a purported lack of sanctions in the international order. The second relates to the absence of a world sovereign. Although these two sources of doubt raise important issues, in the context of Hart's central point of departure, they function to channel the analysis away from the root question of whether there are criteria of legality for the rules of international law.

Curiously, Hart embarks on precisely the sort of adverse comparison of domestic and international law for which he has criticized other scholars.[31] This leads him to view international law as a sort of "primitive" law, since there is no international legislature, nor are there

---

[28]. *The Concept of Law* at 225-26.

[29]. *Id.* at 229.

[30]. *Id.* at 229.

[31]. *Id.* at 210.

courts of compulsory jurisdiction, and centralized sanctions, as there are in advanced municipal legal systems.

Perhaps the most alarming aspect of Hart's treatment of international law is that his own notion of a rule of recognition encompasses not only very simple varieties (e.g., "whatever Rex I enacts is law") but higly complex forms as well, such as may not be immediately evident and comprehensible on a cursory examination. Having set up the concept of a rule of recognition in this way, then, it is a mystery why Hart does not even attempt a search for international rules of recognition.

Hart's denial that there are secondary rules in international law leads him to the assertion that there is only a set, not a system, of international rules. As with primitive law, there are no generally accepted tests of validity for international law. So if states ultimately differ in opinion on the validity of the primary rules comprising international law, those rules are not generally valid. Seen as a set of customary rules, international law can be valid only because the rules are generally acknowledged as such via customary state practice, not because they pass the test of a rule of recognition as the criterion of validity. In Hart's words:

> [O]nce we emancipate ourselves from [*inter alia*, Kelsen's] assumption that international law must contain a basic rule, the question to be faced is one of fact. What is the actual character of the rules as they function in the relations between states? Different interpretations of the phenomena to be observed are of course possible; but it is submitted that there is no basic rule providing general criteria of validity for the rules of international law, and that the rules which are in fact operative consititute not a system but a set of rules, among which are the rules providing for the binding force of treaties. It is true that, on many important matters, the relations between states are regulated by multilateral treaties, and it is sometimes argued that these may bind states that are not parties. If this were generally recognized, such treaties would in fact be legislative enactments and international law would have distinct criteria of validity for its rules.[32]

For Kelsen too, general international law is a kind of primitive law since its rules are created and applied by the subject nations themselves. Particular international law, on the other hand, such as that created by agreements, does not generate general rules of international

---

[32]. *Id*. at 230-31.

law binding on all nations. For Kelsen, even an international agreement signed by all nations would not create general international law since a new state formed after the signing would not have agreed to be bound to its terms.

Kelsen stresses the non-official character of collective state action in international law. Members of the international community must resort to self-help and diffuse "social pressure" to enforce rules.[33] In addition, the principle of *stare decisis* is not strictly followed in international judicial decisionmaking since, according to Article 60 of the Statute of the International Court of Justice, decisions of courts bind only the litigants before them in particular disputes. Kelsen tempers his tone on this point somewhat, however. Although international law lacks a hierarchy of offices, he argues that there is a presupposed hierarchy of norms. Thus, rules instituted by international treaties presuppose more basic rules defining treaties themselves and how they bind parties. So, for Kelsen, although international law *qua* a legal system with normative hierarchy does not require for its existence law-making and law-applying organs, without these organs it is merely primitive law.

Anthony D'Amato, an antiskeptical international positivist, postulates that international law is for all apparent dissimilar law "really law."[34] D'Amato frames his arguments using Hart's vocabulary and general orientation. D'Amato advances two central arguments to support his claim. The first argument, evidently inspired by Austin's quest for "law properly so-called," is that international norms --- specifically human rights standards --- are "law" proper because they are in fact enforceable by "reciprocal entitlement deprivation." The second argument construes international custom as a secondary rule of recognition in Hart's sense, for identifying substantive, or primary, rules of international law.

According to these "primitive-law" analysis of Hart and Kelsen, then, international law lacks a fundamental test of validity. As with the domestic-law models they formulate, however, they suppose that, at least in principle, the identification of international law is an empirical affair, ultimately determined by custom.

But even if the validity of general international law somehow ultimately depends on the identification of international custom, the

---

[33]. H. Kelsen, *General Theory of Law and State* (1945) at 160, 327; *The Pure Theory of Law* (1967) at 323.

[34]. See, A. D'Amato, "Is International Law Really 'Law'?" 79 *Northwestern University Law Review* 1293 (1985); "The Concept of Human Rights in International Law," 82 *Columbia Law Review* 1110 (1982).

validity of construals of international human rights in particular cases involves specialized interpretive and justificatory processes distinct from the "brute" identification of custom. The enterprise of human rights interpretation must be distinguished from journalistic reports on the general opinion of states.

The "Enforceability" Argument

D'Amato advances this argument to defuse the traditional positivistic claim that international law is not really "law" because of its ultimate unenforceability. There is no supranational sovereign to enforce the rules of international human rights law, adversaries allege, so those rules cannot be law. D'Amato's reply challenges the supposition that enforceability is a necessary feature of what is commonly agreed on as domestic law. Much of what passes as "plain vanilla" domestic law is itself unenforceable. For example, it is difficult to see how a judgment for a private citizen against the United States could be enforced if the government chose not to comply with the judgment. In addition, D'Amato argues, along lines similar to Hart's criticism of Austin, that much of what we call "law" concerns private arrangements such as contracts. These arrangements are governed by rules obeyed because they are seen to impose genuine obligations, not entirely out of a sense of being obliged to a superior authority. Further, D'Amato argues that the logical connection between enforcement and law is a contingent, not a necessary one. Supporting this assertion, D'Amato alludes to the famous U.S. Supreme Court case of *Marbury v. Madison*, in which the existence of a right was posited as independent of, and prior to, the existence of an enforceable remedy for a violation of that right. D'Amato's "reciprocal entitlement" thesis forms the Achilles' heel of the enforceability argument. According to this thesis, international law is enforceable in the same sense as domestic law. If nation X violates an international entitlement of nation Y, the violation typically is met by Y depriving X of the same or a different entitlement. When Iran seized American embassy personnel in 1979, the United States' entitlement of diplomatic and consular protection from attack was violated. The United States responded by depriving Iran of its entitlement to thirteen billion dollars of assets in United States controlled banks. D'Amato stresses that a tit-for-a-*different*-tat response is more effective than a tit-for-the-*same*-tat response. If responses were always in-kind the process of custom would erode the very entitlement sought to be protected. Depriving Iran of an entitlemnt other than the one it was deprived of itself, the United States upheld the sanctity of diplomatic and consular inviolability.

A theory of international law requires more than a description of its enforcement. When domestic lawyers disagree about whether a law is valid, it is no answer to simply point out that the law in question is actually being enforced. Similarly, reasonable and competent international lawyers disagree on whether claimed entitlements are provided for under international law. Arguments were made to the International Court of Justice in the Iran Case that United States intervention into the internal affairs of Iran prior to 1979 amounted to unlawful international conduct. If those claims were true it would be arguable that Iran's seizure of American hostages (construed as a tit-for-a-different-tat action) was *ex hypothesi* a lawful reciprocal entitlement deprivation response to that conduct. The possibility of disagreements of this kind --- contested claims about what international law is in particular disputes --- suggests that a theory of international law must account for the appropriate criteria for identifying which claims of international entitlements are valid. D'Amato's second argument attempts to supply such an account.

The "Rule of Recognition" Argument

Two components make up D'Amato's second argument. The first part concerns the role of custom in international law. Custom is conceived of as providing the basis for a style of argument nations employ in asserting claims of right under international law. Custom, *per se*, of course is not a rule. What D'Amato argues is that the practices of nations over time tend to establish an empirical criterion for identifying the content of substantive rules. Although the general language of numerous treaties and conventions constitutes a major source of international law, recourse to customary legal argument is required for a variety of reasons. Resolutions of the United Nations General Assembly are not always seen as binding by non-voting nations. Likewise, countries not parties to a treaty may be reluctant to be bound by its terms. Moreover, differing conceptions of what a treaty means are possible, and disputes arise in which no agreement or treaty is dispositive of the issues. According to D'Amato, primary rules of international law are identified by secondary rules of recognition reflecting customary practices in claim-conflict resolutions. From generalizable provisions of treaties and conventions, rules of customary international law are derived which become binding even on non-signatory nations.

The other part of the second argument describes international entitlements. "Entitlement" refers to a legally recognized right. Enitlements are distinguishable from interests. The interests of a nation, for example, comprise what it wants, which may include illegal aims such as dominating another nation's territory. Entitlements, on the other hand, though expressive of collective interests of nations over time, are logically distinct from interests. Among international entitlements are a nation's right to have its citizens protected abroad, sovereignty over its airspace, jurisdiction over its territorial seas, involability of its borders. D'Amato maintains that human rights are international entitlements in this sense, except that they are predicated, not of nations, but of individuals qua members of the international legal system.

Ad Computum

It is time to tally up D'Amato's arguments. On one hand, he denies that enforceability is a necessary condition for law. On the other hand, he tries to demonstrate that international law in general --- and human rights law in particular --- is "really law" because it is enforceable in a sense commensurate with domestic law. Apart from that dialectical inconsistency, (which is endemic to lawyers' rhetoric) at least D'Amato's enforcement argument serves as a foundation for his claims about reciprocal entitlement deprivation as a secondary rule of recognition. Assuming *arguendo* D'Amato has shown that international law is really law --- that is, that international law is significantly akin to domestic law because it is enforceable and has a rule of recognition as a fundamental test of legal validity --- what is missing?

D'Amato's model of international law distorts how contemporary lawyers and jurists identify, interpret, and argue about human rights in particular disputes arising in United States courts. For most of the human rights cases of the type I discuss in Chapters Four and Five of this study, D'Amato's idea of a basic factual criterion of validity for international law masks the critical role interpretation plays in laying claims to the validity of human rights law in general, and to specific arguments about the meaning and content of human rights possessed by individual claimants in particular.

Summary of Arguments

I will summarize the arguments advanced in this chapter. I have shown how the traditional positivist approaches to the concept of domestic law --- and consequently to international law as well ---are exaggerations which, if adopted, would lead one to wrongly identify the existence (or nonexistence, as the case may be) of human rights law as a brute fact. Consequently, positivism fails to identify an acceptable interpretive context for international human rights law. Thus, Hart's *skeptical* version of positivism assumes a priori that no rule of recognition exists for international law, but doesn't attempt to look for one. D'Amato's antiskeptical rendering of positivism, on the other hand, looks principally at state practice in the form of antecedently unauthorized and nonofficial acts of reciprocal entitlement deprivation for empirical evidence of international law. But D'Amato does not recognize that, more often than not, the authoritative identification of human rights law involves complex interpretive analysis which extends beyond the scope of the crude "international-law-as-plain-fact" model he proposes.

CHAPTER THREE

LEGAL REALISM AND CRITICAL THEORY: HUMAN RIGHTS AS THE "FICTIONS" OF FACTIONS

Introduction

Accounts of the nature of international human rights norms are prone to be contested according to which current of philosophical thought on legal and institutional norms one takes. Thus, whereas legal positivist models (explored in the preceding chapter) generally tend to emphasize the formal, objective, and systemic features of law, realist models concentrate on the nonformal, subjective, and *lebenswelt*-related aspects of law. In this chapter I will argue against the legal realist assumption that judicial interpretations of human rights are fictions which amount to, at worst, mere nonsense, and at best, mythical constructions which are relativized to the subjective moral and cultural values of the interpreter.

At the risk of oversimplifying, briefly put, my premise is that, depending on what institutional features one emphasizes, international human rights standards can be seen to exhibit both systemic (positivistic) and *lebenswelt* (realist/critical sociological) dimensions. However, neither aspect in isolation from the other be said to fully portray the "essence" of such institutional norms. Hence, traditional efforts to force the concept of law into either of these extreme characterizations turns out to be as misleading for institutional human rights as it is for municipal law.

Like positivism, realism and critical theory[1] engender their own sets of skeptics and antiskeptics towards international moral and legal norms. Realist skeptics find the discourse of human rights law to be fundamentally incoherent because of what they take to be intractable moral disagreement stemming from global ethical and/or cultural relativity. Realist antiskeptics accept this subjectivism and relativity, but urge that we look for at least a common "minimum standard" conception of human rights which will be compatible with cultural and moral diversity. As will be seen in Chapter Five, the interpretations of human rights given by contemporary domestic courts involve specialized methods of justification which are tied to traditional methods of legal argumentation (submission of pleadings, court finding of jurisdiction over the dispute, citations of authoritative sources of law, formulation of authoritative opinion undergirded by articualte consistency, and so on). Realists of both the skeptical and antiskeptical variety too often conveniently pass over the conventional institutional "details" involved in technical legal argument when advancing their generalized claims concerning the validity or invalidity of human rights.

Legal Realism
(i) Sociological Jurisprudence

The legal philosophies of Eugen Ehrlich[2] and Roscoe Pound[3] represent two key exponents of the general movement known as sociological jurisprudence, the historical precursor of legal realism. Ehrlich distinguishes between the notion of "positive law" and that of "living law." Positive law is formal law and is not always followed by the living law, which is constituted by the norms which citizens actually are ordered by. To the extent that the positive law is not in step with the "living law," Ehrlich holds that its effectiveness will be diminished.

The insight that a concept of the "living law" is crucial in fully accounting for the nature of law is at least implicit in numerous highly esteemed contemporary construals of human rights as being to some

---

[1]. By "critical theory" I mean chiefly the critical communications theory of society as championed by Jurgen Habermas, which deploys as one of its cardinal notions "communicative action," a form of emancipatory social and political praxis.

[2]. *See*, Eugen Ehrlich, *Fundamental Principles of the Sociology of Law* (1962).

[3]. *See*, Roscoe Pound, *An Introduction to the Philosophy of Law* (1961).

extent relativized to differing levels of economic development of various countries throughout the world.[4] It is unrealistic, the argument goes, to think that all formal (positive) statements of human rights standards in international initiatives can ever be fully actualized, given the limited resources of less developed countries. Therefore, the realist emphasis on what institutions in fact do (or are capable of doing), as opposed to what they ideally should (or could) do, captures much of the thrust of the prevailing inclination to render human rights talk more sensitive to the realities facing different countries.

If law courts in countries such as Chad, Malawi, and Zaire (among the most impoverished in the world[5]) cannot provide free counsel to criminal defendants because such a practice is too costly relative to available resources, then the realist perspective helps us to see why, though we may meaningfully speak of the right to counsel as a basic human right (in the positive/formal sense), we may also acknowledge its lack of implementation in some regions as a characteristic of the "living law" in such locales. A drawback of this point of view is that it does not account for which persistent regional failures to respect human rights (say, on economic grounds) are justifiable from those that are not. If the economic resources of a nation are insufficient to pay for free legal assistance to indigent criminal defendants because the bulk of its wealth is in the hands of an opulent dictator, we ought to be reluctant to accept the "affordability" rationale as a legitimate exuse. What is needed is some way of distinguishing legitimate claims that a purported right is not affordable from illegitimate claims. "Affordable" in such contexts is not a purely descriptive term.

The general notion about the two faces of law (positive and living) as presented in Ehrlich's writings were put forward in the United States

---

[4]. *See, e.g.*, T. Donaldson, *The Ethics of International Business*. In advocating a "fairness-affordability" condition for all assertions of funamental international rights, Donaldson asserts that purported basic human rights must satisfy a threshold criterion of affordability for potential duty-bearers. Thus, he states, in relevant part, that "[E]ach candidate for a right must be tested for 'affordability' by way of the lowest common denominator --- by way, for example, of the poorest nation-state. If, even after receiving its fair share of charitable aid from wealthier nations, that state cannot 'afford' kidney dialysis for all citizens who need it, then the right to receive dialysis from one's nation-state will not be a fundamental international right, although dialysis may consitute a bona fide right for those living within a specific nation-state, such as Japan." Id. at 82. See also, J. Nickel, *Making Sense of Human Rights* at 108-19 (articulation of conditions for fundamental human rights).

[5]. *See, The World Bank Annual Report* 1990 at 105.

largely through the work of Roscoe Pound. The study of the law "in action" is emphasized by Pound. Thus, empirical research, for Pound, is a useful tool for inquiring into whether what the courts said comported with what they in effect did, and whether the intentions behind legislative enactments were ever realized in their actual application. According to Pound, such a study is of value in the determination of the best method for producing laws which promote various social needs and human values.

Pound's reflections are relevant to appreciating the frequently overlooked reality that human rights standards have not been spontaneously generated in lifeless moral laboratories, but have grown out of human experiences in specific historical events. The notorious atrocities taking place around the Second World War, for instance, impelled governments to take cooperative steps in formulating and seeking to promote a number of human rights deemed necessary for insulating the human condition from the real-life horrors of the Nazi Holocaust.[6] Such human rights standards can be comprehended as institutional adaptations to specific orientations of human values. As sociologist Robin Williams observes, shared human experience can lead to collective alignments in value standards:

> Similar repeated and pervasive experiences are often characteristic of large numbers of persons similarly situated in society; such experiences are described, discussed, and appraised by the persons involved. The communication of common appraisals eventually binds value standards, which often become widely accepted across many social and cultural boundaries . . . . [V]alue orientations, repeatedly experienced and reformulated by large numbers of persons over extended periods, will eventually become intellectualized as components of a comprehensive world view.[7]

The elements of such a common view of the world help to structure the basic normative standards formulated in human rights instruments.

An aspect of sociological jurisprudence which has its conceptual roots in traditional natural law theory is represented in the work of Philip

---

[6]. Among the most graphic depictions of such experiences from the (first-person) human perspective is Claude Lanzemann's *Shoah: An Oral History of the Holocaust* (1986).

[7]. Williams, "Change and Stability in Values and Value Systems," in M. Rokeach, *Understanding Human Values* (1979) at 45.

Selznick,[8] which incorporates the idea that law may be evaluated in terms of absolute standards. For Selznick, an important function of the legal sociologist is to examine the nature of law and the conditions under which it tends to develop. Like Fuller, Selznick contends that rules are valid only if they are consistent with the law's "inner morality."

Selznick's methodology for the study of legal validity employs four central notions: (1) the movement from legitimacy to legality, (2) the distinction between rational consensus and civic competence, (3) the institutionalization of criticism, and (4) the institutionalization of self-restraint. Legitimacy requires that the official exercise of power be justified by the derivation of that power from some accepted principle. In addition to legitimacy, the specific decisions of officials exercising power must be critically evaluated to ensure that official decisionmaking takes place in a principled and reasoned manner. Thus, (1) occurs when the authority of officials is justified and their decisions are supportable in terms of reason and principle.

"Rational consensus" as used in (2) occurs when there is a general agreement freely adopted among the members of society that there must be restraint of government, freedom to exchange ideas. Selznick states that the rational consensus necessary to obtain legality "entails deepened public understanding of the complex meaning of freedom under law. This goes beyond passive belief or even commitment. It is an extension of civic competence --- the competence to participate effectively in the legal order."[9]

Considered as embodiments of basic rights, or "moral minimums," though they often extend beyond this extant human rights documents symbolize aspirations and values that are shared by all of humanity. In this sense, such norms reflect a kind of "rational consensus" (in Selznick's sense) of the global community, participation in which cuts across the borders of individual cultures and sovereign states. Admittedly, often only the broad outlines of planetary agreement are discernible. But as the different societies across the world are brought more closely together by economic and technological innovations, the impetus to reach consensus on core, base-line standards is likely to build. And this is apt to be so even though different cultures and nation-states have their own peculiar institutional manifestations of "rational consensus" on the domestic (noninternational) level.

---

[8]. *See*, Philip Selznick, "The Sociology of Law," 9 *International Encyclopedia of Social Science*, 50-58.

[9]. *Id.* at 54.

With regard to (3), Selznick writes: "If the ideas of legality are to be fulfilled, the capacity to generate and sustain reasoned criticism of the rules and of official discretion must be built into the machinery of lawmaking and administration."[10] The requirement of institutionalized criticism is met by the adversary process in existence in this country.

Finally, (4) places upon officials the duty to act in accordance with proper attention to the rule of law. Through the employment of these concepts, Selznick attempts to wed elements of traditional natural law theory --- such as the idea of absolute standards to which the law must conform --- to empirical sociology. In this respect, Selznick's theory of law is very similar to the continental "critical theory" of Jurgen Habermas. I will show later on in this chapter how this approach represents an "antiskeptical" account of human rights.

(ii) American Legal Realism

Much in line with the general thrust of sociological jurisprudence is the relatively recent, and distinctly American school of legal realism, in that both views seek to explain law in terms of extra-legal phenomena. Central to American legal realism is the idea that judges create, rather than discover, the law. One of the most proclaimed writers in the realist tradition is Oliver Wendall Holmes, Jr., whose famous dictum was that "the prophecies of what the courts will do in fact, and nothing more pretentious, are what I mean by the law."[11] For Holmes, law consists of *predictions* of what judges will do.

The predictive theory is a good example of a theory of jurisprudence which might provide a serviceable account of many aspects of municipal law, but gives rise to a relatively feeble portrayal of international law. As Holmes envisions it, knowing law consists of knowing how courts will in fact decide cases. Now, there is a well-known logical problem with this position (articulated by H.L.A. Hart in *The Concept of Law*) which points out the circularity of insisting that law only really exists after the judicial ruling, when it is very natural to speak of law as prexisting that ruling. No matter how discretionary-laden it seems judges articulate their decisions in terms of precedent the judgement does not come out of the air. But in international institutional contexts, a more pronounced problem concerns the predictive theory's excessive tethering of the concept of law to predictions-based-on-past-

---

[10]. *Id.*

[11]. O.W. Holmes, "The Path of the Law," 10 *Harvard Law Review*, (1897) 457-68.

judicial-decisions as such. That is, international law develops out of many nonjudicial institutional arrangements (administrative decisions, arrangements among private organizations, bilateral and multilateral treaties) which are subjected to judicial review much less frequently than counterparts to such arrangements on domestic levels.

Another limitation of a predictive approach to international human rights law is that the method skews inquiry towards the descriptive and conventional facets of "the law" (*i.e.*, what the court in fact will decide --- and for whatever reason, whether justified or not --- regarding a purported claim of right) and away from its prescriptive and postconventional facets (*i.e.*, what the international moral agent ought to do to respect the right in question).

In sum, under American legal realism, if judges wish to sidestep apparently applicable rules which extend to a given case, they are free to do so. What may seem to be a judicial ruling given in conformity with existing law can be interpreted under legal realism as meaning simply that a judge decided that, based upon some personal preference, the contrary result would not be bettter.

(iii) Critical Legal Studies

It is generally accepted that legal realism is in some sense the precursor of the critical legal studies movement. Nevertheless, it must be acknowledged that critical legal theory has an almost overwhelmingly complicated history, and its status as a coherent, unified philosophical "movement" remains highly controversial at the present time. It is probably fair to say that it represents a melange of conceptual approaches from traditional American legal realism, literary criticism, and the New Left (although it is typically distanced from doctrinal Marxist thought). Although it is beyond the scope of the present work to present a detailed account of critical legal studies, some generalities which bear on competing perspectives for interpreting human rights law can be identified at this point. First, whereas legal realism tends to emphasize the idea that judicial interpretation amounts to "policy making," (with the aim of, once recognizing this, attempting to improve on the substance of policy), for instance, rendering it more egalitarian critical theory, tends to seek methods of "emancipation" from the "technocratic" dominance of legal and political institutions at large. Such a project of emancipation may be pursued, as in the case of MacIntyre, through a return to the virtues of the Aristotelian moral tradition or, in the case of Habermas, through an proper appreciation of our "anthropologically deep-seated interests" in liberation from institutions and ideas no longer required for individual or collective survival.

Second, although legal realism points out that there is an irreducible subjectivity, and hence the potential for arbitrariness, in judicial interpretations of rights (which it seeks to replace with the objectivity of scientifically-inspired policy-making) critical theory treats the problem of subjectivity in rights adjudication in a slightly different light. Thus, for MacIntyre, the idea that judges can identify pre-existing rights in pursuit of justice is strongly opposed on the ground that the underlying moral principles upon which judgments of rights are predicated are incommensurable. The incommensurability, in turn, arises from a lack of consensus in contemporary "emotivist culture."[12]

This general theme of a background ethical incommensurability as threatening the objectivity of juridical decisionmaking is prevalent in some more (legally) technical writings of critical legal scholars such as Duncan Kennedy, David Kairys, and Roberto Unger. In the next chapter I will present some of the key challenges that critical legal studies (as distinguished from "critical theory") has posed for the interpretation of legal doctrine.

The Impasses of Realism and Critical Theory

If, as I argued in the preceeding chapter, legal positivism is a poor framework within which to account for human rights law, its antitheses --- legal realism and critical theory --- should be assessed to see if they can produce better results. Though not considered a "legal philosopher" proper, for purposes of situating the most salient philosophical paradigms for human rights interpretation, Alasdair MacIntyre may fairly be regarded as a contemporary partisan of the legal realist/critical legal studies crusade in its most skeptical attitude towards human rights. This is so because MacIntyre stridently argues that human rights simply do not exist at all.

To back up his assertion that there are no human rights, MacIntyre observes that the concept of a right is not found in every society. Further, he states that claims to possessions of rights presuppose the existence of a set of socially established rules. In MacIntyre's view, "[s]uch sets of rules only come into existence at particular historical periods and in particular social circumstances. They are in no way universal features of the human condition."[13] In the interpretive context of this study, it is possible to see how such an objection ignores the

---

[12]. A. MacIntyre, *After Virtue: A Study in Moral Theory* (1984) at 22.

[13]. A. MacIntyre, *After Virtue: A Study in Moral Theory*, 2d ed. (1984) at 67.

special way in which claims to the existence of human rights can reasonably be justified within the milieu of socially established rules, in particular, those rules of law employed by United States federal courts. This is not to say that universal human rights can be mechanically deduced from any such set of rules, nor that all purported human rights norms are supportable by a set of rules. But MacIntyre's argument on this point is obtuse. It fails to appreciate the fact that the notion of universality which underpins the contemporary law of human rights is an *elliptical* one, which need not be straightjacketed into the "standard conception"[14] of human rights in order to remain a meaningful element of juridical discourse.

In addition, MacIntyre advances a linguistically-based argument against the supposition of human rights along the following lines:

> It would of course be a little odd that there should be such rights attaching to human beings qua human beings in light of the fact . . . that there is no expression in any ancient or medieval language correctly translatable by our expression 'a right' until near the close of the Middle Ages. The concept lacks any means of expression in Hebrew, Greek, Latin or Arabic, classical or medieval, before about 1400, let alone in Old English or in Japanese as late as the mid-nineteenth century. From this it does not of course follow that there are no natural or human rights; it only follows that no one could have known that there were. And this at least raises certain questions. But we do not need to be distracted into answering them, for the truth is plain: there are no such rights, and belief in them is one with belief in witches and unicorns.[15]

MacIntyre's logic in this argument is weak. First, although ancient Greek may not have had a single term for 'a right,' there are numerous instances in which the *concept* of *e.g.*, having a claim, is expressed in ancient Greek writings. (The notion that having a claim is part of the complex concept of 'a right' is attributable to the work of Hohfeld, who distinguishes rights as claims, liberties, immunities, and privileges.)[16] For example, in the *Crito*, there is an extended discussion about the morality of breaking one's undertakings and agreements (e.g., the "tacit agreement" that citizens of Athens make to obey its laws by remaining

---

[14]. *See*, Chapter 1, *supra*.

[15]. *Id.* at 69.

[16]. See, W. Hohfeld, *Fundamental Legal Conceptions* (1923).

in the city as adult citizens.)

What is perhaps more important, however, is that the general argument MacIntyre is advancing to the effect that ancient languages did not have the concept of a right is not dispositive on the issue of the existence *vel non* of human rights today. Ancient languages did not have a term for the concept of a photon either. But that does not mean that the contemporary notions of photons and human rights are nonsense.

In addition, the analogy of the existence of human rights to that of witches and unicorns is misleading. Whether the latter two entities exist is an empirical matter. The question of the existence of human rights, however, is not entirely an empirical question, as my refutation of the positivist account of human rights has illustrated.

Finally, it should be noted that even if it were accepted that human beings did not possess human rights simply *qua* humans (i.e., without regard for other particular attributes), it would not follow that such rights could not be attributable to individuals on some other grounds, such as the possession of the property of rationality, or sentience.

So, for purposes of making sense of the law of human rights, MacIntyre's skeptical analysis of human rights is unacceptable in two important respects. First, he sets out to criticize a notion of human rights which is out-of-touch with the current judicial understanding of that idea. Second, the particular arguments he advances to demonstrate the nonexistence of human rights are *non sequiturs*.

"Critical" Theory

Habermas, one of the principal exponents of the "second generation" Frankfurt school of critical theorists, predicates a good deal of his thinking on the nature of human rights with a robust conception of the nature of rationality in the modern post-Enlightenment world. It should be noted that in this regard, Habermas' "critical" approach is akin to that of MacIntyre in *After Virtue*, although the former's conclusions concerning the possibility of human rights are quite clearly not as pessimistic as MacIntyre's. Habermas maintains that it is not possible to return to classical rationality, but he is interested in extracting an "emancipatory" element from modernity by means of the notion of "public space."

As is the case with MacIntyre, Habermas, of course, is not a "legal philosopher" in the traditional sense. Nevertheless, the following discussion will show that Habermas' "theory of communicative action" is associated with a special segment of human rights jurisprudence pertaining to freedom from political domination with respect to normative argumentation.

Habermas wants to advance beyond the pessimistic views of rationality taken by "first generation" critical theorists such as Adorno and Horkheimer. In their book, *Dialectic of Enlightenment*, Adorno and Horkheimer contend that reason, which was supposed to be an agent of human emancipation, became transformed in the philosophy of the Enlightenment into the antithesis of this. Reason became an agent of domination (*e.g.*, the Nazi Holocaust). How did reason come to be associated with human emancipation at all?

In ancient Greek thought *logos* referred to a human capacity for the "good life." This might consist of Aristotelian virtue leading to *eudaimonia*, Platonic contemplation of the Form of the Good, or living in Stoic conformity to the Cosmos. Reason in the Classical sense represented a way of relating human means to human ends. Yet during the Enlightenment, this association of reason with *logos* was abandoned.

Rationality became characterized by instrumentalism --- technical knowledge of how to attain ends but without the emancipatory knowledge of what the ingredients of a good life are. Reason was reduced to calculating about means, not philosophizing about ends. The intellectual project of the Enlightenment period, which held promise for bringing knowledge and enlightenment to humankind, yielded only the former.

Habermas discusses how the sociologist Max Weber, who recognized this "disenchantment" of the modern world, failed to solve the problem of what consequences would in fact result from the loss of reason *qua* enlightenment. For Weber, modernization represents not only a loss of meaning, but also a loss of freedom. In the rationalized modern world, a "new polytheism" arises in which "different value orders of the world stand in insoluble conflict with each other."[17] The contemporary world faces a challenge. A unity not seen in the prevailing orders of the social world must be constructed. But how?

In the ancient world, mythical polythesim solved the problem. Society's competitive strife was personified as a divine struggle. Later on, religion held out another answer by representing reality as a rationally organized hierarchy. ("God's in His heaven, all's right with the world.")

Weber relinquishes such manifestations of naivite, of course. Seeing the legal system as a rationalization of means-end relations, Weber's analysis leads him to conceive of disagreement about the proper ends for society as being a by-product of disillusionment. A plurality of irreconcilable value judgments about social goals leads law to become systematized by specialists who manipulate rules according to desired

---

[17]. J. Habermas, *The Theory of Communicative Action*, (T. McCarthy, trans. 1984) at 245.

ends, whatever those ends happen to be. Habermas expresses this conception of law as follows:

> Weber assimilates to the law an organized means applied in a purposive-rational manner, detaches the rationalization of law from the moral-practical complex of rationality, and reduces it to a rationalization of means-end relations.[18]

So, Weber's theory of law provides no independent justification for the legal order as a whole. For Weber, bourgeois legal systems are characterized by positivity, legalism, and formality. Positivity is the expression of the sovereign's will through law; legalism is sanctioning any behavior which deviates from norms; and formality is the protection of private, free choice through law, plus the principle that what is not prohibited is permitted.[19] Although these conepts express law's function in facilitating bourgeois commerce, they fail to account for the normative dimension of law. Legal norms need justification independently of the particular conventional order or tradition out of which they arise. Habermas finds this post-conventional rational justification missing in Weber's "sheer positivism."[20] There arise at the post-conventional stage a number of concepts which demand some new mode of legitimation. These concepts assume a connection between law and morality. Habermas notes that this fact implicates

> the idea that legal norms are in principle open to criticism and in need of justification; the distinction between norms and principles of action; the concept of producing norms according to principles; the notion of rational agreement on normatively binding rules (as well as that of a compact that makes contractual relations possible); the insight into the connection between the universality and justifiability of legal norms . . .[21]

There is an interesting parallel here to Dworkin's assault on legal positivism (which he also terms "conventionalism" in more recent writings). Dworkin's critique leans heavily on the concept of legal

---

[18]. *Id.* at 262.

[19]. *Id.* at 259.

[20]. *Id.* at 262.

[21]. *Id.* at 260-61.

rights, arguments for which flow from principles of political morality presupposed by the legal order as a whole, and subscribed to by the political community under that order. Similarly, Habermas observes that "[t]he separation of morality and legality effected in modern law brings with it the problem that the domain of legality *as a whole* stands in need of practical justification."[22]

Thus, a legal order conceived of simply as a "model of rules" cannot account for an underlying moral obligation to obey what judges will proffer as their interpretation of the law. Habermas states the matter in the following way:

> The sphere of law, which is independent of the sphere of morality but at the same time demands the readiness of legal subjects to obey the law, must be complemented by a morality grounded on principles.[23]

In Dworkin's writings, idealizations such as the Rawlsian original position, Hercules, and the epistemic presupposition of the one-right-answer thesis that hard cases are uniquely resolvable, serve as master norms for legitimating judicial interpretation in the context of a normative rationality endemic to American constitutional democracy. Similarly, though on a less parochial level, Habermas' "ideal speech situation" supplies a device of legitimation for institutions that engender unrepressed political discourse --- through respect for the human rights of free speech, assembly, and expression --- within a milieu of emancipatory rationality.

Epistemologically, Habermas' analysis has a tripartite structure. Drawing from the notion that there are "anthropologically deep-seated interests," Habermas distinguishes between human interests in prediction and technological control, practical political discourse (which produces individual and group understanding), and emancipation from the "illusion of necessity." According to Thomas McCarthy, these cognitive interests have a "quasi-transcendental status."[24]

Habermas' "theory of communicative action" is deeply democratic. It is within this general political context that Habermas tries to account for the emancipatory facet of rationality in the modern world. This is done with the help of his concepts of the public sphere and universal pragmatics, which form an integral part of his theory.

---

[22]. *Id.* at 261.

[23]. *Id.*

[24]. T. McCarthy, *The Critical Theory of Jurgen Habermas* (1978) at 58.

The Public Sphere

The "public sphere" (*Offentlichkeit*) refers to a social space where consenses emerge on matters of political morality. Habermas notes that from the Renaissance period there evolved a public space, embodying the idea that normative statements must be argued and justified publicly, before an audience. According to one commentator, the public sphere is

> an area of society that arose [during the seventeenth and eighteenth centuries in Western Europe] between the absolutist state and bourgeois society, in which discoursing private citizens could freely and critically discuss practical issues and the role of the state. Institutionally the public sphere took the form of participatory democracy . . . . [25]

The public sphere presupposes an "ideal speech situation" (*ideale Sprechsituation*) in which each individual is recognized as a potential participant in public discourse. This notion is summarized by Habermas scholar Thomas McCarthy in the following passage:

> [S]tructure is free from constraint only when for all participants there is a symmetrical distribution of chances to select and employ speech acts, when there is an effective equality of chances to assume dialogue roles. In particular, all participants must have the same chance to initiate and perpetuate discourse, to put forward, call into question, and give reasons for or against statements, explanations, interpretations, and justifications . . . . [T]he conditions of the ideal speech situation must insure not only unlimited discussion but also discussion which is free from all constraints of domination, whether their source be conscious strategic behaviour or communication barriers secured in ideology and neurosis. [26]

Thus, Habermas argues that there is presupposed in every speech act an idealized communication liberated from domination. Although Habermas concedes that the public space was the product of modern industrialized Western societies, he denies that it was the progeny of any one particular culture. In this way, Habermas is able to sidestep the

---

[25]. R. Kemp, "Planning, Public Hearings, and the Politics of Discourse," in J. Forester, *Critical Theory and Public Life* (1985) at 182.

[26]. T. McCarthy, Introduction to J. Habermas, *Legitimation Crisis* (1975) at xvii.

skeptical challenge of cultural relativists that the public space lacks any claim to universality.

A further claim made by Habermas is that individual speakers in the ideal speech situation are held to a number of underlying validity claims (*Geltungsansprueche*) which flow from what he terms universal pragmatics. He states these requirements in the following way:

> The speaker must choose a comprehensible expression so that speaker and hearer can understand one another. The speaker must have the intention of communicating a true proposition . . . so that the hearer can share the knowledge of the speaker. The speaker must want to express his intentions truthfully so that the hearer can believe the utterance of the speaker (can trust him). Finally, the speaker must choose an utterance that is right so that the hearer can accept the utterance and speaker and hearer can agree with one another in the utterance with respect to a recognized normative background.[27]

In sum, the four underlying validity claims are comprehensibility, sincerity, legitimacy (or appropriateness), and truth. It is now appropriate to consider the implications of Habermas' analysis for the interpretation of human rights.

Human Rights Norms as Presuppositions of Ideal Speech for the International Community

A charitable reading of Habermas would suggest that there is a special correspondence between an identifiable number of international human rights norms and the underlying norms of universal pragmatics for communicative action. My claim that Habermas is an antiskeptical realist with regard to human rights requires that this correspondence be brought out. Habermas' notion of practical rationality, as has been seen, lays emphasis on the idea that members of a society must be able to understand one another by, for instance, sharing common values and a common language. But the universality and objectivity of communicative action is threatened by two extremes: on the one hand it is threatened by technical rationality, which is universal yet tied to instrumental interests; on the other hand, it is threatened by hermeneutics, which are particular --- that is, tied to specific cultural contexts --- and could therefore lead to relativism.

---

[27]. J. Habermas, "What is Universal Pragmatics?," in *Communication and the Evolution of Society*, (trans. T. McCarthy, 1979) at 2-3.

The theory of communicative action presupposes the ideal of communication that is free from domination in every speech act. As such, the charge of ethno-relativism is met with the following response. Although communicative action is evolved and realized in Western industrialized societies, it is not strictly the product of such particular conditions. Rather, specific historical conditions transpired which enabled the ideal of communicative action to be given shape. Thus, modernity has laid the conditions of possibility for emancipatory rationality as embodied in communicative action.

Seen in these terms, it would appear that respect for at least some international human rights, especially those pertaining to due process and to freedom of speech, assembly, and expression, would be required by a "rule of emancipatory reason," as well as from the explicit textual formulations of such rights in international legal instruments. Norms of argumentation appropriate for human rights discourse are, at least in part, universalizable presuppositions of human communication in general.

The universal pragmatics of the ideal speech situation require that all parties have equal opportunity to advance and argue normative statements. Applied to the discourse of international human rights, this requirement translates into the norm of equal respect in court appearances having cognizance of human rights issues.[28] Freedom of thought, speech, and expression would also be considered essential norms.[29] Since normative statements advanced must be proven, the right to be assumed innocent until proven guilty would also be implied.[30] The requirement of comprehensibility would mandate that the accused be able

---

[28]. Article 14 of the International Covenant on Civil and Political Rights provides that "[a]ll persons shall be equal before the courts and tribunals." U.N.G.A. Res. 2200, 221 U.N. GAOR, Supp. (No. 16) 52 U.N. Doc. A/6316 (1967).

[29]. Article 19 of the International Covenant on Civil and Political Rights states, in relevant part:

(1) Everyone shall have the right to hold opinions without interference.

(2) Everyone shall have the right to freedom of expression; this right shall include freedom to seek, receive, and impart information and ideas of all kinds, regardless of frontiers, either orally, in writing, or in print, in the form of art, or through any other media of his choice.

[30]. *See*, Article 14, subsection (2): "Everyone charged with a criminal offence shall have the right to be presumed innocent until proved guilty according to law."

to understand all charges being brought.[31]

Thus, it is arguable that every potential participant within a universal "public space" constructed by international human rights law is entitled to a whole host of such fundamental norms of juridic communication, in both the institutional/empirical sense (*i.e.*, generated by the system of international law) and in a background sense (*i.e.*, generated by Habermas' theory of communicative action).[32]

A principal difficulty with such a "transcendental" grounding for human rights norms lies in its incompleteness. Not all human rights standards are grounded in the ideal of emancipation of language and communication, although that ideal constitutes an important exponent for a number of specific rights referred to in the preceeding discussion.

Another difficulty is that even granting that a range of basic human rights norms are really a priori presuppositions of the emancipatory aspect of communicative action, it does not follow that the concept of such background rights translates into any shared substantive conception of what concrete rights claimants have in particular cases of human rights disputes.

Summary of Arguments

Accepting the central tenets of realism and critical theory as applied to international norms would lead one to wrongly identify the existence of human rights law as a fanciful fiction. Both skeptical and antiskeptical varieties of realism, represented by MacIntyre and Habermas, respectively, were analyzed. If correct, MacIntyre's philosophical perspective would pose a serious threat to any theory of human rights since it asserts that no such rights can possibly exist. But an analysis of MacIntyre's reasoning showed that there are good grounds for rejecting MacIntyre's overly skeptical conclusions about human rights.

---

[31]. *See*, Article 14, subsection (3):

In the determination of any criminal charge against him, everyone shall be entitled to the following minimal guarantees, in full equality:

(a) To be informed promptly and in detail in a language which he understands of the nature and cause of the charge against him . . . .

[32]. Views somewhat similar to the one I take here may be found in some of the writings of Aulis Aarnio, Robert Alexy, and Guy Haarscher. I am not attempting to relate my view to theirs but rather to indicate my direct and indirect debt to these writers.

It was seen that Habermas' theory is constrained by the reality that the "transcendence" of the ideal speech situation cannot serve as a proper foundation for all or even the most fundamental human rights norms. Although there may be good grounds for accepting universal pragmatics as a general theoretical basis for advancing claims about specific human rights norms such as free speech, freedom from arbitary power, and presumption of innocence, as it stands, the theory of communicative action does not provide a bridge between such abstract presupposed conceptions and substantive conceptions of specific human rights. In addition, this aspect of Habermas' theory does not provide a plausible framework for other significant fundamental human rights norms such as the right to freedom from torture, which do not relate to communicative aspects of human interaction.

CHAPTER FOUR

LAW-AS-INTEGRITY: MEDIATING LAW, MORALITY, AND HUMAN RIGHTS IN THE GLOBAL CONTEXT

Introduction

All too often *ethical* theories of basic (or fundamental) rights, in their zeal for maintaining a kind of philosophical purity tied to the abstractness of background moral norms, pass over the special legal and institutional character of the human rights norms they seek to analyze.[1] On the other hand, *legal* theories of human rights frequently present monolithic portrayals of such rights by including for discussion (in the "rhetoric" of "legal language"[2]) only the most firmly established

---

[1]. *See, e.g.*, the essays collected in J. Pennock & J.W. Chapman, *Human Rights: Nomos XXIII* (1981).

[2]. I set these terms in quotes to indicate the special sense they carry in the recent law-as-literature movement, as exemplified in, *e.g.*, J.B. White, *Heracles' Bow: Essays on the Rhetoric and Poetics of the Law* (1985). The following passages express the special usage:

". . .law is in the first place a *language*, a set of terms and texts and understandings that give to certain speakers a range of things to say to each other. . . And the very fact that the lawyer speaks a *legal language* means that he or she inhabits a legal culture and is a member of a legal community, made up of people who speak the same way. For this

standards which have been clearly "incorporated," into (a) the domestic authority of a national legal order such that they have (municipal) validity;[3] or (b) the multinational authority (*erga omnes*) of the international legal system.[4] The unfortunate result of such dissociations of moral from legal theory in the field of human rights is that the advances made in jurisprudential thought concerning the *systematic interconnectedness* of law and morality[5] have remained at the parochial (as distinguished from the global) level (essentially, rooted in problems of constitutional hermeneutics).

What is needed is a theoretical forum that will provide for an integrated treatment of the unique legal and institutional dimensions of human rights on the one hand, and their singular moral dimensions (*e.g.*, their embodiment of "egalitarian universalism"[6]) on the other. To date, the law-as-integrity model of law is unparalleled in its power to articulate the complex interplay between law and morality, at least as concerns the

> 'language' is not just a set of special-sounding words, but a set of intellectual and social activities, and these constitute both a culture --- a set of resources for future speech and action, a set of ways of claiming meaning for experience --- and a community, a set of relations among actual human beings."
>
> "To characterize this activity [of speaking legal language] as '*rhetorical*' . . . I mean not merely the art of persuasion --- of making the weaker case the stronger, as the Sophists were said to do --- but that art by which culture and community and character are constituted and transformed."

Id. at xi (emphasis added).

[3]. *See, e.g.*, Schluter, "The Domestic Status of Human Rights Clauses of the United Nations Charter, 61 *California Law Review* 110 (1973); Scoble, "Enforcing the Customary International Law of Human Rights in Federal Court," 74 *California Law Review* 127 (January, 1986); Randall, "Federal Questions and the Human Rights Paradigm," 73 *Minnesota Law Review* (1988).

[4]. *See, e.g.*, Ian Brownlie, *Principles of Public International Law* (4th ed., 1990), Chapter XXIV.

[5]. *See, e.g.*, D.A.J. Richards, *Toleration and the Constitution* (1986); E. Pincoffs, *Philosophy of Law* (1991), Chapters 8-12.

[6]. This terminology is Alan Gewirth's. *See, Human Rights: Essays on Justification and Applications* (1982) at 4.

limited range of institutional material (that is, British and North American municipal law) to which it has been applied by its author.

In this chapter, I show how several tenets of critical legal studies (law is riddled with contradictions, indeterminate, incoherent[7]) counterpoised with law-as-integrity (law is a controversial interpretive concept, yet ideally coherent and determinate in hard cases) provide rival frameworks for voicing competing attitudes towards moral and legal responsibility vis a vis international human rights guidelines. Applied to international moral agents, these dual jurisprudential perspectives engender alternative dogmas. One claims that uncertainty about the obligations of international actors (such as multinational corporations) defeats attempts to take the international rule-of-law tied to human rights standards seriously. (As a moral/legal agent, global corporations are seen as ethically "footloose;"[8] ethical/juridical relativism.) The other holds that uncertainty, part and parcel of "constructive" rights interpretation, is not necessarily at odds with a global rule-of-law conception of global moral and legal responsibility. (Although interpretations of international rights can be touchy in multi-country settings, global actors are everywhere bound to respect some base-line standards, period; ethical/juridical centrism.)

Andrew Altman denies that "soft-core" critical legal studies (which does not, as more radical versions do, deny an objective structure to legal doctrine) is ultimately a foe of liberal theory. In a sense, the feud between soft-core CLS and liberalism (including Altman's defusing of the conflict) is a no-win conflict: we can't really tell how much doctrinal determinacy and coherence is necessary for the rule of law (national or international) to be regnant. Both perspectives are, however, of some value in that each lends warrant to a different genre of international obligations for MNCs. Some human rights and well-settled norms of the law of nations (entitlements to airspace, *pacta sunt servanda*) attract a high degree of consensus in the global community and are fairly determinate in terms of the obligations they impose on international agents. These norms may be best accounted for under an "integrity-style" model. Other human rights (right to a paid vacation) and norms relating to practices such as bribery, advertising, and environmental regulation do not attract worldwide agreement and are significantly less determinate, given the varieties of levels of economic development and

---

[7]. *See* A. Altman, *Critical Legal Studies: A Liberal Critique* (1990).

[8]. *See* D. Windsor, "Defining the Ethical Obligations of the Multinational Enterprise," in W.M. Hoffman *et al*, eds., *Ethics and the Multinational Enterprise* (1986).

cultural and religious values obtaining in multi-country environments. A soft-CLS approach is perhaps more appropriate for the latter institutional guidelines.

The "Third Theory of Law" (Early Dworkin)

Ronald Dworkin's theory of law[9] explicitly challenges the legal positivist position with respect to the court's role in deciding a hard case where no clear rule of law exists to resolve the case. In addition, Dworkin's theory sets out a rights thesis which distinguishes between arguments of principle and arguments of policy and defines their role in the determination of the rights of litigants in hard cases. Principles perform an important function in Dworkin's theory with respect to the determination of the rights and obligations of litigants in hard cases. Principles may be distinguished from rules in that principles carry "gravitational" weight and often require the invocation of value judgments when applied in individual cases. Thus the issue of whether a given principle is appropriate in a given case is not decided in as formal a manner as, say, the issue of whether a given rule is in agreement with a rule of recognition.

The main emphasis in Dworkin's theory is on adjudication. Dworkin accuses positivism of giving an inadequate characterization of judicial discretion. By identifying law merely in terms of official pedigree, positivism limits the law to a finite set of rules which, under certain factual circumstances, may "run out." In such circumstances, positivism holds that a judge exercises discretion which is not under antecedent legal control. Dworkin rejects that notion, arguing that relevant legal arguments of principle which carry legal weight never run out, even in the hardest cases. Thus, according to Dworkin, there is never a case where judicial decisionmaking will be left uncontrolled by law. Although there may be substantial disagreement among competent lawyers as to what the correct decision should be in a given case, there is nevertheless always a right answer to that case.

Dworkin does not claim that judges have no discretion at all, only that the sense in which they do have discretion is a weak one. The relevant legal standards to which a judge may turn go beyond mere rules to include principles and policies which ultimately determine the limits of judicial discretion.

In framing his arguments against the positivist view that law may be identified in terms of pedigree, that rules with adequate pedigree will be valid legal rules, and that a rule's legal validity is sufficient to

---

[9]. Ronald Dworkin, *Taking Rights Seriously* (1977).

establish an obligation to obey that rule, Dworkin draws upon moral-sociological material to augment the meaning of "the law." Judges, in reaching their decisions, look to the political morality which runs through the legal system. "Law" encompasses not only a closed set of official pronouncements but also the conventional practices of society and the social rules to which they give rise.

It is through the judicial decision that law and morality become connected. Principles and policies of law exist as a part of a political morality which is internal to the legal system. By adding principles and policies as standards which are available for judicial decisionmaking, Dworkin is able to reject the positivist claim that judges have discretion in the "strong sense." What is meant by a "strong sense" of discretion? According to Dworkin:

> An official's discretion [in the 'strong sense'] means not that he is free to decide without recourse to standards of sense and fairness, but only that his decision is not controlled by a standard furnished by the particular authority we have in mind when we raise the question of discretion.[10]

For Dworkin, although a judge might be constrained by the texts of rules and statutes, this does not mean that the judge will be completely bound by them. Rather than being strictly confined to precedent, judges find support in principles and policies for their decisions. By "principles," Dworkin intends the sort of arguments that are generally associated with courts. Principles relate principally to considerations of justice, fairness, and standards of morality. "Policies," on the other hand, represent the sort of arguments that are generally associated with the executive and legislative branches of government. Policies relate to considerations of collective societal goals.

Dworkin's theory posits the process for determining what the best justification for a law as a two-step methodology. First, the political and moral traditions of the community which support the clearly valid rules of law are identified. It is these traditions which lend support to the rules by providing an institutional and an historical context for formulating specific interpretations of the rules and for resolving inconsistencies or contradictions that may exist among them. Second, the political and moral traditions are critically examined from the standpoint of independent standards of normative political theory, such as the principles of justice and fairness. (In his later works, Dworkin adds the

---

[10]. *Id.* at 32.

principle of due process to the list.) The most adequate theory of law will be based upon the most adequate political theory.

To say, as Dworkin does, that there is always a right answer with regard to what the rights of the litigants are in a hard case, is not to say that extant legal standards are necessarily clear and unambiguous. The assertion refers instead to the judge's duty in a hard case to go beyond standards which have previously been set down and look to whatever principles may constitute the most satisfactory justificatory theory. Dworkin concedes that there is no morally neutral way to determine what the law is. A judicial decision as to the legal rights of litigants in a hard case will be controversial, and will only be as good as the arguments regarding the content of the community morality that are offered in support of it.

The positivist separation of law from morality is, for Dworkin, fundamentally untenable. Dworkin holds that judgments of political rights are a necessary condition for applying the law. This is dubbed the "rights thesis," which according to Dworkin is "that judicial decisions enforce existing political rights."[11] This does not mean, of course, that the political rights to be enforced by the judicial decision clearly appear on the face of the text of the "black letter law." What is meant is that the political rights are found in the political theory which will best justify, on the basis of some conception of political morality, the relevant settled law. Thus, common law, statutes, and the Constitution do not by themselves provide the answer as to what the political morality would consider to be an individual's right in a case. An apparent tension between "judicial originality" --- the focus of legal realists --- and "institutional history" --- the focus of legal positivists --- falls away for Dworkin because although "judges must make fresh judgments about the rights of the parties who came before them," nevertheless, "these political rights reflect, rather than oppose, political decisions of the past."[12]

Since the validity of a judicial decision is based upon the strengths of the arguments that support it, the subjective biases of individual judges are of no major significance for Dworkin. Moreover, even though judgments of political morality are involved in judicial decisions, judges have a political responsibility to conform to the various rules of institutional competence which shape their professional role. The legal traditions of the community provide the conditions of "fit," that is, judicial holdings must conform to the body of existing law, whatever may

---

[11]. *Id.* at 87.

[12]. *Id.*

be their ultimate "appeal," or reasoned justification, in the sense of conformity to principles of justice, fairness, and due process.

Law-as-Integrity (Later Dworkin)

In Dworkin's recent book, *Law's Empire*, law-as-integrity is presented with the following central tenets:

(I) Legal positivism (conventionalism) does not adequately justify "hard cases" because it (a) permits the exercise of extra-judicial discretion in their resolution; (b) mistakes theoretical questions of law for questions of "plain fact."

(II) Pragmatism (*e.g.*, the law-and-economics paradigm, legal realism) fundamentally misconstrues legal interpretation by denying that rights exist as such (although it concedes that sometimes judges speak "as if" individuals really had rights).

(III) Law is an interpretive concept; background legal concepts (*e.g.*, justice, fairness and due process) are also interpretive concepts that engender reasoned disagreement.

(IV) Legal interpretation is a "constructive" enterprise, analogous in its hermeneutical methods to literary and artistic interpretation.

(V) Integrity in legal interpretations is a mandate of an idealized "associative" political community "personified" (a "community of principle").

(VI) The idealized judge, Hercules, if committed to integrity, still tries to find the "one right answer" to hard cases. In justifying the best possible legal solution, Hercules employs "constructive interpretations of settled doctrine in an effort to render it consistent with the scheme of principle that are presupposed and endused by that body of doctrine."

Integrity Internationalized

Can one cogently speak of an international "community" whose commitment to human rights is justified by a principle of integrity? Dworkin's important insight that individuals might not agree about precisely what is required by justice, fairness, or due process (Tenet III *supra*) while still remaining bound by a community consensus embodied in their political institutions (Tenet V) is extendable to the global human rights context.

That there is an emerging transnational human rights "culture," as evidenced by proliferations of international guidelines and codes of conduct, is hard to deny. We may, however, expect continued disagreement about precisely what is required (and feasible) with respect to realizing human rights standards. Yet it seems reasonable to suppose that at least the outlines of a transnational community constituted by a shared allegiance to a core scheme of principles generated by human rights is currently in place. Dworkin speaks of an individual's obligations as having been instituted by a scheme of common principles which

> arise from the historical fact that his community has adopted that scheme, which is then special to it, not the assumption that he would have chosen it were the choice entirely his. In short, each accepts political integrity as a distinct political ideal and treats the general acceptance of that ideal, even among people who otherwise disagree about political morality, as constitutive of political community.[13]

In the international arena, so far as human rights obligations are concerned, not only individuals, but also corporations and nation-states are to be counted as members of a "political community" in this sense.

There are two central aspects to Dworkin's notion of integrity to be distinguished. The first aspect concerns the maintenance of consistency in both adjudication and legislation.[14] As Dworkin puts it:

> Integrity demands that the public standards of the community be both made and seen so far as this is possible, to express a single, coherent scheme of justice and fairness in the right relation. An institution that accepts that ideal will sometimes, for that reason, depart from a narrow line of past decisions in search of fidelity to principles conceived as more fundamental to the scheme as a whole.[15]

It is probably fair to say that this general view is largely consistent with the attitudes of lawyers, jurists, and scholars towards adjudications of international legal issues. Indeed, when international tribunals (such as the World Court at The Hague) adjudicate cases they explicitly endorse principles associated with the so-called "rule of law:" *stare decisis, pacta sunt servanda*, right of appeal, presumption of innocence,

---

[13]. *Law's Empire* at 211.

[14]. It is unclear what would be demanded of executive and administrative activities. Arguably consistency is mandatory for these as well, since both are in principle subject to judicial review.

[15]. *Law's Empire* at 219.

etc.. Many such legal principles are codified in international initiatives, such as those developed by the International Commission of Jurists.[16]

The second aspect of integrity relates to the existence of the community of principle. In Dworkin's words:

> Members of a society of principle accept that their political rights and duties are not exhausted by the particular decisions their political institutions have reached, but depend, more generally, on the scheme of principles those decisions presuppose and endorse.[17]

One notable consequence of taking such a view towards human rights standards would be that the textual expression (or "codification") of human rights norms does not itself provide a complete list of the relevant rights and duties of moral agents in the world community. That is, one could presumably point to a more abstract collection of background moral principles that are presupposed by the enterprise of interpreting human rights issues in particular cases. An authoritative declaration of a universal right not to be tortured, in other words, carries with it the supposition of a more general universal right to human dignity.

We may succinctly express the provisional framework established by appropriating the concept of law-as-integrity to the human rights context by reformulating the core tenets set out above as follows:

(I) *International conventionalism* (legal positivism) misconstrues the nature of human rights in international law as an exclusively factual matter.

(II) *International pragmatism* (legal realism, critical theory) misconstrues the nature of human rights in international law as fictions (i.e., "as if" assertions) constructed to serve ideological, political, and economic objectives, not as genuine rights (*i.e.*, trumps over a community's goals legitimated on grounds of principle).

(III) *The concept of human rights* is an interpretive concept. Concepts related to the implementation of human rights in institutional settings (e.g., international law, consensus, universality, jurisdiction, world community) are also interpretive concepts.

(IV) *Authoritative human rights interpretations* take place within a "constructive" (albeit objective) enterprise (like literary/artistic interpretation).

---

[16]. See, e.g., *The Rule of Law and Human Rights* (1966).

[17]. *Id.* at 211.

(V) *Integrity in human rights interpretation* is a mandate of an idealized "associative" *international community* "personified" (a global "community of principle").

(VI) *An idealized jurist* (I'll name this person Grotius) charged with interpreting human rights cases, if committed to integrity, will seek to find the best possible fit for established institutional material and political morality by employing "constructive interpretations" in the form of *justifying theories of human rights*.

Is Integrity's Concept of Law Too Narrow for a Cosmopolitan Model of Human Rights Adjudication?

In a key passage in *Law's Empire*, Dworkin renders an abstract account of the concept of law as the scheme of rights and responsibilities that licenses either the deployment or withholding of collective force, where such force is construed as governmental coercion on behalf of a single nation-state. This formulation of the concept of law (a) incorrectly binds the concept of law to the separate concept of coercion and (b) overrestricts that concept to the rights and responsibilities of single-nation communities. But many authoritative interpretations of international human rights do not directly involve the legitimation or constraint of coercion. Accordingly, Dworkin's canonical expression of the concept of law is too narrow for a cosmopolitan model of human rights adjudication. I suggest a modified formulation of the concept of law as the principled justification for authoritative conduct: policymaking, decisionmaking, and action (or forebearance) on behalf of officials of national and international communities. In an abstract sense, law consists of justifying theories of standards for official conduct, which may or may not ever be manifested as deployments of political force or coercion as such. Often legal norms are constituted, interpreted, applied in particular cases, and obeyed on a regular basis independent of utilizations of coercive mechanisms such as sanctions (*e.g.*, fines, incarceration, payment of damages). The logical connection between coercive force and law is a contingent, not a necessary one. My account of the concept of law better explains why the effective institution of and regular compliance with legal norms need not involve essential reference to official sanctions or governmental force at all. Moreover, the revised account lends greater cogency both to the notion of international law as a primary form or exemplar of law and to the nonpositivistic, "constructive natural law" conception of domestic law (the interpretive personification of a community) that Dworkin articulates in *Law's Empire*.

One might see the spirit of this analysis as analogous to, yet the inverse of, what Kelsen had in mind by his famous "pure" theory of law. Kelsen sought to render an (empirical) account of the nature of law --- viewed as a system of coercive norms --- apart from what he took to be the separate (nonempirical) phenomenon of a philosophy of justice. But the polarity of Kelsen's approach needs to be reversed and the voltage of Dworkin's decreased a bit. A philosophy of justice (theory of rights) is integral, not accessory, to law. And whereas coercion is undoubtedly a prominent and highly visible means of ensuring compliance with justified legal norms, it is in no way either the exclusive or the necessary method that the law provides for preserving and expanding its "empire" within a national community, between national communities, or on behalf of the world community.

Again, I would stress that the concept of law I am here defending is largely consistent with the sophisticated and detailed conception of law as an interpretive literary and rhetorical personification of a community that Dworkin puts forth in *Law's Empire*, and may be seen as ultimately helping to buttress the position that many positivistic approaches to law have both overstated the connection between law and coercion, and underestimated the predominantly legal character of international norms such as human rights.

Initially, it will be helpful to take a look at Dworkin's expression of the concept of law. Here is what he says:

> Governments have goals: they aim to make the nations they govern prosperous or powerful or religious or eminent; they also aim to remain in power. They use the collective force they monopolize to these and other ends. Our discussions about law by and large assume, I suggest, that the most abstract and fundamental point of legal practice is to guide and constrain the power of government in the following way. Law insists that force not be used or withheld, no matter how beneficial or noble these ends, except as licensed or required by individual rights and responsibilities flowing from past political decisions about when collective force is justified. The law of a community on this account is the scheme of rights and responsibilities that meet that complex standard: they license coercion because they flow from past decisions of the right sort. They are therefore "legal" rights and responsibilities.[18]

My contention is that this formulation --- which explicitly identifies law with rights and responsibilities that "license coercion" --- is

---

[18]. R. Dworkin, *Law's Empire* (1986) at 93.

misleading and underinclusive. It is misleading because it suggests that law is concerned only with state coercion. It is underinclusive because it ignores international law, which is instituted not by a single domestic community but by a variety of overlapping communities. Law concerns the ordering and legitimation of many variant social moral, and economic relations in a community, not just deployments (and suppressions) of political force *qua* coercion. The concept of law is captured better by the following modification:

Law is the principled justification (scheme of rights and responsibilities) that licenses authoritative conduct: policymaking, decisionmaking, and action (or forebearance) on behalf of the officials of national, international, and global communities.

One crucial way in which this reformulation is superior to Dworkin's phraseology is that it preserves the important "rule of law" facet, while also expanding the concept of law to include both key noncoercive aspects of domestic law and international law (institutionalized authority of the world community) as well. Suc noncoercive aspects would encompass familiar legal forms of social undering such as legislation, contract, mediation, arbitration, adjudication, and elections. An example will help illustrate the improvement achieved through such an expansion of conceptual scope.[19] Consider the problem of rendering a general concept of romantic love. One might express the concept abstractly as "affectionate relations between a man and a woman expressed in acts of sexual intercourse." Clearly, such a formulation includes what a lot of people deem central to romantic love. Yet it is equally clear that this account is much too narrow since it excludes platonic, homosexual, juvenile, and other significant types of romantic involvement between persons.[20]

---

[19]. I concede that it is controversial whether more expansive or less expansive formulations of general concepts are preferable. One is led to ask what we expect from an abstract depiction of the concept of law. Is the best formulation so expansive that it becomes overinclusive? Is it preferable to give a more restrictive account that borders on underinclusiveness? Or is some compromising midpoint between extremes the ideal (as it might be for the wording of a piece of legislation)?

[20]. A study of female same-sex platonic love relationships from the Sixteenth through the Twentieth centuries is given in L. Faderman, *Surpassing the Love of Men: Romantic Friendship and Love Between Women from the Renaissance to the Present* (1981).

The law-as-integrity conception lays great emphasis on the interpretive dimension of law, the idea of moral integrity in legislation and adjudication, and the notion of law as a personification of a "community of principle." Throughout *Law's Empire* the essential nature of legal interpretation is portrayed as a "constructive" endeavor analogous to projects of literary and artistic interpretation. One might naturally wonder why, given such an orientation, Dworkin includes the coercion element in the concept of law at all. I think at least part of the reason lies in a kind of intellectual *stare decisis* --- an effort to follow the tendency of modern theories of jurisprudence to stress the connection between law and force. After all, the liberal ideal of the "rule of law" involves the notion that law is a constraint on the illegitimate exercise of political power. However, while the rule of law may embody control on the exercise of power as an important function of law (it certainly has been historically significant, especially since the *ancien regime*), it is not obviously true that this is either the defining or the most salient characteristic of law as such. Of course, Dworkin's formulation of the concept of law in *Law's Empire* departs from positivist conceptions in many important respects. For instance, Dworkin's understanding of legal obligation as a genre of fraternal (associative) obligations, and his restatement of the rights thesis originally developed in *Taking Rights Seriously* is at odds with Austin's "command" thesis, Hart's "internal point of view" hypothesis, and Kelsen's "coercive system of norms" account. As such, it may be said in support of Dworkin that this is what we want from a concept of law: an "umbrella" concept that allows important theories of law to share at least something in common, in this case, the law-as-legitimate-coercion notion. That might be a worthy aim, but unfortunately to come under the positivist's conceptual tent is to perpetuate the mistake of placing the concept of law on the same plateau as the concept of a national legal system, with reference only to the centralized command mechanisms of the same. It may be (though I doubt it) that the concept of a legal system ought to include coercion as an essential element. The fact that most (though not all) legal norms are in principle capable of being backed up by the deployment of state force (*e.g.*, garnishment procedures, imprisonment) or that some of them require that the state not exercise its force in specific areas (*e.g.*, the establishment clause, constraints on privacy invasion) does tend to underscore the gravity of the authoritative decisionmaking process. Citizens do often have a lot at stake in legal outcomes. But the measure of practical importance of official conduct manifested as coercive force is ancillary to the question of its legitimacy. And not all material official conduct is expressed, or is even expressible, as coercive force.

It might be thought that Dworkin's formulation can be immunized from my attack if we stipulate that whatever the government does pursuant to law, whether it be policymaking, decisionmaking, symbolic display, and so on, is by definition either an exercise or withholding of the sort of "force" to which he alludes in the excerpt under discussion. The problem with this line of thought is that the "force" of law (scheme of rights and responsibilities) behind governmental conduct is much broader than the "licence for coercion" that Dworkin depicts. The force of law is ultimately authoritative force, yet it is highly nuanced. It encompasses not only brute forms of coercion (physical and economic sanction) but also complex forms of moral and psychological sanctions, as well as positive incentives and rewards. Law is often as effective through persuasive, symbolic, and recommendatory modes as through muscle flexing, though admittedly the former tend not to get as much press as the latter. It should also be noted that forms of coercion operable in legal contexts are themselves typically instrumentalities, not ends-in-themselves, aimed at attracting voluntary, peaceable compliance with norms and at promoting an attitude of respect for legitimate authority.

Another explanation for Dworkin's inclusion of the power element in the concept of law relates to the parochial nature of his theoretical focus. Dworkin's theory of law is fundamentally a theory of North American and British law. Yet it is not clear that the law of those two countries --- or for that matter national law in general --- ought to be considered paradigmatic of the concept of law.

International law is law too, after all. It ought to come within the purview of an abstract portrayal of the concept of law. Instead, it largely falls outside the scope of Dworkin's formulation due to the narrow "license for coercion" wording he employs.

The idea of law as a form of formal coercion implies that enforcement mechanisms are a key ingredient in any recipe for legal standards. However, the relatively less enforceable (and less enforced) character of international norms such as human rights does not diminish their legal status. As was argued in Chapter Two, legal positivists such as Austin, Hart, and Kelsen rather misleadingly portray domestic legal systems as paradigmatic of the concept of law, with the result that such theories tend to take exaggerated stances on the legal status of international law, including human rights standards.

One might object to my proposed reformulation of the concept of law by asserting that the sort of authoritative conduct involved in the enterprise of law is, if not proximately connected to single-state coercion, at least ultimately so tied. My response is that we need not strain so hard to make sure that all of what we count as legal affairs are completely traced to coercive sources. Here are just a few samples of law from everyday occurrences which illustrate that one may comprehend the principled justifications (structures of rights and responsibilities) for authoritative conduct at hand quite independently of any reference to coercion or force.

Examples:
(1)   Executive Order proclaiming "national mental health week." (The governmental "force" involved in this kind of directive is largely symbolic, not coercive. It is nevertheless a "legal" directive since it directs official conduct according to statute.)

(2)   Declaratory judgments in civil litigation proceedings.

(3)   Publication of violations of canons of professional responsibility by attorneys without imposition of jail time or fine. Note that the publication may still be viewed as a "sanction," yet it does not involve a deployment of force, except in a psychological sense.

(4)   Unenforced court judgments. (Such judicial decisions have legal force and effect, and may figure into future adjudications as precedential authority, yet no money need actually be exacted from the defendant as a prerequisite for this.)

(5)   Many features of a standard civil trial. (Granted, there are rules and procedures involving force at play on many levels, there are just as many levels at which force is irrelevant to the official decisionmaking process. Certainly, if the defendant or counsel disobeys directives of a trial judge, they may be sanctioned for contempt. But the overwhelmingly widespread noncontemptuous behavior of defendants and attorneys comes more from attitudes of respect, conformity, and social conditioning than as a direct response to state force.)

(6)   Opinions and judgments from the World Court, the Commission on Human Rights, and obligation-imposing initiatives promulgated by regionally- and globally-instituted bodies, such as the United Nations and its sub-entities.

The important point to be gleaned from these examples is that much of what we properly comprehend as law does not involve any essential connection to coercion or enforcement. It is hard to see how a judgment for a private citizen against the United States government under the Federal Tort Claims Act could be enforced if the government opted not to comply with the court order.[21] Moreover, a good deal of what we normally call law concerns the nonviolent, background facilitation of private arrangements such as commercial investments, contracts, powers of attorney, wills, negotiable instruments, and the like. These sorts of legal arrangements are governed by rules and principles complied with because they are either seen to impose genuine obligations or to produce mutually beneficial outcomes for affected parties, not out of a sense of being coerced by power-wielding officials.

Another objection might doubt that my references to international law are fair, since Dworkin's focus is exclusively on American and British (domestic) law. Accordingly, it might be thought that such domestic legal systems provide the most apt paradigms for the concept of law. The concept of international law, the argument would go, is but a weak facsimile of the concept of domestic law. But that would be a bad argument because it assumes a primacy for national law with no supporting rationale. The question of which is more basic --- national or international law --- reflects a deep "interpretive" issue (in Dworkin's sense). Kelsen expressed this conceptual problem well through his distinction between "pluralistic" and "monistic" construals of international law. The former theory holds that international law and national law are distinct and mutually independent orders regulating different subject matters and having separate sources (basic norms). The latter theory, however, deems the international legal order as itself authorizing various spheres of validity of national legal orders. For Kelsen, one embraces the monistic hypothesis (as a "free" matter of values and attitudes) if one intends to interpret international social, economic, and political relations as genuine legal relations.

Justifications of deployments of coercive force --- authorized violence on the part of a government --- or the withholding of such deployments are not the absolute telos of law. Violence and official responses to violence are undoubtedly on the rise in many contemporary societies and in the international community at large. It may be that the United States is an excessively legalistic culture in part because it is also a culture of warring political and economic factions which often require the use of coercion as an intermediary. But as a conceptual matter, it is simply wrong to exaggerate the link between law and coercive power as Dworkin's quoted passage does.

---

[21]. An argument to this effect is given by Anthony D'Amato in "Is International Law Really 'Law'?," 79 *Northwestern University Law Review* 1293 (1985).

Critical Legal Studies Versus Integrity

In a recent work, Andrew Altman has given an exceptionally clear analysis of recent critical legal studies (CLS) scholarship.[22] Professor Altman characterizes the CLS indictment of incoherence and contradiction against the liberal theory of law (the Anglo-American rule of law,) in terms of three central doctrines: the "patchwork" thesis, the "duck-rabbit" thesis, and the "truncation" thesis. Collectively, one might think of these three hypotheses as affording a means of examining alleged internal difficulties with the integrity model of law --- a way of mounting, as it were, a "Critique of Judicial Reason."

The "Patchwork" Hypothesis

According to the patchwork hypothesis, the prevalence of conflicts, gaps, and ambiguities in legal rules requires the deployment of general principles to "patch together" (*i.e.*, render consistent and coherent) the resultant imperfections in the fabric of legal doctrine. However, since principles remain indeterminate due to their generality, the patchwork thesis maintains that no "rational reconstruction" for legal doctrine so as to render it as consistently integrated by one moral outlook is possible. Hence, the high degree of indeterminacy about the law is criticized as unacceptable for liberal proponents of the "rule of law."[23] Moreover, the contradictions in legal doctrine embodied in its patchwork normative texture are grounded in "starkly incompatible ethical viewpoints,"[24] as reflected, for instance, in the extremes of "individualism" on the one hand and "altruism" on the other.[25]

The kind of international legal doctrine associated with human rights interpretations is susceptible to critique along the lines of the patchwork hypothesis. For instance, gaps in doctrine do occur when, say, one country ratifies human rights legislation while another does not. A recent instance of this was the United States' refusal to subscribe to the World Health Organization's infant formula code, which regulates marketing practices for breast milk substitutes in less developed countries, despite its acceptance by 118 other nations. Conflicts exist

---

[22]. A. Altman, *Critical Legal Studies: A Liberal Critique* (1990).

[23]. Altman, *Critical Legal Studies*, at 117-20.

[24]. *Id.* at 105.

[25]. *Id.* at 120.

when a single moral agent or legal personality (such as a multinational corporation) is faced with contradictory mandates depending on which country (home or host) it is operating in. A case involving Dresser Industries, a company based in the United States with a subsidiary in France, illustrates this situation. U.S. law imposed sanctions against subsidiaries of U.S. firms for selling equipment to the former Soviet Union for a gas pipeline from Siberia to Western Europe. French law, on the other hand, ordered Dresser of France to honor its contract to supply twenty-one gas compressors.[26]

Other instances involving conflicts require judgment concerning the respective weighing of opposing norms, such as the principle of *pacta sunt servanda* (*e.g.*, honor GATT obligations not to restrict trade) versus the principle of treatment as an equal (*e.g.*, honor Black South Africans' rights to freedom from apartheid by refusing to transact business with systematic rights-violators). The Comprehensive Anti-Apartheid Act of 1986 provided for trade sanctions against South Africa and against commercial transactions by U.S. nationals in that country. In addition Section 402 of the Act provided for special international trade law remedies.[27] However, had the President of the United States ever opted to enforce this section, say, against Japan (the dominant trader with South Africa after the Act was passed) such would conflict with well-settled international obligations with Japan imposed by GATT.

Ambiguities appear when human rights standards (for instance, those relating to "privacy," "fair conditions of employment," disclosure of "likely environmental harm") are broadly stated and hence amenable to differing interpretations, depending on ideological orientation, level of economic development, and the national legal environment of the host country.

The problem of uncertainty has a special significance in interpretations of international law. Where there is substantial uncertainty about the conventions of nation-states concerning, *e.g.*, the exercise of diplomatic asylum, courts will find that no custom exists upon to which to predicate a binding obligation. It should be noticed in this regard that the concept of uncertainty is a relative one, used to

---

[26]. *See*, G. Steiner and J. Steiner, *Business, Government, and Society: A Managerial Perspective* (5th ed., 1988) at 117-18.

[27]. "The President is authorized to limit the importation into the United States of any product or service of a foreign country to the extent to which such foreign country benefits from, or otherwise takes commercial advantage of, any sanction or prohibition imposed by or under this Act." 22 U.S.C. 5002.

distinguish binding custom from practices which do not have substantial uniformity.

The "Duck-Rabbit" Hypothesis

The "duck-rabbit"[28] hypothesis asserts that "the structure of legal doctrine can be organized in radically different ways, depending upon which of two incompatible ethical viewpoints (*e.g.*, individualism vs. altruism) one adopts."[29]

In "internationalizing" CLS critique, it is perhaps more accurate to identify the dominant tension between rival ethical traditions in the international human rights context not so much as a tug-of-war between the poles of individualism and altruism (as in the Kennedy and Unger works), but rather as a fundamental conflict between the standards of developed versus developing countries.[30]

For example, part of the debate surrounding the proposed United Nations Code of Conduct for Transnational Enterprises (which articulates a body of human rights standards for both nation-states and multinational corporations) is dominated by a conflict over the issue of whether international norms from the traditional conception of "international law" (*i.e.*, customary law of state responsibility) and from "international obligations" (*i.e.*, treaties, conventions, and agreements based on the express consent of the concerned states) --- which would supply background principles for resolving disputes (expropriation of alien property) --- would tend to favor the interests of developed market-economy countries, or the interests of developing countries. In general, developing nations tend to agree on the need to stimulate their economies by permitting free trade and private enterprise to flourish, but they are skeptical about the perceived ability of developed nations to manipulate "international law" to their own benefit, with a resultant prejudicial impact on less developed countries. The counterargument sometimes advanced by representatives of developed countries is that the sheer number of less developed countries gives them great ability to actively shape the evolution of international law to their benefit, and that the trend

---

[28]. The terminology follows Wittenstein's example. *See*, L. Wittgenstein, *Philosophical Investigations*, 3d ed., trans. G.E.M. Anscombe (1958) at 194.

[29]. Altman, *Critical Legal Studies* at 105.

[30]. The recent debates at the United Nations Environmental Summit are a notable example of this.

in emerging international law has been to accord developing countries increasing protection.[31]

Regardless of exactly how splits in international ideologies are described, it is clear that this form of CLS hypothesis has an important bearing in the global human rights context. Interpretations of human rights and their correlative duties can be construed in widely divergent ways, according to which of multiple possible legal, ethical, and cultural perspectives are taken. (This problem appears concretely in situations in which multinational companies operate in different host countries such as Japan, Saudi Arabia, Mexico, and so on.) Granted that a multinational firm has a *prima facie* duty to provide "fair conditions of employment," whose moral and legal standards, those of the home country (*e.g.*, the United States) or those of the host country (*e.g.*, Mexico) should be used in deciding whether a given employment policy or practice (*e.g.*, comparatively low wage rates in *maquiladoras*; extremely hot, unairconditioned assembly lines) is permissible? Members of a community living under a lower level of economic development will view the right to an adequate wage (entailed by the right to fair employment conditions) less stringently than members of an affluent community would.

International agents which would seek to take seriously human rights obligations instituted under a code of conduct would confront the following obstacle. Interpretations of human rights and their correlative duties can be construed in widely divergent ways, according to which of multiple possible legal, ethical, and cultural perspectives (reflected in the different host countries in which the firm is operating) are taken. Granted that a firm has a duty to provide "fair conditions of employment," whose standards, those of the home country or those of the host country, should be used in deciding whether a given employment policy or practice (*e.g.*, wage rates in *maquiladoras*) is permissible under the code? Obviously, a community living under a lower level of economic development will view the right to an adequate wage less stringently than an affluent community.

This situation may be characterized as an internationalized form of the duck-rabbit hypothesis in the following way. Whereas the domestic form of the duck-rabbit thesis deals with the question of which parts of legal doctrine are core and which are peripheral in interpretation, the international form of the thesis deals with the question of which standards

---

[31]. *See*, D.F. Vagts, "The Question of a Reference to International Obligations in the United Nations Code of Conduct on Transnational Corporations: A Different View," UNCTC Current Studies, Series A, no. 2 (1986).

(home or host) are applicable. Thus, saying that host country standards (lower wage rates permitted under Mexican law) prevail is one way of structuring existing doctrine (which consists of a universal human rights vocabulary --- "fair wages" --- yet realized in variant local standards) according to the ideological viewpoint of developed countries (this interpretation works to their own advantage). Whereas saying that home country standards (higher wage rates dictated by U.S. minimum wage laws) prevail is a say of structuring norms according to the ideological perspective of developing countries (this alternative interpretation redounds to their advantage).

Indeterminacy and Global Obligations

The concept of indeterminacy central to CLS critique is relative to some assumed degree of determinacy tied to a legal order and its decisionmaking institutions. But it is important to keep in mind that a globalized rule of law need not (though presumably it may) be as "strong" of a rule of law conception as that obtaining in classical views of national legal orders.

The closest thing I know of to a liberal account of international legal and moral responsibilities for MNCs in the "conventionalist" camp (to borrow Dworkin's term) is Thomas Donaldson's "moral minimum" theory. Donaldson's method handles indeterminacy in conflict of norm situations facing the MNC with an "ethical algorithm."[32]

---

[32]. The conflict situation arises when the MNC follows a practice that is legal/moral in the host country, yet illegal/immoral in the home country. The MNC might face strict EPA regulations for firms doing business in the U.S., yet also operate in a host country with relatively lax environmental standards. The ethical algorithm distinguishes Type 1 conflicts from Type 2 conflicts. In a Type 1 conflict, the lower level of economic development of the host country plays a role in the host's view that the practice is legally/morally permissible. For Type 2 conflicts, however, the moral reasons underlying the host's view that the practice is permissible are independent of the host's level of economic development. Instead, the moral reasons are grounded in religious or cultural values of the host country, for instance, those which condone nepotism, or low-level bribery, in some countries. If the conflict is Type 1, a "rational empathy" test is used by the multinational manager. Under this test, the practice is impermissible if members of the home country would not, under conditions of economic development relevantly similar to those of the host country, regard the practice as permissible. If, on the other hand, the conflict is Type 2, the practice is impermissible if either of the following are true: (1) it is possible to conduct business successfully in the host country without undertaking the practice; (2) the practice is a direct violation of a fundamental international human right. T.

Methodologically, the ethical algorithm resembles Hart's rule of recognition.[33] The interpreter (for Donaldson, the multinational corporate manager; for Hart, the municipal jurist) consults a master norm to remove uncertainty about what the relevant authoritative standards are.

As I see it, Donaldson's algorithm is a bit too crude as it stands, and needs modification in at least the following ways to render it compatible with an integrity framework: (i) an idealized jurist/moral philosopher ("Grotius;" not a multinational manager or executive) must be taken as the appropriate interpreter of "final appeal" for MNC obligations. Interpretations of obligations by the MNC itself will likely be self-serving, toeing pragmatist objectives of limited justification such as economic efficiency and maximization of wealth,[34] rather than staying in line with integrity's principles of justice, fairness, and due process. (ii) In conflict-of-norm situations, Grotius bases interpretations of rights and responsibilities not on a law-as-plain-fact-algorithm (international rule of recognition), but instead on (a) justifying theories[35] of international rights; that are (b) sensitive to *intra*national interpretive divergence, as well as the obvious *inter*national conflict of norm

---

Donaldson, *The Ethics of International Business* (1989).

[33]. For Hart, rules of recognition cure the defect of uncertainty attending primary rules of obligation. *The Concept of Law* (1961) However, it should be kept in mind that Hart denies that there is any rule of recognition for the international legal order. For a contrary view, see, D'Amato, "Is International Law Really 'Law'?," 79 *Northwestern University Law Review* 1293 (1985).

[34]. Far too many corporate executives and managers subscribe to Boddewyn's dictum that "law obedience is to a considerable extent a matter of costs and benefits."

[35]. Justifying theories, as I see them, are philosophically-based theories which aim to legitimate, *i.e.*, provide the best possible moral and legal justifications for, interpretations and applications of international rights that impose correlative obligations on individuals, nation-states, and other organizations such as corporations. Justifying theories provide a philosophical *ratio decidendi* for contemporary interpretations of international rights and responsibilities in institutional settings involving such variant forms of social ordering (Fuller's term) as adjudication, mediation, contract negotiation, and managerial direction.

situations; and which are (c) tied to conceptions from general moral theory, such as global distributive justice, sufficient to assess cost/affordability rationales involved with interpretations under both the "rational empathy" test (for Type 1 conflicts) and the "fundamental international rights" proviso (for Type 2 conflicts).

Consider whether a U.S.-based MNC is obligated not to discriminate against its employees on the basis of race when operating in countries where domestic folkways permit such practices. From a home perspective, the issue may be framed as a problem of interpreting whether Title VII of the Civil Rights Act applies extraterritorially. Prior to a recent U.S. Supreme Court opinion, there was a split of interpretations even within the U.S. (among various federal circuits; also the EEOC) on whether U.S.-based firms must follow the nondiscrimination requirements of the Act with regard to U.S. citizens working abroad. Donaldson's procedure wrongly assumes we can put our finger on a clear national home country norm that competes with a clear national host country norm. If such were the case, the only problem would be deciding which of the two extant national norms to prefer. But one could conclude, for instance, that although Title VII does not apply extraterritorially (the actual interpretation given by the Supreme Court in *Boureslan v. Aramco*), and that at least some identifiable host country norms (in Saudi Arabia) permit discrimination on the basis of race and gender, that nevertheless, an MNC is bound to respect an international human right to nondiscrimination which "trumps" any need to entertain interpretations flowing from the conflict-resolving algorithm.[36] This approach follows the lines of what Kelsen calls the "monistic," as opposed to the "pluralistic" interpretation of international law. For Kelsen, choosing between the two interpretations means postulating a basic "hypothesis of juristic thinking" that is a "free" (*i.e.* metascientific) matter of values and attitude.[37]

---

[36]. There may be conflicts with other international rights established by *e.g.*, bilateral treaties to be resolved. Thus, in *MacNamara v. Korean Air Lines*, the court held that the Friendship Commerce and Navigation Treaty (allowing a country's corporations to hire persons "of their choice" in another country) overrides Title VII of the Civil Rights Act and the Age Discrimination in Employment Act. 45 Fair Empl. Prac. Cas. (BNA) 384 (E.D. Pa. 1987), rev'd 48 Fair Empl. Prac. Cas. (BNA) 980 (3d Cir. 1988).

[37]. *See*, H. Kelsen, *Principles of International Law* at 587. Thus, for Kelsen, one accepts the monistic hypothesis (i.e., that the international legal order determines the territorial, personal, and temporal spheres of validity of various national legal systems; international legal order comprises a universal

Moreover, Grotius must refer to some background moral theory of distributive justice (apt to be controversial) in applying the "rational empathy" test part of the algorithm. Grotius needs guidance in deciding (even in the context of the home country) what rights need to be traded off when they compete with considerations of cost and affordability.

Grotius' Task

Interpretations of MNC obligations pose "patchwork" and "duck-rabbit" situations in the CLS sense. But the indeterminacy associated with such interpretations is not necessarily incompatible with an "integrity" conception of international law and ethics --- especially as regards institutional rights buttressed by authoritative corporate and international guidelines.

The cosmopolitan jurist, Grotius, seeks the best possible fit for institutional material and appeal to political morality by employing "constructive interpretations" geared to justifying theories for MNC obligations. Some key tasks of justifying theories are to indicate appropriate weighing (priority/"gravity" relative to other standards), scope delimitation (exceptions to application), "booting," (abstract, initial postulates for rights: "original position," "social contract," etc.) and entailment relationships (derivation of basic rights from assumed possession of other rights) for applicable international rights addressed to MNCs *qua* global moral agents. We may expect that Grotius' interpretation of rights and responsibilities in the face of conflicting and uncertain standards for MNCs must transcend conventionalist ("plain fact") international jurisprudence, embracing moral concepts and legal argument a good deal more sophisticated than any single ethical formula can definitively adjudicate.

A Decisionmaking Schemata for Conflicting Interpretations

Assuming that a global code of conduct specified a list of fundamental human rights and their correlative corporate obligations, situations would arise in which Grotius would be faced with following either the home country's interpretation of a right --- which might view a morally questionable practice as acceptable --- or the host country's interpretation of that right --- which might deem the same practice as unacceptable. Therefore, it might be desirable for such a code to also set

---

normative order) if one wishes to interpret international (social, political, economic) relations as legal relations.

out a decisionmaking schemata --- as an general canon of interpretation, not a rigid "rule of recognition" --- which could be used by Grotius to choose from among competing rights interpretations in duck-rabbit situations.

Again, from the perspective of the MNC's home country, applicable provisions of a human rights code, such as the right to a "livable environment" and the right to "physical security" might be interpreted as prohibiting certain practices (dumping of hazardous/toxic wastes; lax safety standards for factory workers). However, some would argue that the lower level of economic development of the LDC is a factor which lends justification to giving less weight to such rights than they would be accorded in the home country.

So, the critical question is whether lower levels of economic development justify business practices which would be interpreted as basic rights violations if undertaken in the company's home (*i.e.*, developed) country?

With respect to human rights standards for which the relative level of economic development is a factor in justifying theories that offer less stringent interpretations for such rights a code of conduct could provide a counterfactual test, or interpretive schema. An example of such a formula for Grotius to use as an interpretive aid is the following modification of the ethical algorithm:

Would community A, if situated under a hypothetically similar level of economic development, accept community B's justifying theory for the human rights obligation in question?

--If so, then the company based in community A should deem practices that would be permissible under community B's interpretation of the right as permissible within that jurisdiction.

--If not, then the practice should be deemed impermissible within that jurisdiction.

Example:
Lower wage rates paid to workers in *maquiladoras* (assembly plants) in Mexico are typically justified by U.S.-based firms on the grounds that, relative to the level of economic development of Mexico, they are fair. By U.S. standards, however, the wages would be considered exploitative.[38] It is commonly noted in this connection, that

---

[38]. *See, e.g.*, James Russell, "U.S. Sweatshops Across the Rio Grande," *Business and Society Review*, No. 50 (Summer 1987) 17-20.

the lower wages paid to Mexican workers are not prohibited by Mexican law. In determining whether a firm's rate of compensation violates the basic right to fair employment conditions, the interpretive scheme asks whether the U.S. community would consider the wage level violative of that right if situated in a level of economic development similar to that of the Mexican community.

It should be noted that the deployment of a conceptual tool such as the reformulated "ethical algorithm" above need not definitively settle particular disputes over what constitutes an acceptable minimum standard. In effect, this device works to shift dispute away from the question of whether host or home standards should apply *simplicitur* (under the actual facts of existing institutional arrangements) towards a counterfactual inquiry into whether members of the home country *would* find host standards acceptable under various hypothetical assumptions.

The Truncation Hypothesis and Corporate Duties to Aid in Less Developed Countries

The "truncation" hypothesis of CLS holds that "the principles that underlie legal rules are not consistently applied to all of the cases over which they claim moral authority but are truncated well short of the full range of cases over which they claim authority."[39]

In the domestic Anglo-American context, examples of such truncation typically cited are the following: constitutional theory's divisions between "strict scrutiny" (for racial classifications) and "intermediate scrutiny" (for gender classifications), common law rules denying legal duties to give aid to those with whom no statutory or contractual obligation exists.[40]

Briefly, Altman's rejoinder to the CLS truncation attack is that the truncation hypothesis squares with the kind of robust pluralism to which the liberal rule of law is committed.[41]

---

[39]. Altman, *Critical Legal Studies* at 105.

[40]. The common law rules have two exceptions. The defendant owes a duty to aid, even absent preexisting statutory or contractual duties if: (i) the defendant's actions helped create a perilous situation (*Montgomery v. National Convoy & Trucking Co.*, 195 S.E. 247 (1937)); or (ii) the plaintiff and the defendant are in a "special relationship" (*Tarasoff v. Regents of the University of California*, 551 P.2d 334 (1976)).

[41]. *Id.* at 147.

What are some instances of truncation in the international human rights context? Professor Donaldson's recent book on international business ethics provides a good example of a purported justification for truncation of a particular class of duties correlative to human rights --- the duty to aid, or "class (iii)" obligations[42] --- as concerns multinational corporations.[43] The issue somewhat parallels the familiar *domestic* legal/moral issue of the scope of the *individual's* duty to render aid to "strangers,[44]" as well as the classic *international* moral issue of the scope of duties to render aid to "distant peoples".[45] It will be helpful to critically examine the grounds asserted for this truncation, to see if the truncation hypothesis is compatible with the integrity paradigm for human rights.

Donaldson's claim runs as follows. Multinational corporations, as opposed to nation-states and individuals, do not in general have duties to aid those deprived of basic rights, except for two circumstances: (i) a corporation itself has caused the rights deprivation, (ii) "exceptional circumstances" exist.[46] In support of this contention, Donaldson argues (a) that corporations, unlike nation-states and individuals, are "economic animals" which have "limited economic missions;" (b) that considerations of "fairness" and "affordability" dictate that governments --- and not corporations --- bear responsibility for aiding those deprived of fundamental rights; and (c) that to the extent that corporations do have duties to aid the deprived, they represent "maximal" not "minimal" obligations. A minimal duty is construed as one which, if not honored, results in the loss of a corporation's "moral right to exist."

---

[42]. *See,* Chapter One, *supra,* "Duties Correlative to Human Rights."

[43]. T. Donaldson, *The Ethics of International Business* (1989) at 85. This view is shared by Richard DeGeorge. *See, Business Ethics* (3rd ed., 1990) at 434.

[44]. *See,* Feinberg, "The Moral and Legal Responsibility of the Bad Samaritan," in J. Feinberg & H. Gross, *Philosophy of Law* (4th ed., 1991), 579-91.

[45]. *See,* James, "The Duty to Relieve Suffering, 93 Ethics (October, 1982) 4-21; Singer, "Famine, Affluence and Morality 1 *Philosophy and Public Affairs* (1972) 229-43.

[46]. An example of such a circumstance would be the devastation of a host country by earthquake, and a company is capable of providing blood to victims, while a local government is not able to do so.

The "Limited Economic Mission" Rationale

One can see, however, how arguments might be advanced against the grounds Donaldson offers for truncation of duties to aid with respect to corporations. It is not clear, for instance, that corporations really are, in the relevant moral sense, limited economic agents with limited economic objectives. Thus, contrary to the view that the corporation is merely an economic entity, a popular article widely respected even in business circles, for instance, emphasizes the appropriateness of analogizing, for purposes of responsibility-ascription, the corporation to the individual in the sense that corporations evince both rationality and respect in their goal-setting and decision making capacities.[47] Moreover, in addition to supporting numerous charitable and humanitarian causes, many corporations routinely contribute to political election campaigns, form political action committees (PACs), provide honoraria to members of Congress and so on.[48] As such, they assume noneconomic roles as well as economic ones. A critic may retort that such noneconomic roles are ultimately taken on to further the corporation's special and paramount economic objectives such as generating profits for shareholders and investors, creating jobs for employees, and providing goods and services for consumers. However, the same charge could analogously be leveled at the frequently obsessive life goals of many materialistic people who seek to amass obscene personal fortunes. Surely it does not follow that upper-crust "yuppies" have managed to shed basic humanitarian responsibility for aiding others in virtue of their choice for a distorted priority of values.

The "Fairness-Affordability" Rationale

Further, saying that considerations such as "fairness" and "affordability" militate against holding corporations responsible for duties to aid does not resolve the deeper --- and key --- moral question of what one may objectively claim to be "fair" and "affordable" in particular cases in which we inquire about whether a duty to aid exists. Donaldson states flat out that

---

[47]. Goodpaster & Matthews, "Can a Corporation Have a Conscience," *Harvard Business Review* (January-Februrary, 1982).

[48]. *See*, M. Weidenbaum, *Business, Government, and the Public* (1990) 423-37.

[W]hile it would be strikingly generous for multinationals to sacrifice some of their profits to buy milk, grain, and shelter for persons in poor countries, it seems difficult to consider this one of their minimal moral requirements, since if anyone has such minimal obligations, it is the people's respective governments, or perhaps, better-off individuals. This is another way of saying that it is an unfair arrangement --- and hence would conflict with the fairness-affordability criteria to demand that multinational corporations, rather than national governments, shoulder such [type III] burdens.[49]

There are some underlying problems connected with the notions of fairness and affordability involved here that must be highlighted. Saying, for instance, that a multinational corporation cannot "afford" to help shelter the homeless, feed the hungry or perhaps simply encourage its legal department to handle *pro bono* cases for indigents in a country that systematically deprives human rights (as many firms have done on behalf of *apartheid* resistors in South Africa), or saying that it is "unfair" to ask them to undertake these sorts of actions, amount to controversial assertions. It is likely to be disputed, for instance, whether corporations are really morally obligated to engage directly in actions intended to decrease the incidence of disease, homelessness and malnutrition in countries in which they do business. Ought multinational firms become health care providers, erect houses and set up soup kitchens?[50]

However one comes out on such issues, there is something artificial and arbitrary, not to say disingenuous, about Donaldson's general disclaimer that obligations to render aid are not affordable for multinational enterprises as a class (absent causal involvement in rights deprivations and/or out-of-the-ordinary circumstances). Donaldson's general exemption of corporations from shouldering type III duties amounts to a shorthand way of collectively rendering conclusory judgments in advance of the kind of reflective casuistical deliberations that are needed to support meaningful decisions in many particularly hard and debatable cases. So what can be the point of assuming beforehand (as a general rule) that charitable obligations are not "affordable" for multinational enterprises as a class? Given the prevalence of poverty, chronic malnutrition, and inadequate health care throughout developing

---

[49]. Donaldson, *The Ethics of International Business* (1989) at 85.

[50] I am indebted to Professor Thomas White for raising this question in his commenting on a paper I delivered on this topic at the American Philosophical Association Pacific Division Meeting, April, 1993.

countries, it would be more accurate to describe the very real conditions that mandate international charitable duties as "the rule," rather than relegating them to the sort of hypothetical "exceptional conditions" Donaldson's model of truncation supposes them to be.

I should say at this point that I concur with George Brenkerts observation in a recent criticism of another argument from Donaldson's book that the concept of affordability ought to be replaced by a broader concept of capability that would encompass not only a corporation's financial resources but other non-monetary resources at its disposal as well.[51] Once this substitution is in place, the question in the present context arises: how much assistance can we reasonably expect a corporation to provide to those deprived of basic rights? Most would agree it is highly dubious to assert that a corporation alone must bear full responsibility for aiding the deprived. We expect governments and wealthy individuals to share that responsibility. Yet in many run-of-the-mill situations a poor host country's government (and similarly poor neighboring nation-states) are incapable of providing enough much needed aid, making corporations which profit from operations in the country or region plausible candidates for rendering assistance.

I emphasize that these circumstances are today all-too-ordinary and do not reflect the sort of "exceptional circumstances" Donaldson's model appears to contemplate. Of course, corporations cannot reasonably be expected to discharge duties of aid to the extent that they would manifestly lose a competitive advantage in their markets or be led into outright bankruptcy. (Obviously, we do not expect nation-states to go belly-up from giving humanitarian assistance either.) And I would caution that the claim that corporations have duties to aid should not be overblown into the much less plausible assertion that corporations must be blamed for not completely elevating all individuals deprived of basic rights to a completely deprivation-free existence. But all of this is not to say (as Donaldson does) that corporations do not have the type III duties in question. Instead, it is to allow that we would rightly excuse the corporation for not being capable of absolutely discharging those duties, given the host of other obligations owed to other stakeholders (shareholders, employees, customers, and so on) that it must satisfy as well.

In fact this is where an abstract Rawlsian-based justifying theory for human rights becomes useful. Such an approach provides a yardstick for the fairness--affordability criterion calibrated in terms of the

---

[51]. G. Brenkert, "Are International Human Rights Affordable?" *11 Journal of Business Ethics* 515-21 (1992).

background dimension of international distributive justice passed over by Donaldson's account.

Modifying the precise details of Rawl's specifications of the original position for present purposes, we may imagine individuals situated under an internationally encompassing veil of ignorance. That is, individuals do not know what nation they belong to; they do not know whether they are an employee in a maquiladora in Juarez, a CEO of a multinational corporation in Manhattan, or whether they are unemployed and without means of subsistence, perhaps even starving to death in Lima. Nor do they know the relative affluence or impoverishment of the country in which they live. The crucial point here is that they need to reach an agreement (under the supposition that they will make a rational choice in the face of uncertainty) on the principles that will govern the social, political, and economic relationships between individuals, nations, and other globally-active institutions --- including multinational corporations.

Importantly, the principles of justice thus derived need not be conceived of as dependent upon the presence of either conventional business practices or extant schemes of cooperation, centrality of operations, and sustained reciprocity among international agents --- even though the latter clearly exist to a limited degree amongst both governments and multinational firms. One may reasonably suppose that individuals in an international original position would accept a modification of Rawl's own version of the difference principle addressed not only to nations, but also to productive organizations that have reasonable capacities for distributing resources to less developed countries which would reduce human suffering. I would venture to postulate that the sort of vast economic inequalities obtaining as between, say, the holdings of a highly profitable business enterprise and the abject poverty of the inhabitants of a host underdeveloped country are justified only if they are reasonably expected to work to the advantage of the least advantaged. My argument is that a robust conception of the corporation's duty to aid the deprived as a *prima facie* obligation of distributive justice flows from the modified circumstances of the original position. As a *prima facie* obligation it may well be that in particular cases, considerations of cost will render it unfair to expect that a corporation will respect it. But one need not suppose beforehand that, as a general rule, considerations of cost and affordability necessarily would always be dispositive of the corporation's obligation to render humanitarian assistance from the perspective of contractors in the original position.

The Minimal-Maximal Distinction

In saying that I take the corporate duty to aid as a *prima facie* obligation of global distributive justice I must hasten to add that I do not intend to attribute (as Donaldson does) the special senses of "minimal" and "maximal" moral duties to the obligation to aid. The reason is simple: it is doubtful whether the notion of a corporation loosing its "moral right to exist" is sufficiently cogent to support drawing a bright line between "minimal" and "maximal" corporate obligations. (And frankly, if this kind of normative corporate "death" were to be the transcendental sanction for malfeasances of minimal moral duties, the modern corporation would either be extinct or else on the endangered species list in the noumenal world.) I assume that, like the related notion of the "social contract for business," the idea that corporations forfeit their moral right to exist by neglecting their minimal moral obligations is at bottom a heuristic device.[52] That being the case, I fail to see why, by simply redrawing the lines that divide minimal from maximal duties, this concept of an abstract moral sanction may not be deployed towards the advocacy to greater, rather than lesser, redistribution of economic and humanitarian assistance to the poor in less developed countries, who could be assisted at comparatively slight cost and effort to the corporate moral agent.[53]

Is Poverty an "Exceptional Circumstance"

Given the widespread poverty, chronic malnutrition, and lack of access to health care through out the hundreds of developing countries in which multinational businesses chart their markets, I doubt the cogency of the "exceptional circumstances" proviso for third-class corporate

---

[52]. *See*, Donaldson, "Social Contracts and Corporations: A Reply to Hodapp," 9 *Journal of Business Ethics* (February, 1990) 133-39.

[53]. It should be noted that in many civil law systems it is an actionable offence (for individuals) to fail to assist those in need of aid --- even strangers ---- unless rendering aid would imperil one's own life or well-being or would demand unreasonable cost or effort. *See*, J. Feinberg, "The Legal and Moral Responsibility of the Bad Samaritan," in J. Feinberg and H. Gross, *Philosophy of Law* (1987). And some have argued that the common law reluctance to legislate such a natural duty of aid is unwarranted and at odds with a principle of benevolence that undergirds common-law patterns found in, for instance, the law of contract. *See*, E. Weinrib, "The Case for a Duty to Rescue," *The Yale Law Journal*, Vol. 90 (1980).

duties. If unusually dire circumstances (Donaldson's example of earthquake victims) genuinely warrant the ascription of a corporate duty to aid as an exception to a general rule, regrettably, throughout most of the developing nations the situation is the reverse. The Donaldsonian exception ought therefore to be the rule.

Moreover, Donaldson's analysis of the "exceptional circumstances" prong of corporate third-class duties confuses the broad notion of a duty to aid the deprived with the much narrower sub-concept of a duty to rescue those temporarily in distress. This latter aspect of my argument can best be elaborated with the help of Henry Shue's distinctions between different categories of type III duties. According to Shue, type III duties include, first, obligations to aid those deprived of basic rights where the moral agent stands in a certain role or special relationship to the victim (*e.g.*, a nurse or lifeguard). These are called type III-1 duties. Second, there are obligations to aid stemming from the failures of social institutions to aid, termed type III-2 duties. Finally, Shue distinguishes obligations to aid those deprived of basic rights as a consequence of disasters, labeled type III-3 duties.[54]

Thus, the typical rescue situation involves a person or group of persons falling away from a *status quo*. A cyclone hits a village; a baby falls into an unguarded swimming pool. Normally, such situations are seen to give rise to what Henry Shue terms type III-3 duties to render aid to those deprived of basic rights as a consequence of some natural disaster. But whereas the rescue situation involves some antecedent enjoyment of a basic right which is deprived by a perious occurrence, duties to aid the deprived also arise in circumstances in which a person or group of persons may have never had a prior enjoyment of the basic right. The latter situations give rise to type III-1 duties (in which, according to Shue's construal, the duty to aid is tied to particular roles or relationships) and type III-2 duties (in which aid is needed due to deprivations resulting from social failures to perform type I and type II duties). What Donaldson's framework does not provide, however, is an acceptable principled basis --- which integrity would demand --- for drawing the bottom line for corporate dutes to aid at type III-3 duties to the exclusion of type III-1 and III-2 duties unless the narrowly drawn exceptions exist.

A couple of possible criticisms need to be considered at this point. First, some may object that it is just contrary to our common sense intuitions about the conventional roles of business to blame the profit-driven corporate entity for not giving up some of its revenues or

---

[54]. H. Shue, *Basic Rights: Subsistence, Affluence, and U.S. Foreign Policy* (1980).

resources for "charitable" purposes. Such critics ought to bear in mind not only the sobering fact that our common sense in moral matters is fallible and often in need of enlightened revision, but, in addition, that the corporate duty of aid is often a background norm intimately bound up with and presupposed by familiar direct legal duties of the corporation which are themselves widely accepted in the business community. This helps to explain why we would be especially justified in blaming the multinational corporation for unlawfully evading its fair share of taxes imposed on it by the government of a developing host country. The host government will have pro tanto less revenue available to assist its own indigent citizens in need of aid as a consequence of the corporation's delict.

Second, I expect that the aspect of my analysis most likely to upset those affiliated with international business enterprises is its apparent ideological bent in favor of the interests of the poor in developing countries at the expense of corporate wealth held in developed countries. In response I would refer opponents to a salient underlying feature of the internationalized original position: the hypothetical model directs one toward an honest and unbiased reflection on how one would opt to be treated were one's own social and economic circumstances to be reversed with, for instance, an inhabitant of a less developed host country confronted with scarcity, malnutrition, poverty, and so on. Thus, the goal here is to approach the philosophical ideals of political neutrality and moral universalizability rather than sanctifying the corporate quest for maximizing profits, power and advantage.

The central point which I hope has emerged from this discourse is that it is a controversial interpretive issue whether duties to aid are properly truncated along the lines advanced by Donaldson. Saying that class (iii) duties are truncated for multinational corporations but not for nation-states and individuals amounts to a *normative* ethical claim. Now, while that normative claim may well be true, as a *metaethical* matter, it is fair to say that cogent arguments can be given on both sides of this issue. According to Altman, the capacity for ongoing disputation over just how legal norms ought to be truncated is a strength of liberal legal theory rather than a deathblow to its vitality, as CLS critique would have it. (In fact, Altman disagrees with Dworkin's inference that one of the ultimate goals of law should be to "purge" all of its truncations.) So, Altman's (liberalist) response to the CLS truncation charge applies a fortiori to the human rights paradigm. Existing truncations in human rights theory represent the "front lines" of "internal" critique (matters debatable within the interpretive enterprise at hand, whether it be Anglo-American liberalism, or "globalized integrity") about the proper extension of background moral norms across institutional norms. It is more prudent to deem the issue of the scope of corporate duty to aid as a casuistical question dependent on specific contextual interpretation, instead of as a matter fit for the kind of rigid classificatory regime Donaldson proposes.

Integrity in the Widening Gyre

What is required to shore up the viability of the integrity model in the face of the CLS hypotheses is a demonstration that competing accounts of human rights doctrine remain compatible with the tenets of the international counterpart of liberal legal philosophy. Most likely, those who remain aligned with the CLS attack on liberal legal philosophy will be skeptical about the suggestion that the integrity model facilitates our understanding of human rights in their emerging institutional guise. I hope that, at a minimum, this chapter has indicated how part of the underlying tension that has developed between CLS and liberal jurisprudence may be mapped onto the global arena as a prolegomenon for further reflection in this field. The next chapter will attempt to lend greater detail to our inquiry by framing a set of more elaborate institutional contexts for human rights.

CHAPTER FIVE

INTERPRETIVE CONTEXTS FOR GLOBAL RESPONSIBILITIES

Introduction

The positivist analyses of the legality of international norms discussed in Chapter Two share a false assumption (which Dworkin dubs, in the municipal legal habitat, the "semantic sting") that the paramount object of a theory of law is to give criteria of meaning for the term 'law.' But the legal status of international human rights norms is indeterminate and uncertain. Attempts to give necessary and sufficient conditions for the concept of law, whether it be that of domestic, international, or human rights law, are of little help in answering puzzling yet pressing questions such as the following: How are the appropriate texts of various human rights identified by courts? What fixes the meaning of human rights in such texts? How do United States courts render interpretations about the weighing, scope and applicability of specific human rights in particular cases? What roles do international consensus and acceptance of human rights standards play in human rights adjudication? Are there any objective grounds for preferring one interpretation of human rights law to another in controversial cases? Answers to these sorts of questions simply cannot be deduced in an all-or-nothing fashion from general philosophical conclusions about whether international law really is or is not 'law.'

Likewise, the realist analyses of law harbored the mistaken hypothesis that law is merely a fiction relativized to moral and cultural values. The realists wrongly assume that all legal meaning is made up out of whole-cloth.

Thus, having rejected the positivist and realist portrayals of international law has cleared the air for inquiring into the above questions with a fresh conception of international human rights law. I will be setting the stage in this chapter for testing whether the law-as-integrity model is a satisfactory paradigm for the human rights obligations of nation-states, individuals, and multinational corporations. Since law-as-integrity addresses law as an interpretive concept which is pronounced by the United States judiciary, I will direct my attention in the first part of this chapter ("Adjudicative Contexts") to international human rights as norms in United States courts and in regional and international legal institutions. I will take an empirical approach here --- setting out the principles and rules governing judicial decisionmaking in several key international human rights cases.

The integrity model's approach to treating issues of legality as "interpretive" questions seems promising because so many of the central issues involved in contemporary human rights adjudication are highly controversial. They pose hard cases, to follow Dworkin's terminology. Integrity suggests that in resolving such hard cases, courts will be rendering decisions which will, as far as possible, fit with the relevant existing sources of law. Where the rules from such sources do not clearly dictate a result, integrity assumes that courts will fashion decisions with the assistance of general principles which are presupposed by, or which serve to justify, the extant institutional material.

Adjudicative Contexts

Initially, we will examine some significant human rights decisions of United States courts. An advantage of selecting domestic adjudications of human rights as an interpretive context for the present study is that the context places human rights squarely within the scope of the three central paradigms of legal philosophy (positivism, realism, and integrity) which are directed at the law of domestic courts. A further advantage of this context is that it facilitates discussion of human rights in a practical way by centering debates around real adjudicative issues which federal courts will be confronting with increasing frequency in future.

Human Rights Law in United States Courts

In the latter part of the twentieth century, significant portions of the Universal Declaration of Human Rights and other international human rights documents, have developed into both conventional and customary law binding, at least in principle, on all nations. Indeed, in the past decade or so in particular, United States courts have played a leading role in developing, and in some instances, enforcing, this body of international human rights law.

In article VI, section 2, the United States Constitution refers to international law by providing that "all Treaties made, or which shall be made, under the Authority of the United States, shall be the supreme Law of the Land; and the Judges in every State shall be bound thereby, any Thing in the Constitution or Laws of any State to the Contrary notwithstanding." Pursuant to this provision, the only one in the Constitution which addresses the relation of international law to municipal law in domestic courts, a self-executing treaty proclaimed by the President, or a non-self-executing treaty when implemented by Congress, will supersede all inconsistent state and local laws. In addition, under the so-called "last-in-time" rule, a self-executing treaty will supersede prior inconsistent federal laws.[1]

Although the other principal source of international law, customary international law, is not treated in the text of the Constitution, the Supreme Court has held that it is "part of our law, and must be ascertained and administered by the courts of justice of appropriate jurisdiction, as often as questions of right depending upon it are duly presented for their determination."[2] Since customary international law has the same status as treaty law it supersedes all inconsistent state and local laws and, theoretically, it supersedes prior inconsistent federal laws and international agreements. "[A]s in the case of treaties, American courts will give effect to the obligations of the United States under customary international law; at the behest of affected private parties, courts will prevent violations of international law by the States or by lower federal officials."[3]

The Evolution of Human Rights as Legal Standards

The idea that all human beings are entitled to at least some basic human rights stems from the traditional law of nations pertaining to State Responsibility for Injuries to Aliens. Eventually a body of law grew up around state practice and various arbitral decisions in the nineteenth and early twentieth centuries which bound all states to an "international minimum standard" of procedural and substantive justice with regard to the treatment of aliens. The "minimum standard" required that aliens be treated in accordance with ordinary standards of civilization, and was

---

[1]. *See, Asakure v. Seattle*, 265 U.S. 332 (1924); *Whitney v. Robertson*, 124 U.S. 190 (1888).

[2]. *The Paquete Habana*, 175 U.S. 677 at 700 (1900).

[3]. L. Henkin, *Foreign Affairs and the Constitution* (1972) at 223.

interposed by the United States to protect its own citizens overseas in cases involving extended imprisonment, arbitrary expulsion, and cruel and inhuman punishment.

In 1945 the United States signed the United Nations Charter, including the human rights provisions in articles 55 and 56, thus expanding the scope of its adherence to the "international minimum standard" for all human beings, instead of just for aliens. Moreover, by being a signatory to other international human rights documents including the Universal Declaration of Human Rights, the American Convention on Human Rights, and the United Nations Covenant on Civil and Political Rights, the United States made further commitments to the fundamental civil and political rights provided by those documents.

Regarding domestic interpretations and applications of international human rights norms as contained in human rights texts, it has only been in recent decades that United States courts have been deployed as part of customary or conventional international law.

Since the United Nations Charter was ratified by the United States government, it is the supreme law of the land. Article 1(3) of the Charter sets out as one of the United Nations central aims the attainment of cooperation among nations "in promoting and encouraging respect for human rights and for fundamental freedoms for all without distinction as to race, sex, language, or religion." According to article 55(c) the United Nations is obligated to advance "universal respect for, and observance of, human rights and fundamental freedoms for all without distinction as to race, sex, language or religion." And pursuant to article 56 the members of the United Nations "pledge themselves to take joint and separate action in cooperation with the Organization for the achievement of the purposes set forth in Article 55."

According to *Foster v. Nielson*, the legal status of such human rights provisions of the United Nations Charter in the domestic context depends on whether the provisions were intended by their authors to be self-executing.[4] In the words of a court which followed this approach, "[i]t is only when a treaty is self-executing, when it prescribes rules by which private rights may be determined, that it may be relied upon for the enforcement of such rights."[5] However, the *Nielson* approach, as with other such attempts to divine the actual framers' intent (this is discussed in more detail in the next chapter) is misled. Looking at the

---

[4]. 27 U.S. (2 Pet.) 253 (1829).

[5]. *See, Dreyfus v. Von Finck*, 534 F.2d 24 (2d Cir.), *cert. denied*, 429 U.S. 835 (1976).

documents of the San Francisco Conference which instituted the United Nations in 1945, one scholar notes that "[n]othing . . . indicates that the framers even considered the direct legal impact of the human rights clauses on the domestic law of the members."[6]

Consequently, it has been suggested that the intent of the parties to an international treaty is irrelevant to the issue of self-execution. As one commentator has said:

> The intent of the parties to an international treaty is relevant only to the question of whether private individuals shall have the right of protection in domestic courts against violations of a treaty provision. Whether this result is to be achieved by legislation or by the treaty itself is a question of constitutional law and not within the purview of the intent either of all parties to the treaty or of a particular ratifying power.[7]

American courts have ruled consistently that human rights clauses of the United Nations Charter are not self-executing. In *Sei Fujii v. California,* a part of the California Alien Land Law (which provided that land transferred to an alien ineligible for citizenship escheated to the state) was invalidated by the District Court of Appeals of California on the ground that it violated the nondiscrimination clauses of article 55(c) of the Charter.[8] This judgment was affirmed by the California Supreme Court, though on the basis that the state law was violative of the fourteenth amendment's equal protection clause. In dismissing the District Court's rationale, the Supreme Court noted that it saw noting in articles 55 and 56 that would show

> that these provisions were intended to become rules of law for the courts of this country upon the ratification of the Charter. The language used in Articles 55 and 56 is not the type customarily employed in treaties which have been held to be self-executing and to create rights and duties in individuals. . . . [Articles 55 and 56] lack the mandatory quality and definiteness which would indicate an intent to create justiciable rights in private persons immediately upon

---

[6]. Schluter, "The Domestic Status of the Human Rights Clauses of the United Nations Charter," 61 *Calif. L. Rev.* 110 (1973) at 130.

[7]. Riensenfeld, "The Doctrine of Self-Executing Treaties and U.S. v. Postal: Win at Any Price?," 74 *Am. J. Int'l L.* 892 (1980).

[8]. 217 P.2d 481 (1950), *aff'd*, 242 P.2d 617 (1952).

ratification. . . . The humane and enlightened objectives of the United Nations Charter are, of course, entitled to respectful consideration by the courts and legislatures of every member nation, since that document expresses the universal desire of thinking men for peace and for equality of rights and opportunities. The Charter represents a moral commitment of foremost importance, and we must not permit the spirit of our pledge to be compromised or disparaged in either our domestic or foreign affairs. We are satisfied, however, that the Charter provisions relied on by plaintiff were not intended to supersede existing domestic legislation, and we cannot hold that they operate to invalidate the alien land law.[9]

Other cases have indicated that the principle of nondiscrimination of article 55(c) is not a legal norm for domestic tribunals. Thus, in *Camacho v. Rogers*, a federal district court held that "the very wording of Article 55 shows that it is not intended to be self-executing."[10] Moreover, another district court in *Diggs v. Dent* stated that although the Charter places international duties on the United States government, it found that

> [T]reaties do not generally confer upon citizens rights which they may enforce in the courts. It is only when a treaty is "self-executing" that individuals derive enforceable rights from the treaty, without further legislative or executive action . . . . The provisions of the Charter for the United Nations are not self-executing and do not vest any of the plaintiffs with any legal rights which they may assert in this court.[11]

The *Diggs* ruling was affirmed by the United States Court of Appeals for the District of Columbia. That court held that any obligation placed on the United States by the Charter "does not confer rights on the citizens of the United States that are enforceable in court in the absence of implementing legislation."[12]

---

[9]. 242 P.2d 617 (1952) at 621-222.

[10]. 199 F. Supp. 155 (S.D.N.Y. 1961) at 158.

[11]. 555 F.2d 848 (D.C. Cir. 1976).

[12]. 555 F.2d at 850.

Criticism of Fujii and its Progeny

The "skeptical" approach to the legality of the human rights clauses of the United Nations Charter has come under attack by several writers. In addition, since the issues raised in *Fijii* have not been appealed to the United States Supreme Court, strictly speaking, it remains unsettled whether the Charter's human rights provisions are in fact self-executing.

I will now advance arguments against the various aspects of the excessively skeptical interpretation embodied in the *Fijii* opinion. The skeptical view, as has been shown, limits the construction of the human rights clauses in the Charter to the actual intent of the framers of the Charter. However, in actual practice, the judiciary typically does, and indeed often must, go beyond actual intent in construing, e.g., constitutional provisions. I will discuss this general "constructive" approach to legal interpretation in detail in Chapter Six. At present it should be noticed that one can plausibly analogize the domestic approach to the interpretation of constitutional law to the interpretation of international human rights law, and specifically with respect to the issue of interpreting self-executing rights provisions. This proposal is advanced in the following passage:

> Section 1 of the Fourteenth amendment . . . is "self- executing" in the sense that courts apply the Due Process clause or the Equal Protection clause without legislative implementation. But note, on the other hand, that Section 5 of that amendment gives Congress the power to enforce it "by appropriate legislation." that is, the same text at once constitutes applicable "law" upon which private parties may rely in litigation, and provides a basis for federal legislation.[13]

Another aspect of the skeptical position taken in *Fujii* is the claim that the human rights provisions of the Charter fail to constitute valid legal obligations for domestic courts because of their apparent vagueness and indefiniteness. But that objection cannot stand. The human rights provisions of the Charter are actually no more vague or indefinite than a host of well-established constitutional and statutory formulas which courts routinely apply. Perhaps more importantly, however, since the adoption of the Charter, a number of international human rights documents have arisen which give a good deal more content to articles 55 and 56. For example, the Universal Declaration of Human Rights embodies an extensive array of some very specific human rights the

---

[13]. H. Steiner & D. Vagts, *Transnational Legal Problems* (2d ed., 1976) at 584.

United Nations considers fundamental. In addition, the International Covenant on Civil and Political Rights has contributed significantly to an increasing international consensus concerning the concept of human rights.[14]

A further dimension of the *Fujii* approach which is suspect is its lumping together of all of the various human rights provisions in the Charter without regard for differences in degree of international consensus and support for the separate provisions. Thus, even if it were true that some of the provisions in articles 55 and 56 were so general as to not be self-executing, it simply does not follow that all such human rights norms share the same fate. The latter view is held by a number of legal scholars who, citing the Advisory Opinion of the International Court of Justice in the Namibia case, maintain that the nondiscrimination provision clause of article 55(c), at least, is generally binding on all states.

Should Fujii Be Overturned?

The continued viability of the *Fujii* case has been called into question by cases which suggest that the United States Supreme Court may in future overturn that decision. In *People of Saipan ex rel. Guerrero v. United States Department of Interior*, the 9th Circuit Court of Appeals formulated an alternative test for deciding whether a treaty is self-executing. *Guerrero* involved a challenge to the execution of a lease alleged to be violative of the United Nations Trusteeship Agreement Over Micronesia. Finding that the agreement afforded "judicially enforceable rights" the court stated that

> The extent to which an international agreement establishes affirmative and judicially enforceable obligations without implementing legislation must be determined in each case by reference to many contextual factors: the purposes of the treaty and the objectives of its creators, the existence of domestic procedures and institutions appropriate for direct implementation, the availability and feasibility of alternative enforcement methods, and the immediate and long-range social consequences of self- or non-self-execution.[15]

Pursuant to the *Guerrero* standard, it is certainly arguable that articles 55 and 56 are self-executing provisions. Even if determining the

---

[14]. *See*, Note, "Individual Enforcement of Obligations Arising Under the United Nations Charter," 19 *Santa Clara L. Rev.* 195 (1979) at 209.

[15]. 502 F.2d 90 (9th Cir., 1974) at 97.

actual intentions of the "creators" of the Charter *vis a vis* the issue of self-execution is futile, there are other indicia of the objectives of the Charter. For example, article 1(3) sets out as among the central purposes of the Charter that of "promoting and encouraging respect for human rights and for fundamental freedoms for all without distinction as to race, sex, language, or religion." Because the "alternative enforcement methods" referred to in the *Guerrero* test are not yet fully developed in the international arena, a failure of domestic courts to interpret the human rights clauses of the Charter as self-executing will likely allow the perpetuation of international human rights violations.

Another case which could eventually provide a grounding for a Supreme Court reversal of *Fujii* is *Diggs v. Shultz*,[16] which involved a challenge to the Byrd Amendment under United Nations Security Council Resolution 232. Although the Court of Appeals for the District of Columbia found that the Byrd Amendment prevailed under the "last-in-time" rule, it rejected the lower court's judgment that the plaintiffs lacked standing for the action. This ruling is significant in that it opens the way for plaintiffs to challenge, without dismissal for lack of standing, statutory violations of treaty obligations by the United States, and in so doing present test cases premised upon the theory of the self-executing nature of human rights provisions.

Customary International Human Rights Law

Traditionally, treaties have formed the dominant part of international human rights law. Nevertheless, customary law is becoming a significant factor in the development of international human rights norms. This is particularly noteworthy since customary law is binding on all states and not only the parties to an individual treaty, as some classical views held.

For example, Oppenheim maintained that conventions and treaties only establish contractual rights and duties for participating parties.[17] This "limited contract" view is premised on a peculiarly narrow conception of the legal effect of contracts.

But there are significant differences between standard municipal contracts and international treaties and conventions which make the restrictive contract view dubious. Municipal contracts are typically intended to the exclusive to the parties themselves. Do the signatories of human rights treaties intend its provisions to be limited only to

---

[16]. 470 F.2d 461 (D.C. Cir. 1972), *cert. denied*, 411 U.S. 931 (1973).

[17]. *See*, L.F.L. Oppenheim, *International Law: A Treatise*, (1955), Vol I at 28.

themselves? In the case of universalized human rights standards such a restrictive reading of the parties' intent would be seriously mistaken.

Another traditional view of international custom alleges that specific human rights provisions in treaties eventually "gel" into customary international law over time. A variant of this position adds the requirement that actual practices of nations in acquiescing to the provisions are needed as evidence of this gelling into customary law.

But what constitutes the sort of empirical evidence necessary for interpreting customary practice? The traditional norm-gelling approach cannot settle all issues in interpreting custom. Must actual violations of human rights provisions first occur and then be halted voluntarily by a non-signatory nation in deference to the treaty provisions for the gelling to become effective? Must the signatory nations make a demand on the non-signatory nation in accordance with the treaty provision? If so, then their demand would come from the treaty provision itself, in which case it already has antecedent legal effect, which is what the norm-gelling view denies.

A third approach holds that multilateral treaties and conventions "automatically" pass into international law since they are *ipso facto* customary law themselves binding on non-signatory nations. But if that is true, then controversy would still erupt in the process of interpreting those human rights provisions. Suppose a dispute arises about what the parties intended a provision in a convention to mean. Do they intend a human rights provision prohibiting acts of torture to be universally generalizable or do they intend it to be exclusive to themselves? Perhaps the plain meaning of the language in the provision is not dispositive. In that case the *travaux preparatoires* could be looked at to determine their intent. Positivists such as D'Amato think that the intent of the parties in such cases provides the rule of recognition for identifying what the law is. But a specific intent found in the *travaux preparatoires* may not cover all the issues raised in a difficult case either. In fact, a court might find that the best interpretation of a human rights provision requires disregarding the specific intentions of the parties altogether. It is hard to see how that kind of an interpretation of the law could be based on a rule of recognition.

In the law of the United States today, although customary international law is not referred to in the Constitution, it is the "law of the land" which must be interpreted and applied when appropriate for rendering a judicial decision.[18] The question of precisely which human rights are constitutive of customary international law is obviously of critical importance when domestic courts must render judgments on the basis of that law. The assertion that the Universal Declaration of Human Rights is a part of customary international law has been a continuous source of controversy. When the Declaration was adopted, the United States maintained that insofar as it was not a treaty, it did not establish international legal obligations.[19] A contrary view, however, has been gaining increasing allegiance among international legal commentators,[20] international resolutions,[21] and judicial opinions.[22] Perhaps one of the more ambitious claims that various portions of the Declaration evidence customary international human rights law was advanced before the International Court of Justice in the context of the Hostages Case. In its memorial, the United States discussed the existence of fundamental human rights norms in the international community as follows:

---

[18]. This doctrine was set out in The Paquete Habana, where the Supreme Court declared that customary international law is "part of our law, and must be ascertained and administered by the courts of justice of appropriate jurisdiction, as often as questions of right depending upon it are duly presented for their determination." 175 U.S. 677 (1900) at 700.

[19]. See, 3 U.N. GAOR 934, U.N. Doc. A/177 (1948).

[20]. See, Humphrey, "The International Bill of Rights: Scope and Implementation," 17 Wm. & Mary L. Rev. 527, 529 (1976). According to the author, the Universal Declaration of Human Rights constitutes "part of the customary law of nations and therefore is binding on all states. The Declaration has become what some nations wished it to be in 1948: the universally accepted interpretation and definition of the human rights left undefined by the Charter." Id. See also, Waldock, "Human Rights in Contemporary International Law and the Significance of the European Convention", in *The European Convention on Human Rights* 1, 15 (Brit. Inst. Int'l & Comp. L. Ser. No. 5, 1965).

[21]. The Montreal Statement, for example, proclaimed that the Declaration "has over the years become part of customary international law." Montreal Statement of the Assembly for Human Rights 2 (1968), reprinted in 9 J. Int'l Com. of Jurists 94, 95 (1968). In addition, the Proclamation of Teheran asserted that the Declaration "constitutes an obligation for members of the international community." Declaration of Teheran, Final Act of the International Conference on Human Rights 3, at 4, para. 2, 23 U.N. GAOR, U.N. Doc. A/CONF. 32/41 (1968).

[22]. See, Filartiga v. Pena-Irala, 630 F.2d at 882.

. . .[R]ecognition of the existence of certain fundamental human rights has spread throughout the international community. The existence of such fundamental rights for all human beings, nationals and aliens alike, and the existence of a corresponding duty on the part of every State to respect and observe them, are now reflected, inter alia, in the Charter of the United Nations, the Universal Declaration of Human Rights and corresponding portions of the International Covenant on Civil and Political Rights.

In view of the universal contemporary recognition that such fundamental human rights exist . . . Iran's obligation to provide "the most constant protection and security" to United States nationals in Iran includes an obligation to observe those rights.[23]

Although the doctrine of *The Paquete Habana* indicates that insofar as the Universal Declaration manifests customary international law it is, in principle, enforceable in domestic courts as the "law of the land," efforts to implement that law before 1980 typically were dismissed.[24] However, in 1980, the case of *Filartiga v. Pena-Irala*[25] broke new ground in the implementation of customary international human rights law in domestic courts.

Filartiga v. Pena-Irala and Its Progeny

Filartiga involved a wrongful death action based on acts of torture committed by the Inspector General of Police in Paraguay against Joelita Filartiga, a citizen of Paraguay. The United States Court of Appeals for

---

[23]. Memorial of the Government of the United States of America at 71, Case Concerning United States Diplomatic and Consular Staff in Tehran (U.S. v. Iran), 1980 I.C.J. 3. The memorial refers to articles 7, 9, 12, and 13 of the Declaration, and articles 7, 9, 10, and 12 of the United Nations Covenant on Civil and Political Rights as the universal fundamental human rights which every state must respect. The human rights included within these articles include the right to life, liberty and security of person; the prohibition of torture and cruel, inhuman or degrading treatment or punishment; the right to be treated with humanity during detention; the right to equality before the law and to nondiscrimination in its application; the prohibition of arbitrary arrest and detention; the right to privacy; and the right to freedom of movement.

[24]. *See*, e.g., *Jamnr Prods. Corp. v. Quill*, 51 Misc. 2d 501, 509-10, 273 N.Y.S. 2d 348, 356 (Sup. Ct. 1966).

[25]. 630 F.2d 876 (2d Cir. 1980).

the Second Circuit applied the Alien Tort Claims Act,[26] which gives federal courts jurisdiction of lawsuits by an alien in tort for violations of the law of nations.

The court construed the apposite tort as a violation of international human rights law rather than only the law of Paraguay. The court interpreted international law as establishing a right not to be tortured by officials of one's own government. Because the plaintiffs did not allege that their claim arose out of a treaty to which the United States was a party, the jurisdictional issue under the Alien Tort Claims Act involved whether torture is violative of the "law of nations," that is, customary international law. This interpretation included a finding of international consensus on the prohibition of torture sufficient to render the right not to be tortured a universalizable human rights norm. In relevant parts of its opinion, the court argued that "[t]orture is viewed with universal abhorrence; the prohibition of torture by international consensus and express international accords is clear and unambiguous; and 'for purposes of civil liability, the torturer has become --- like the pirate and the slave trader before him --- hostis humani generis, an enemy of all mankind.'"[27] In addition, the court stated that "[i]f the courts . . . are to adhere to the consensus of the community of humankind, any remedy they fashion must recognize that this case concerns an act so monstrous as to make its perpetrator an outlaw around the globe."[28]

Included in the sources of international law upon which the court based its decision was article 5 of the Universal Declaration. The Chief Judge indicated that the right to freedom from torture "has become part of customary international law, as evidenced and defined by the Universal Declaration . . . which states, in the plainest of terms, 'no one shall be subjected to torture.'"[29]

The *Filartiga* court did not refer to any ultimate empirical test of validity for international law in reaching its decision. Granted, the court initially looked to empirical textual sources of international and domestic law. The court noted, for instance, that torture was prohibited by the

---

[26]. 28 U.S.C. 1350. The Alien Tort Act dates back to the original Judiciary Act of 1798, and provides that "The district courts shall have original jurisdiction of any civil action by an alien for a tort only, committed in violation of the law of nations or a treaty of the United States."

[27]. 577 F.Supp. 860 at 863 (1984).

[28]. *Id.*

[29]. *Id.* at 882.

following legal documents: the Paraguayan Penal code, article 337; the American Convention on Human Rights, of which Paraguay was a signatory; and the Declaration on the Protection of All Persons from Being Subjected to Torture.

But the court had to justify its interpretation that the right not to be tortured, expressed in these texts, was a universalized legal right that would apply to a government's torture of one of its own nationals. In making this determination, the court did not, as D'Amato's thesis suggests, consult a rule of recognition for international law; rather, it advanced an interpretation about the scope of applicability of a specific human right based ultimately on a theory of international consensus about that norm.

It might be objected that the *Filartiga* court interpreted the right not to be tortured as universalizable on the basis of an empirical finding of international consensus for that proposition. This consensus, then, might be construed as just the sort of rule of recognition that I deny exists for settling human rights cases. But that would be a bad account of the meaning of the court's decision. The court did not consult a global Gallup poll. Indeed no such empirical test for international consensus could definitively resolve the matter. Questions such as the following would remain unanswered: How much international consensus would suffice? Would unanimity be required, or would a majority or a plurality consensus among nations do?[30]

Clearly, the *Filartiga* court's finding of consensus makes more sense as an authoritative interpretation of what international legal scholars term custom. But this claim seems to raise a new difficulty. For if I am right in claiming that custom fails as a rule of recognition for international human rights law, how is custom identified and what is its role in validating human rights interpretations? The specific character of this interpretive process will be elaborated in Chapters Six and Seven.

---

[30]. *Cf.* a parallel in Dworkin's writing, in the context of cases in statutory construction of domestic law, of what he terms the "speaker's intent" conception. Dworkin cites a number of cases in which a common problem haunts the conversational model of interpretation (discussed in Chapter 4). In the quest for an empirical discovery of the particular intentions of the authors of a statute (e.g., the Endangered Species Act in Tennessee Valley Authority v. Hill, 437 U.S. 153 (1978)), an impasse is met. Specifically, it is unclear just whose intentions --- the overall average, the majority, or a plurality --- of those voting for a bill must be consulted. Moreover, if the issue at bar is not covered by the text of the legislative history of the bill, one must ask hypothetically how the "author" (as established by one of the above formulas) *would have* resolved the issue if he or she had actually thought about it. The requisite empirical information will usually be absent or inconclusive. *Law's Empire* at 327.

Limitations on Filartiga

Filartiga is highly significant not only in its holding that torture is a violation of the customary international law of human rights, but in its engendering of other suits predicated on international human rights law.[31] However, cases decided after *Filartiga* indicate, as Chief Judge Kaufman himself advocated in a *New York Times* article, that the *Filartiga* ruling is limited in scope, and ought not to be taken as an authoritative determination that every human right contained in the Universal Declaration has become a part of customary international law actionable in United States courts.[32]

One limitation on the use of the law of customary international human rights arose from Fernandez v. Wilkinson, which involved an indirect application of that law in ascertaining a Cuban refugee's protection under domestic law.

Fernandez began with an I.N.S. determination that a member of the "freedom flotilla" from Cuba was ineligible for admission to the United States due to a past conviction of a crime involving moral turpitude. Pending the proceedings for Fernandez's deportation, he was detained in a federal penitentiary without bail and without having been charged with or convicted of a crime in the United States. Finding that such detention was a violation of "fundamental human justice as embodied in established

---

[85]. LaRue Tone Hosmer, "A Focus for Ethical Responsibility," in W. Michael Hoffman *et al*, (eds.) *Corporate Governance and Institutionalizing Ethics* (Lexington, MA: D.C. Heath, 1984) at 234.

principles of international law," a United States district court held, in the spirit of Filartiga, that

> Our review of the sources from which customary international law is derived clearly demonstrates that arbitrary detention is prohibited by customary international law. Therefore, even though the indeterminate detention of an excluded alien cannot be said to violate the United States Constitution or our statutory laws, it is judicially remedial as a violation of international law.

Accordingly, the *Fernandez* district court ruling employed customary international human rights law in order to further enhance rights existing under domestic law from federal statutes and the Constitution.

The Court of Appeals for the Tenth Circuit offered a somewhat different approach by interpreting the apposite federal statutory law to mandate termination of the alien's detention. As to the role of customary international law, the appellate court stated that the relevant federal statutory law was harmonious with the former in the sense that its construction of the statutory provisions was "consistent with accepted international law principles that individuals are entitled to be free of arbitrary imprisonment." Thus the court of appeals placed primary emphasis on its construal of domestic law, while acknowledging the "supporting" role of customary international human rights law in that construal.

Another case which represents a qualification of *Filartiga is In re Alien Children Education Litigation*, involving the right to free elementary school education. The case originated with a challenge to a Texas statute which withheld free primary education to children of undocumented aliens. The court noted that documents such as article 26(1) of the Universal Declaration, as well as like provisions in a number of international human rights sources, evince an emergent right to free elementary education in customary international law. However, the court found that at the present time such a right was merely an "important international goal" which fell short of acquiring the status of customary international law.

International Human Rights Standards as a Normative Interpretive Chart for Domestic Law

It is arguable that even if international human rights law is not "directly incorporated" into domestic law via self-execution of human rights clauses of the United Nations Charter and through rules of decision from customary international law, it is nevertheless "indirectly incorporated" in the sense that it assists courts in their normative exegesis of statutory and constitutional provisions. Thus, domestic courts sometimes look to international human rights law as a basis for normative argumentation against the validity of inconsistent state or federal laws, while denying that such incongruity per se is sufficient to automatically invalidate the domestic law.

This approach was taken in a concurrence to the United States Supreme Court decision in *Oyama v. California*, when it ruled that a provision of the California Alien Land Law was unconstitutional. Finding the state law violative of the fourteenth amendment, a pair of justices declared that the Alien Land Law's "inconsistency with the Charter, which has been duly ratified and adopted by the United States, is but one more reason why the statute must be condemned." In addition, various court opinions have alluded to the Universal Declaration in support of the position that economic and social rights ought to be expanded.[33]

Fundamental Human Rights Obligations of Multinational Corporations

In contrast to fundamental human rights such as freedom from torture, which are properly addressed to nation-states and individuals in the sense that they impose obligations on the addressee not to deprive the claimant of the right, there are a number of fundamental rights which are properly addressed directly to multinational corporations (though they are also addressed to nations). One of the most important of these rights in terms of evolving legal doctrine is the right to freedom from employment discrimination. The activities of both nations and corporations fall within the scope of this right: nations have the capability of ratifying and implementing legislation promoting respect for nondiscrimination in employment consistent with international law as articulated by the United Nations and the International Labor Organization; multinational corporations have the responsibility for formulating their employment practices when operating in host countries.[34]

---

[33]. *See, Copeland v. Secretary of State*, 226 F. Supp. 20, 31 n.16 (S.D.N.Y.), vacated and remanded, 378 U.S. 588 (1964); Pauley v. Kelley, 255 S.E.2d 859, 864 (W.Va. 1979).

[34]. Many countries have ratified and implemented bilateral Friendship Commerce and Navigation (FCN) treaty agreements. Such agreements allow a country's corporations to hire persons "of their choice" in another country.

Thus, an FCN treaty between the United States and South Korea gives foreign and U.S. companies reciprocal trade rights while operating in each other's countries. This includes a reciprocal right to fill its executive positions with persons "of their choice" without regard for domestic employment or labor laws. Thus, in *MacNamara v. Korean Air Lines*, the court held that the FCN Treaty overrides Title VII of the Civil Rights Act and the Age Discrimination in Employment Act, even when the foreign enterprise is present but not incorporated in the United States. In *MacNamara*, a United States citizen working for a Korean company's branch office in the United States filed suit against his foreign employer alleging age, national origin, and race discrimination in violation of the Age Discrimination in Employment Act of 1967 and Title VII of the Civil Rights Act of 1964. The employer moved for summary judgment on the ground that the employee failed to state a claim upon which relief could be granted. The Korean company's motion was based on its interpretation of Article VIII(1) of the Treaty of Friendship, Commerce and Navigation. The *MacNamara* court concluded that the plaintiff was an "executive within the meaning of the FCN Treaty" and that "engage" entitles a transnational employer to terminate employees. The court held that the "of their choice" language is "an absolute rule which confers on the treaty party an unconditional freedom of choice in the selection of certain personnel to manage the investment of the party in the host country."

In *Fernandez v. Wynn Oil Company* the court considered the issue of what legal rights American women have when working abroad for an American employer. Although the court did not resolve the issue of how women working abroad must be treated when applying for work overseas with American companies, the case shows how sex stereotypes and customer preferences may play a part in employment practices. That is, American corporations operating overseas often seek to adhere to the foreign standards of a host country in regard to employment practices.

In *Seville v. Martin Marietta Corporation*, the court held that American women employees hired in Germany by an American company may bring a sex discrimination action against their American employer. The women employees alleged that their employer's policy discriminated against women with regard to compensation, terms, conditions, and privileges of employment. The case is noteworthy because the court addressed the issue of the extraterritorial coverage of Title VII.

In *Boureslan v. Aramco*, the Fifth Circuit departed from an EEOC Policy Statement concerning the extraterritorial applicability of Title VII in cases involving discriminatory practices against U.S. citizens by foreign subsidiaries of U.S.-based firms.

In September, 1988, the United States Equal Opportunity Commission issued a clarification of its position on employment discrimination involving foreign and United States transnational firms. Before that time, the Commission had remained silent on the issue of how Title VII should be applied to cases like *Seville, Fernandez, Sumitomo Shoji,* and *MacNamara*. In its Policy Statement

The United Nations has declared that all nations should strive to achieve nondiscrimination in employment. And in the World Labor Report, issued by the International Labor Organization, the following recommendation was given:

> There are three major priority areas for action in the future: (1) women's work should be perceived in even more countries as an essential component of the development process; (2) special measures should be taken to ratify and implement under national legislation ILO and United Nations standards, especially on equal employment opportunities, equal pay for equal work, working conditions, job security and maternity protection; and (3) there is a need to formulate national policies to accelerate the creation of productive and equal employment opportunities for women so as

---

relating to discrimination in the international workplace, the EEOC stated that Title VII would apply to charges brought by U.S. citizens and other individuals in the U.S. charging discriminatory practices by a foreign or multinational corporation abroad. *See* Application of Title VII to American Companies Overseas, Their Subsidiaries and to Foreign Companies, EEOC Release No. 88-P-15 (September 2, 1988). The Boureslan court ruled against a U.S. citizen who brought an action under Title VII alleging that his company mounted a campaign of discrimination in the form of racial, religious, and ethnic insults. *Boureslan v. Aramco*, 857 F.2d 1014 (5th Cir. 1988). The Fifth Circuit rejected the view taken in *Bryant v. International School Services* (Bryant v. Int'l School Services, 502 F. Supp. 472 (D.N.J. 1980) *rev'd on other grounds*, 675 F.2d 562 (3d Cir. 1982)) and instead applied the presumption against extraterritoriality. In the Boureslan dissent, it was pointed out that the majority opinion leads to the inconsistent result that "one U.S. citizen assigned to [a foreign] office of a U.S. corporation, and another U.S. citizen working for the same company in [the United States] could experience identical acts of discrimination, but only the latter [would] have a remedy . . . ." 857 F.2d at 1027. The dissent offered an analysis of Title VII, principles of statutory construction, international law, and Sections 402 and 403 of the Restatement (Third) of the Foreign Relations Law of the United States to support its position that the presumption against extraterritoriality did not have to be applied in as stringent a manner as the majority held. The majority distorted the presumption, according to the dissent, by requiring "a more explicit statement by Congress that it intended Title VII to apply so broadly . . . . [N]ot every exercise of extraterritorial jurisdiction violates international law. . . ." *Id*. at 1022-23.

to enable them to participate more fully in economic growth and social progress.[35]

Provisional Analysis

This portion of the chapter has allowed me to develop an empirically-based interpretive context centered around adjudication which facilitates discussion of the legality of international human rights beyond the constraints imposed by traditional philosophical analyses.

A number of interpretive questions emerge from the foregoing exposition of international human rights law.

First, it was seen that as yet unresolved issues surrounding intent vis a vis the self-executing nature of the human rights provisions in the United Nations Charter will dictate how the judiciary --- in particular the United States Supreme Court --- will treat future cases.

Second, it remains to be seen how domestic courts will view customary international law in the wake of *Filartiga* and the post-*Filartiga* case law.

Thus, the nature and extent of the legality of international human rights norms, as interpreted by domestic courts, is a highly technical interpretive matter which is still being formulated by the judiciary.

Some Skeptical Objections

A number of objections might be raised against my exposition of the body of human rights adjudications so far. First, it might be argued that such judicial decisions represent an inappropriate attempt to use the rhetoric of human rights as a vehicle for resolving what are essentially international political matters, as a legal matter instead. A more appropriate response to alleged mistreatment of a foreign national by his or her own country would be through diplomacy or appeal to public opinion, such an objection might hold. Second, someone might object that this body of law at best is evidence of parochial norms which have legal effect only within the borders of the United States. Thus, such judicial decisions are in no way representative of international human rights law, much less of universal human rights norms. A third objection might claim that the parochial norms of other nations on similar cases involving similar issues might conflict with the decisions of U.S. courts.

---

[35]. United Nations International Labor Organization, World Labour Report. vol. 2 at 232 (1985). The ILO also issued statements regarding equality of opportunity in its "Tripartite Declaration of Principles Concerning Multinational Enterprises and Social Policy," 15 BN 92-2-101896-2 (1978) at 9.

The legal systems of other countries may not recognize the rights that U.S. courts declare to be human rights. The same may be said of an internationally-instituted tribunal charged with deciding human rights issues. It might reach different conclusions altogether about the substance of the human rights at issue. Thus, the overall integrity of human rights adjudication, when faced with the possibilities of such differing interpretations, is called into doubt. It is presumptuous, such an objection would point out, to think that the decisions of the courts of this country provide the "best answer" to all human rights issues. Why should we take them seriously at all?

Replies

I maintain that the above skeptical objections can be most suitably responded to within the framework of integrity's own division of "internal" and "external" skepticism. The internal/external analysis offered by the integrity model is especially appropriate for dealing with skeptical arguments addressed to the claims in the present study since the centerpiece of the study is the integrity model itself. According to Dworkin, internal skepticism in general is skepticism "*within* the enterprise of interpretation, as a substantive position about the best interpretation of some practice or work . . . " which "addresses the substance of the claims" to which it is opposed.[36] It "relies on the soundness of a general interpretive attitude to call into question all possible interpretations of a particular object of interpretation."[37]
External skepticism, on the other hand, is skepticism "*outside and about*" an interpretive enterprise. An external skeptic denies, for instance, that "moral values can be part of what he calls . . . the 'fabric' of the universe."[38] As applied to legal interpretation, external skepticism amounts to "a metaphysical theory, not an interpretive or moral position," which "insists that [interpretive claims] are not descriptions that can be proved or tested like physics" and that opinions about such claims "are projected upon, not discovered in, 'reality.'"[39]
Thus, the internal skeptic might challenge an ethical assertion such as "slavery is wrong" by disagreeing with specific arguments that might be

---

[36]. R. Dworkin, *Law's Empire* at 78.

[37]. *Id.*

[38]. *Id.* at 80.

[39]. *Id.*

advanced in support of such a moral position. One such argument might allege that slavery is not considered wrong everywhere, and attempt to back up that statement "by moral arguments of some kind, for example by appealing to a form of moral relativism that holds that true morality consists only in following the traditions of one's community."[40] Whereas external skepticism might challenge the assertion by simply denying that there is any objectivity to moral beliefs at all.

How does the distinction between internal and external skepticism bear on my claims about domestic interpretations of human rights norms? I would suggest that the three skeptical objections to the interpretations by United States courts brought up in the previous section may be understood as either internal or external varieties of critique. How they are to be replied to depends, in part, on which way they are understood. The precise delineation between an internal and an external skeptic may not always be present in respect to particular arguments, especially when the arguments are relatively complex. And it is at least conceivable that an argument advanced as a variety of internal skepticism can be recast as an example of external skepticism. Nevertheless, I take it that the distinction is a reasonably serviceable one for the purpose at hand. The counterpart to Dworkin's internal skeptic in regard to the interpretive context presented in this chapter might, in principle, accept the kind of enterprise of human rights interpretation that I have shown United States courts are increasingly committed to, yet seek to challenge the substance of the theoretical claims advanced by those courts by arguing that their account of human rights law is, in some specific and identifiable way, mistaken.

The counterpart to the external skeptic, on the other hand, would be adverse to any proposed interpretation of international human rights on the ground that, at best, such an interpretation will only express, say, the subjective ethical and cultural biases of the interpreter. To such a skeptic, the variety of different possible interpretive positions on human rights law represented by the world's legal systems indicates that no one of these interpretive positions could yield a superior account of that law. One popular version of an "external" objection is to charge that the judicial decisions of United States courts on human rights issues are ideologically biased. They are Western-liberal-industrialist and do not reflect the views of the majority of nations.

The integrity model clearly prefers internal to external critique, often treating the latter as inevitably giving rise to intellectual cul de

---

[40]. *Id.* at 82.

sacs, at least in the realm of legal and moral debate.[41] This preference may be viewed as both an important virtue --- and a vice --- of the integrity model. The advantage is that the resultant exchanges between Dworkin and his anticipated critics on the level of "insider" legal discourse are, as is usual for Dworkin, fruitful and illuminating. The disadvantage, however, is that any possibility of productive dialogue with the more "radical" segments of the intellectual community are foreclosed in a somewhat *a priori* fashion. Dworkin pays little heed to critical legal studies writers, neglecting a vast literature which seems to be fueled by precisely the kind of internal interpretive critique he himself recommends,[42] in favor of giving quick, trenchant stabs at only the most popular names associated with the movement.[43] It is beyond the scope of the present study to resolve the epistemological questions associated with opting for one or the other of these methodologies as a general practice for argumentation. Since this study seeks to explore the applicability of the integrity model to the human rights milieu, however, I will follow Dworkin's lead in taking the three skeptical objections as internal interpretive assertions, and respond to them accordingly.

Suppose we take the first skeptical objection to human rights decisionmaking by United States courts as a form of "internal" criticism. It would seem plausible to suppose that someone advancing an argument of that sort might generally accept the cogency of the enterprise of domestic legal interpretation, even as regards the interpretation of some human rights issues, yet be opposed to its deployment for what it takes to be "political" (or "foreign policy") matters rather than "legal" matters. Although the employment of this sort of vocabulary is too crude for legitimate legal argumentation, it is easy to translate the spirit of the first objection into the appropriate linguistic formulae for that purpose. Thus, the objection to domestic courts adjudicating international human rights violations can be rephrased as an objection premised on "lack of jurisdiction" or the "act-of-state" doctrine. "Internal" objections in this sense can be readily be found directly within the pleading of the litigants in human rights cases, and consequently also in the court opinions, when

---

[41]. *See, e.g.*, Dworkin at 83-86.

[42]. *See, e.g.*, the literature listed in "A Bibliography of Critical Legal Studies," 94 *Yale Law Journal* (1984) 461.

[43]. For a much more sympathetic effort at explaining and summarizing the salient theories of critical legal studies, see J. Boyle, "The Politics of Reason: Critical Legal Theory and Local Social Thought," 133 *University of Pennsylvania Law Review* (April, 1985) 685-780.

the challenges are ultimately ruled on. For instance, in *Trajano v. Marcos*,[44] a recent 9th Circuit decision which involved the consolidation of five cases claiming that Ferdinand Marcos and others committed international human rights violations by torturing, abducting, and killing the plaintiffs and their decedents, the defendants argued that the act-of-state doctrine constituted a complete defense to the suit. (This argument was initially accepted by the district court, which dismissed the action. However, the 9th Circuit reversed that dismissal.) In addition, the defendants argued that the original Congressional intent of the Alien Tort Claims Act was narrowly limited to grant domestic jurisdiction for actions by foreign dignitaries for assaults by United States citizens, not to establish jurisdiction for international human rights violations. However, the 9th Circuit rejected that construction, following the path taken by *Filartiga v. Pena-Irala* in upholding jurisdiction under the Act for human rights violations against aliens.

These two objections to international human rights adjudication by United States courts --- the act-of-state doctrine and the jurisdictional challenge --- are examples of internal skepticism in Dworkin's sense because they are based on arguments framed within the interpretive enterprise that genre of adjudication is premised upon, and advancing them reflects the notion which the account of legal practice they provide is a better one. The replies to such objections, which appear in the judicial opinions that justify the interpretations at hand, are effective (or ineffective as the case may be) to the extent that they reasonably meet the substance of the disputed point.

A good example of the second skeptical objection, which downplays the significance of domestic interpretations of international human rights relative to international contexts, on the grounds that they are mere parochial determinations, is found in an important article by Louis Henkin.[45] In reviewing the efforts of national courts in implementing human rights standards, Henkin states that "strictly there is no international law of human rights." Since international law ultimately depends on the judgments of domestic law, his argument continues, it is thereby reducible to the latter. But Henkin's argument confuses the employment of international legal procedures for the promotion and protection of human rights law (which he claims are defective) with the substantive law of international human rights itself, which may be

---

[44]. 878 F.2d 1439 (9th Cir., 1989; Unpublished Disposition, Text in Westlaw, No. 86-2448, 86-15039).

[45]. L. Henkin, "International Human Rights as 'Rights,'" 1 *Cardozo Law Review* 425 (1979).

interpreted by a variety of tribunals. What Henkin does not acknowledge is that the theoretical integrity of such interpretations is distinct from the question of their global political efficacy. An interpretation *of* international law need not ultimately result in an effective enforcement as a precondition to being deemed a statement of "law." The preceding chapter showed how such confusions about the concept of law can distort one's perspective on the legal status of international law. Moreover, to identify international law, in the subdued sense Henkin proposes, with domestic judgments raises the following problem. The domestic judgments of human rights he discusses are predicated on interpretations of a variety of human rights texts. Although the domestic courts employ a number of their own regional legal doctrines and background understandings, their interpretations are not entirely self-referential. Their human rights decisions are interpretations of international law, and the rights which are determined from those decisions have a distinctly international dimension: they are addressed to individuals and states of other nations, and the claimants of such rights are non-citizens, relative to the adjudicating body.

What I want to emphasize is that Henkin's objection does not amount to a condemnation of any claim I am advancing in this study. I would concede that domestic courts from other legal systems as well as internationally-constituted tribunals may propose different interpretations of international human rights law. In addition, I would grant that the decisions of United States courts on human rights issues are not necessarily binding on the addressees of those rights from the perspective of other legal systems. It is of course possible that other legal systems might accept the decisions as binding, however. Henkin's point is misleading since it supposes that the only "strictly" international human rights law would have to issue from, and be enforceable by, a court which was the adjudicative incarnation of a world order, representing a common juridic denominator of all of the world's legal systems. The fact that such a tribunal is nonexistent poses no more of a threat to the significance of regional interpretations of human rights law than the lack of a divine being does to the authority of secular moral codes.

An "internal" form of the third skeptical argument might be framed as follows. The possibility of conflicting interpretations arising from particular interpretations given by the courts of different legal systems indicates a lack of coherence for the concept of international human rights law. This objection may be answered with the observation that the mere existence of inconsistent rules of law (*e.g.*, between different states within the U.S.) in the area lawyers term "conflict of laws" does not remove the legality of such rules. It obviously does pose specialized problems for resolving the conflicts in particular cases of interstate adjudication, however. Typically, one or the other state's laws will be deemed controlling in specific cases according to general principles such as *lex loci delictus*, or *lex loci contractus*. The possibility of different legal interpretations which might result in effectively inconsistent judgments or pronouncements of human rights norms need not lead to skepticism about the integrity of individual interpretations of those norms.

Summary

It should be clear that my argument is *not* that United States court interpretations of international human rights are automatically entitled to be deemed legally binding norms in every conceivable corner of the world. It is no part of my thesis to maintain that human rights decisions of United States tribunals are to be considered the political equivalent of internationally-constituted adjudicators of the law of human rights in the sense discussed in Chapter One.[46] Rather, I am claiming that such interpretations have an objective theoretical content which is not vitiated by the regionally-based *pedigree* of its institutional context. (The theoretical underpinnings of the interpretations are contained within justifying theories of human rights, discussed in Chapter Eight, *infra*.) Obviously, any possible interpretation of human rights must be given on the basis of some particular set of background conceptions. It is the acceptability of the substantive theoretical claims of the interpretations which justifies or fails to justify those interpretations, not the self-proclaimed political credentials of the particular institutional authors of them.

Non-Adjudicative Contexts

In the preceding section of this chapter, two fundamental international human rights --- freedom from torture and freedom from employment discrimination --- were examined within the interpretive context of rights adjudication. The right to freedom from torture was taken as a paradigm illustration of a human right addressed primarily to nation-states (as well as to individuals in certain instances). The right to freedom from employment discrimination, on the other hand, was shown to be legitimately addressed, not only to nation-states (and individuals), but also to multinational corporations. This section will focus on nonadjudicative interpretive contexts involving human rights standards established by legislation, treaties, and transnational codes of conduct. Two specific human rights isolated for discussion in connection with such

---

[46]. *See* the section entitled "Human Rights and Civil Rights."

initiatives will be the right to nutrition (protected by, *inter alia*, the WHO Code on Marketing Breastmilk Substitutes) and the right to freedom from apartheid (protected by, *inter alia*, the United States' Comprehensive Anti-Apartheid Act of 1986). This interpretive context will accordingly serve as a complement to the previous one.

To support my claim that nonadjudicative legal contexts, including "informal" ones which involve interpretations of "voluntary" instruments such as codes of conduct, are integral to a theory of international human rights law, I will apply a number of concepts from the legal philosophy of Lon Fuller to the analysis. Unlike Dworkin, Fuller's philosophy of law incorporates an extremely wide range of institutional legal (and quasi-legal) sources in an effort to explain not only the substantive normative underpinnings of contemporary legal orders, but also the *procedural* dimensions of such orders.[47] Shifting attention to international legal process in this way is necessary to illuminate the way in which human rights standards are becoming integral to corporate and governmental responsibility in the global marketplace, even in the absence of judicial pronouncements of such rights in formal adjudicative proceedings. For example, consider the obligations imposed on a corporation by international codes pertaining to the transfer of hazardous technology. Although the codes themselves make no explicit reference to the notion of a fundamental human right, at least two basic human rights threatened by dangerous technology --- the right to a livable environment and the right to physical security --- are implicit in such international regulations.

Moreover, the Comprehensive Anti-Apartheid Act, which authorizes a variety of international trade remedies against transnational businesses as a means of enforcing the right to freedom from apartheid in South Africa, has not yet been the subject of formal adjudicative interpretation. Nevertheless, since the Act does establish a number of innovative legal rights and obligations in the international realm, in order to make sense of such a law it is necessary to consider the special interpretive issues surrounding its potential application outside of a formal adjudicative setting. A number of practical decisions facing international business actors, such as the decision by Japanese firms to sell computers to the South African police, have been influenced in part by their interpretations of the Act's apparent legitimacy (and, in some instances, illegitimacy) as an international human rights enforcement mechanism. Consequently,

---

[47]. In other general respects, however, the theories of Dworkin and Fuller are remarkably similar, at least in spirit and purpose. Both philosophers, for instance, are largely successful in their efforts to mediate between the extremes of legal positivism and legal realism.

the question of the normative justifiability of the Act must be addressed within the context of the various domestic and international legal obligations that bear on transnational business activities with systematic rights violators such as the government of South Africa.

Beyond the Institution of Adjudication: Law and the Different Forms of Social Ordering

Lon Fuller has indicated the dangers of associating the concept of law with only one particular form of social ordering, such as adjudication. In Fuller's mind, it is misleading to identify the concept of law with only one institutional mechanism, as many philosophers of law have done. Thus, John Chipman Grey proclaims that law is what the courts say it is, and in doing so, directs attention to adjudication as the essence of law. John Austin, on the other hand, identifies law with managerial direction and legislation in defining law as the command of the sovereign. Similarly, Savigny connects the concept of law with custom by suggesting that custom, as a reflection of the common consciousness of the community, constitutes the essence of a legal system. Finally, Rousseau, Locke, and Kant locate the essential nature of legal and political obligation in contract as a form of social ordering.

In Fuller's mind, law is a compilation of many different kinds of social ordering, such as *adjudication* (involving presentations of proofs and reasoned argumentation, impartial decisionmaking); *legislation* (involving voting directed at the formulation of and governing by rules, detached and impersonal regulation of individual behavior); *contract* (involving reciprocal bargaining and agreement); *mediation* (involving negotiations and compromise, settlement of conflicts), and *managerial control* (involving issuance of commands/orders, efficient hierarchical direction). In addition, Fuller describes how "mixed" forms of the above are sometimes involved in the legal process.[48]

Law-as-Process

Fuller criticizes the view that law can be adequately defined exclusively in terms of duties, powers, and entitlements.[49] In Fuller's

---

[48]. *See*, Fuller, "The Forms and Limits of Adjudication," in K. Winston, *The Principles of Social Order* (1981) 86-124.

[49]. The position that law consists of duties, powers, and entitlements is taken by Anthony D'Amato in "Lon Fuller and Substantive Natural Law," 26 *American Journal of Jurisprudence* 202 at 209 n.24.

thinking, this view misleadingly excludes the implicit elements of both the creation and interpretation of law --- what he terms the "inner morality" of law. For Fuller, there are "implicit laws of lawmaking" which exist as principles which must be adhered to in order to be successful in creating any sort of law whatsoever. Fuller's position, influenced by his emphasis on the "social aspects" of law, is developed as an attack on positivist methodology. His departure from positivism leads him to examine the nature of the legal process in the pragmatic spirit of such thinkers as John Dewey and G.H. Mead.[50]

The Implicit Laws of Law-Making

One of the most serious flaws of positivism, in Fuller's mind, is its blanket association of law with explicit, deliberately enacted legislation. Whereas the counter-tendency of legal realists to reduce the notion of law to custom or *Volksgeist*, he feels, is likewise mistaken. Taken by themselves, each of the two extreme positions --- law as conscious legislative enactment, and law as "spontaneously ordered" custom[51] only provide partial truths about the nature of law. To support this claim, Fuller distinguishes between "made law" and "implicit law."

The Aspirational Dimension of Law

As has been shown, Fuller's attention to the implicit aspects of law are a consequence of his depiction of law as a process rather than as a static set of rules. Such a perception of law as process also enables Fuller to reject the conventional doctrine subscribed to by both Kelsen and Dworkin (among others) that neither laws nor legal systems may partially exist.[52] By construing law, *qua* legal process, as an aspirational enterprise, Fuller is able to speak intelligibly about degrees of legality, as in the following passage:

---

[50]. *See*, R. Summers, "Professor Fuller's Jurisprudence and America's Dominant Philosophy of Law," 92 *Harvard Law Review* 433 (1978).

[51]. The legal sociologist Henri Levy-Bruhl appropriates the notions of the "collective conscience" of Emile Durkheim and the *Volksgeist* of F. von Savigny in his portrayal of law as a dynamic process. For Levy-Bruhl, law is a "product of the collective conscience." *See*, L. Fuller, *Anatomy of the Law* (1968) at 48.

[52]. *See*, H. Kelsen, General Theory of Law and State (1945); R. Dworkin, "Philosophy, Morality, and Law --- Observations Prompted by Professor Fuller's Novel Claim," 113 *University of Pennsylvania Law Review* 668 at 677 (1965).

A recognition that laws may vary in clarity would entail . . . that laws can have varying degrees of efficacy, that the unclear statute is, in a real sense, less a law than the clear one.[53]

Such a process-oriented approach to law permits one to claim that, given that the aspiration of a legal system is to attain justifiability or legitimacy, any given system of laws will be more or less successful in that effort. To attribute such an implied quest for legitimacy to the notion of a legal system represents a strong challenge to ever-present attempts to tie the concept of law exclusively to brute deployments of coercive power by the state.[54]

Interpreting Global Responsibilities in the Absence of Formal Adjudications of Human Rights Standards

Fuller's insights on the notion of law as a cluster of different forms of social ordering and their corresponding institutional mechanisms, together with his analysis of the process-related aspects of law are directly relevant to understanding global legal responsibility towards international human rights standards.

Fuller's analysis of law suggests that it is misleading to construe law as a set of preexisting rules. Such a narrow conception of law excludes the broader sense in which law, as manifested by the presence of administrative agencies, mediation panels, arbitration boards, and the like, is a process for making social policy.

The second implication of Fuller's view is that there is not a clear distinction between coercive obedience to law on the one hand, and voluntary choice on the other. This insight is expressed by Susan Foote (independently of any reference to Fuller) in the following passage:

> [t]he existence of law does not inevitably lead to coercion; nor does voluntary action occur only in its absence. For example, an institution may possess the legal authority to coerce but may choose not to exercise that power. A regulatory agency may

---

[53]. L. Fuller, *The Morality of Law* (1966).

[54]. *See*, R.C.L. Moffat, "The Perils of Positivism or Lon Fuller's Lesson on Looking at Law: Neither Science Nor Mystery --- Merely Method," 10 *Harvard Journal of Law and Public Policy* 295 at 342 (Spring, 1987). The author presents an interpretation of Fuller's process approach to law which locates it as a middle ground between positivism and "romanticism."

hesitate to act in the face of public mistrust or countervailing social pressures.[55]

Taking International Human Rights Codes Seriously

Looking at the non-adjudicative dimension of human rights standards must include a critical examination of the possibilities and limitations surrounding written human rights codes of conduct for governments and international business.[56] Such codes might be thought of as voluntary "Geneva conventions" for multinational moral agents. A confluence of the following trends indicates that the time may be ripe for seriously considering the development of such initiatives: (1) increasing demands for observance of human rights, especially in LDCs; (2) a movement towards institutionalization of business ethics;[57] (3) continued globalization of business; and (4) emphasis on what Sethi terms "proactive," or anticipatory strategic management with respect to international markets.[58] As regards the question of possibilities for human rights codes, I will first focus on some existing codes which either

---

[55]. S. Foote, "Corporate Responsibility in a Changing Legal Environment," in A.P. Iannone, Contemporary Moral Controversies in Business (1989).

[56]. The growing importance of international codes of conduct for multinational corporations is emphasized in the following passage by George Trisciuzzi:

> There is little likelihood that multinational enterprises will be subject to the authority of an international regulatory agency in the near future. A great amount of attention, however, is being paid to the establishment of codes of conduct [which] have been seen as an alternative means to constitute an international moral authority by agreements among governments and to provide guidelines for multinational business activities.

"Multilateral Regulation of Foreign Direct Investment," in B.S. Fisher & J. Turner, eds., *Regulating the Multinational Enterprise* (1983) at 147.

[57]. *See, e.g.*, W. Michael Hoffman, et al (eds.), *Corporate Governance and Institutionalizing Ethics: Proceedings of the Fifth National Conference on Business Ethics* (Lexington, MA: D.C. Heath, 1984).

[58] *See* Sethi, "A Conceptual Framework for Environmental Analysis of Social Issues and Evaluation of Business Response Patterns," in s.P. Sethi and C.M. Falbe, *Business and Society* (Lexington, MA: D.C. Heath, 1987), 39-52.

directly or indirectly prescribe a limited number of human rights standards for governments and for multinational enterprises. One notable task that human rights-related provisions in extant codes of conduct have accomplished is that of specifying various substantive duties of their addressees that are correlative to the human rights in question. Accordingly, I argue that future codes of conduct could play an important role in charting basic global responsibilities for international moral agents by bridging abstract and general human rights formulations (such as those contained in the U.N. Declaration, *e.g.*, the right to adequate nutrition) to specific and concrete corporate obligations (such as those delineated in the WHO Infant Formula Code, *e.g.*, restrictions on marketing breastmilk substitutes in LDCs).

On a somewhat broader level, such codes would be a means by which MNCs could indicate a commitment to a base-line "moral minimum," and also establish a "level playing field" which would reduce the competitive disadvantage currently borne by individual firms which opt to forego rights-violating practices. Finally, by subscribing to human rights codes of conduct, multinationals would be demonstrating a commitment to a "common discourse" (in Aristotle's sense[59]) as moral agents in the world community.

International Codes of Conduct[60] in General

There is a growing corpus of formalized standards and guidelines for nation-states and corporations in the international realm. Such

---

[59]. The term derives from Aristotle's reflections on the notion of a commonality existing amongst friends. For Aristotle, friendship, especially the political friendship associated with a *polis*, is constituted and maintained more by common discourse and thought than by consensus. See, *Nichomachean Ethics* 1170b 9-12.

[60]. The UN Group of Eminent Persons (which was established in 1972) defines "code of conduct" as

> a consistent set of recommendations which are gradually evolved and which may be revised as experience or circumstances require. Although they are not compulsory in character, they act as an instrument of moral persuasion, strengthened by the authority of international organization and the support of public opinion.

UN Department of Economic and Social Affairs, *The Impact of Multinational Corporations on Development and on Industrial Relations* (E/5500/Rev. 1 St/ESA/6) (1974) at 55.

initiatives range from guidelines developed by businesses and consumer groups,[61] to regimes undertaken by nation-states *inter se*,[62] to instruments developed jointly between business and government for regulating international commerce,[63] to instruments developed by various global organizations.[64]

Human Rights-Related Provisions in Existing Codes

Two important extant codes of conduct for MNCs from the perspective of human rights obligations are: (i) the Comprehensive Anti-Apartheid Act of 1986, and (ii) the World Health Organization's Code of Marketing for Breastmilk Substitutes.

(i) Freedom from Apartheid and the Comprehensive Anti-Apartheid Act

The purpose of the Comprehensive Anti-Apartheid Act of 1986 was "to set forth a comprehensive and complete framework to guide the efforts of the United States in helping to bring an end to apartheid in South Africa and to lead to the establishment of a nonracial, democratic form of government."[65] The Act provides for trade sanctions against South Africa and against commercial transactions by United States nationals in that country. The Act also addresses employment practices of United States firms. The statute states that Congress passed the legislation because it found apartheid "abhorrent and morally repugnant."[66]

---

[61]. *E.g.*, The Sullivan Principles, and the World Health Organization Code of Marketing Breast Milk Substitutes.

[62]. *E.g.*, The General Agreement on Tariffs and Trade (GATT).

[63]. *E.g.*, The European Community and Andean Common Market.

[64]. *E.g.*, The International Labor Organization's Tripartite Declaration of Principles Concerning Multinational Enterprises and Social Policy (1977), and the Organization for Economic Cooperation and Development's Declaration on International Investment and Multinational Enterprise (1976).

[65]. 22 U.S.C. s 5002 (Supp. IV 1986).

[66]. 22 U.S.C. s 5020(b) (Supp. IV 1986).

The Anti-Apartheid Act mandates that United States companies operating in South Africa actively oppose employment practices engendered by apartheid. Section 110(b) states that "it is the sense of Congress that United States employers operating in South Africa are obliged both generally to actively oppose the policy and practices of apartheid and specifically to engage in recruitment and training of Black and colored South Africans for management responsibilities."[67]

Another section of the Act states that employment practices of the United States Government in South Africa ought to operate as a model for the labor practices of United States nationals in South Africa.[68] Further, the Act provides for the enforcement of employment-related rights of United States citizens as well as foreign nationals working in South Africa. According to Section 5032(b):

The Secretary of State and any other head of a department or agency of the United States carrying out activities in South Africa shall promptly take, without regard to any provision of law, the necessary steps to ensure that the labor practices applied to the employment of services described in paragraphs (1) through (3) of subsection (a) of this section are governed by the Code of Conduct.[69]

Section 5035 is the Code of Conduct portion of the Act.[70] This

---

[67]. 22 U.S.C. s 5020(a)(1) (Supp. IV 1986).

[68]. 22 U.S.C. s 5032 (a) (Supp. IV 1986).

[69]. 22 U.S.C. s 5032(b) (Supp. IV 1986).

[70]. The Code of Conduct reads, in pertinent part, as follows:
(a) Principles; enumeration
(1) desegregating the races in each employment facility; (2) providing equal employment opportunity for all employees without regard to race or ethnic origin; (3) assuring that the pay system is applied to all employees without regard to race or ethnic origin; (4) establishing a minimum wage and salary level which takes into account the needs of employees and their families; (5) increasing by appropriate means the number of persons in managerial, supervisory, administrative, clerical, and technical jobs who are disadvantaged by the apartheid system for the purpose of significantly increasing their representation in such jobs; (6) taking reasonable steps to improve the quality of employees' lives outside the work environment with respect to housing, transportation, school, recreation, and health; and (7) implementing fair labor practices by recognizing the right of all employees, regardless of racial or other

section encourages firms to desegregate job facilities, establish a minimum wage, and promote affirmative action programs to increase the number of Black South Africans in various skilled or unskilled positions.[71]

Compared to domestic civil rights legislation such as Title VII of the Civil Rights Act of 1964, the Anti-Apartheid Act contains rather lax enforcement provisions. The 1986 Act provides that "United States businesses in South Africa which refuse to report on their progress in complying with the Sullivan Principles[72] (Code of Conduct) are subject to a $10,000 fine."[73] Section 5113(d) of the 1986 Act also limits its enforceability by stating that "[n]othing in this section may be construed to authorize the imposition of any penalty for failure to implement the Code of Conduct."[74]

Consequently, individual complainants of job discrimination are without significant legal remedies under the Anti-Apartheid Act. The Act

---

distinctions, freely and without penalty or reprisal, and recognizing the right to refrain from any such activity.

It is the sense of the Congress that in addition to the principles enumerated in subsection (a), nationals of the United States subject to this section should seek to comply with the following principle: taking reasonable measures to extend the scope of influence on activities outside the workplace, including -

(b) Principles for employer nationals of United States
(1) supporting the unrestricted rights of black businesses to locate in urban areas; (2) influencing other companies in South Africa to follow the standards of equal rights principles; (3) supporting the freedom of mobility of black workers to seek employment opportunities wherever they exist, and making provision for adequate housing for families of employees within the proximity of workers' employment; and (4) supporting the rescission of all apartheid laws.

---

[71]. *Id.* at 5035(a)(1), (4)-(5).

[72]. The Sullivan Principles, which were initially formulated, yet subsequently abandoned, by Reverend Leon Sullivan with the objective of promoting nonracist practices by U.S.-based MNCs in South Africa, included provisions requiring desegregation of employment facilities, elimination of discrimination against the rights of Blacks to form or belong to government-registered unions, and so on.

[73]. 22 U.S.C. 5113(d) (Supp. IV 1986).

[74]. 22 U.S.C. 5113 (d)(3) (Supp. IV 1986).

does not afford a legal basis upon which an individual or group may demand damages, nor does it address discriminatory practices associated with recruitment, assignment, and promotion. Moreover, the Act contains no mandatory scheduled reporting system which would promote voluntary compliance on behalf of United States firms. Accordingly, without the coercive threat of significant sanctions, some critics of the Anti-Apartheid Act doubt its efficacy in reducing the discriminatory effect that apartheid has on United States employment practices in South Africa.[75]

In addition to requiring that United States employers follow fair employment practices, the Anti-Apartheid Act restricts exports,[76] imports,[77] and finance and investments between the United States and South Africa.[78] Sections 402 and 403 of the Anti-Apartheid Act provide

---

[75]. *See, e.g.*, Comment, "United States Labor Practices in South Africa: Will a Mandatory Fair Employment Code Succeed Where the Sullivan Principles Have Failed?" 7 *Fordham International Law Journal* 359 (1984); *See also*, Schmidt, *Decoding Corporate Camouflage: U.S. Business Support for Apartheid* (1980).

[76]. Some examples of prohibited exports are computers, software, technology for the government's military, police, apartheid-enforcing agencies, and penal institutions. 22 U.S.C. 5054 (Supp. IV 1986). Other prohibited exports include items on the United States munitions list, 22 U.S.C. 5007; crude oil and petroleum products, 22 U.S.C. 5071; and nuclear materials and technology, 22 U.S.C. 507.

[77]. Examples of prohibited imports include: Krugarrands and other gold coins minted or offered for sale by the government of South Africa, 22 U.S.C. 5051; arms, ammunition and military vehicles, 22 U.S.C. 5052; articles grown, produced, manufactured by, marketed or otherwise exported by parastatal organizations (*e.g.*, corporations, partnerships, or other entities owned, controlled, or subsidized by the government) of the South African Government, 22 U.S.C. 5053; uranium ore, uranium oxide, coal, and textiles, 22 U.S.C. 5059; agricultural commodities, products, byproducts, or derivatives, ar articles suitable for human consumption that is a product of South Africa, 22 U.S.C. 5069; iron or steel, 22 U.S.C. 5070; and sugar and sugar products of South Africa, 22 U.S.C. 5073.

special international trade law remedies. Thus, Section 402 states that "[t]the President is authorized to limit the importation into the United States of any product or service of a foreign country to the extent to which such foreign country benefits from, or otherwise takes commercial advantage of, any sanction or prohibition imposed by or under this Act."[79] After the Act was passed, Japan became the dominant party in international trade with South Africa. However, the discretionary sanctions authorized by Section 402 were not invoked by the United States.

Another section of the Act, Section 403, creates a private civil right on behalf of United States nationals against individuals, partnerships, or corporations which take commercial advantage of, or otherwise benefit from, the restricted business activities of the United States national.[80] Though never effectively enforced, this portion of the Act permitted private United States parties to police the global marketplace for actions of foreign corporations which tend to support the rights-violating activity of the Government of South Africa.[81]

---

[79]. 22 U.S.C. 5002.

[80]. Section 403(a) states that:
Any national of the United States who is required by this chapter to terminate or curtail business activities in South Africa may bring a civil action for damages against any person, partnership, or corporation that takes commercial advantage or otherwise benefits from such termination or curtailment. 22 U.S.C. 5003(a) (Supp. IV 1986).
The cause of action must be maintained in the United States District Court for the District of Columbia or in the Court of International Trade. Successful plaintiffs may be awarded lost profits, costs of bringing the action, and attorney's fees. *See*, 22 U.S.C. 5003(b) (Supp. IV 1986).

[81]. The legislative history of Section 403 is expressed in the following passage:
U.S. firms may bring a private action for damages against any firm that takes commercial advantage of any sanction imposed by this Act. For example, if a U.S. company had been selling computers to an agency of the South African Government and was prohibited by this Act from continuing to sell computers, it could bring an action for lost profits against any foreign firm which deliberately intended to injure the U.S.

A key point that should be kept in mind concerning the relatively "defective" enforcement mechanisms of the Anti-apartheid Act is that its limited enforceability does not imply that the underlying international human right it seeks to protect from deprivation (*i.e.*, the right to freedom from apartheid) is not a high-priority institutional right.

(ii) The Right to Adequate Nutrition and the WHO Code of Conduct

The connection of the WHO Code, whose stated aim is "to provide safe and adequate nutrition for infants," to such basic human rights as the rights to adequate food, nutrition, and physical security, is evident from the text of the Code, which provides, in relevant part, that: "infant malnutrition is part of the wider problem of lack of education, poverty, and social injustice" and that "in view of the vulnerability of infants in the early months of life and the risks involved in inappropriate feeding practices, including the unnecessary and improper use of breastmilk substitutes, the marketing of breastmilk substitutes requires special treatment, which makes usual marketing practices unsuitable for these products."[82]

Beginning in the 1950s, and continuing thereafter for several decades, a number of companies (such as Nestle, Abbott Laboratories, Borden, Bristol-Myers, American Home Products) promoted the sale of infant formula to Third World countries. The companies perceived underdeveloped countries as potentially lucrative markets for restoring a decline in domestic sales. Many companies marketed infant formula through aggressive promotional campaigns which included (i) the provision of free promotional samples to new mothers, (ii) uniformed "milk nurses," who were actually sales representatives compensated by commission, advocating to new mothers the primacy of bottle feeding over breast feeding, (iii) billboards portraying plump, healthy babies next to the product, suggesting that formula fed babies are the healthiest.[83]

---

company by replacing it. The U.S. company is entitled to costs and attorney's fees if it prevails. S. Rep. No. 370, 99th Cong., 2d Sess., 132 Cong. Rec. S9890 (daily ed. July 30, 1986), reprinted in 1986 U.S. Code Cong. & Admin. News at 2350.

[82]. World Health Organization, *International Code of Marketing of Breastmilk Substitutes*.

[83]. The infant formula controversy is discussed in detail in R. Buchholz, et. al., *Management Response to Public Issues* (2d ed., 1989) 149-63.

Numerous problems were overlooked by the infant formula companies in marketing their product to the less developed countries. Some consumers were not able to read the instructions for properly mixing the formula and for sanitizing bottles and nipples. Many others overdiluted formula, due to the extremely high cost of the product relative to the consumers' budgets. Often the formula was mixed with impure water, and not adequately refrigerated. Such problems led to high incidences of infant diseases (such as gastroenteritis), malnutrition, and death.

A series of public and institutional pressures led the infant formula companies to "voluntarily" alter their marketing activities so as to effectively respect the right of nutrition of infants in less developed countries which was being deprived. The World Health Organization (WHO) and the United Nations Children's Fund (UNICEF) carried on a joint meeting concerning the problem of infant malnutrition, which was followed by meetings established under the aegis of the Protein Advisory Group (PAG), a United Nations entity. Shareholder resolutions were initiated at the companies' annual meetings, coordinated by organizations such as the Interfaith Council on Corporate Responsibility (ICCR). The Infant Formula Action Committee (INFACT) initiated a boycott of Nestle products in the U.S..

Nestle helped form the International Council of Infant Food Industries (ICIFI), a coalition of formula manufacturers, to institute self-regulating standards, which were eventually incorporated into a code of marketing ethics. Finally, in 1981, after being endorsed by the World Health Assembly, the WHO international code for marketing infant formula was adopted.[84]

Charting Global Institutional Human Rights

The rights discussed so far in this chapter represent but a few examples (somewhat arbitrarily selected) of human rights which have been instituted by international initiatives. Though not necessarily exhaustive, the following charts are intended to be illustrative of the range of textual sources of human rights, the extent of rights instituted within the global community, and the international forms of social ordering connected with their implementation and interpretation by legal institutions:

---

[84]. World Health Organization, *International Code of Marketing Breast-Milk Substitutes* (1981). The United States cast the only dissenting vote against the code.

Chart 1

TEXTUAL SOURCES OF HUMAN RIGHTS:

Universal Declaration of Human Rights
International Covenant on Civil and Political Rights
Optional Protocol to the International Covenant on Civil and Political Rights
International Convention on the Elimination of All Forms of Racial Discrimination
International Convention on the Suppression and Punishment of the Crime of Apartheid
Convention on the Elimination of All Forms of Discrimination Against Women
Convention on the Prevention and Punishment of the Crime of Genocide
Convention on the Non-Applicability of Statutory Limitations to War Crimes and Crimes Against Humanity
Slavery Convention of 1926
1953 Protocol Amending the 1926 Convention
Slavery Convention of 1926 as Amended
Supplementary Convention on the Abolition of Slavery, the Slave Trade, and Institutions and Practices Similar to Slavery
Convention for the Suppression of the Traffic in Persons and of the Exploitation of the Prostitution of Others
Convention Relating to the Status of Refugees
Protocol Relating to the Status of Refugees
Convention on the Reduction of Statelessness
Convention Relating to the Status of Stateless Persons
Convention on the International Right of Correction
Convention on the Nationality of Married Women
Convention on the Political Rights of Women
Convention on Consent to Marriage, Minimum Age for Marriage and Registration of Marriages
Convention Against Sexual Exploitation

Chart 2

INSTITUTIONAL HUMAN RIGHTS NORMS (PREINTERPRETIVE STAGE):

- --dignity
- --due process, fair trial, freedom from ex post facto laws, juridical personality
- --nondiscriminatory treatment
- --fair employment conditions
- --fair wages
- --physical security
- --livable (decent) environment
- --autonomy
- --privacy
- --adequate food and nutrition
- --basic education
- --ownership of property
- --freedom of speech, expression, thought, conscience, association, religion, political participation
- --freedom from arbitrary detention
- --freedom from slavery
- --freedom from torture and genocide
- --freedom from apartheid
- --freedom of movement
- --freedom from sexual exploitation

Chart 3

INTERNATIONAL FORMS OF SOCIAL ORDERING ASSOCIATED WITH THE IMPLEMENTATION AND INTERPRETATION OF HUMAN RIGHTS NORMS

FORM OF SOCIAL ORDERING

Adjudication
Example: *Filartiga*, et al

Legislation
Example: Anti-Apartheid Act; ILO Conventions; WHO Code

Contract
Example: International Convenant on Civil and Political Rights

Mediation
Example: EEOC conciliations

Managerial Direction
Example: ICIFI; advising boards of directors in response to shareholder resolutions (*e.g.*, disinvestment)

It is important for international moral agents to know (i) which among currently accepted human rights impose obligations on them, as opposed to other international moral agents, and (ii) the specific kind of obligations such rights impose on their activities so that they will be able to make decisions that will honor those normative burdens.

The basic human right of freedom from torture, appears to be properly addressed exclusively to nation-states and individuals since acts of torture are usually perpetrated by agents of governments seeking an efficient means of law enforcement. Similarly, there are a number of human rights which are rather obviously properly addressed directly to multinational corporations (though they are also addressed to nations and individuals). One such right is the right to freedom from employment discrimination. Whereas nations have the capability of ratifying and implementing legislation promoting respect for nondiscrimination in employment consistent with international law as articulated by the UN and the ILO, multinational corporations have the responsibility for formulating their employment practices when operating in host countries. The hiring and promotion practices of MNCs will have a significant part to play in the evolution of employment rights in the international workplace. They have the capability of either aggravating or alleviating employment discrimination worldwide.

Human rights codes of conduct, then, help to identify, in a systematic and comprehensive way, those fundamental rights which can cogently be said to be addressed to corporations in the obvious sense in which the right to nondiscrimination in employment is so addressed, and freedom from torture not.

My point is that there is often an important heuristic role played by codes of conduct in clarifying and delineating the ways that international agents might respect human rights standards.

Complexity of Ethical Interpretation

Even if human rights norms and correlative duties for MNCs are incorporated into codes of conduct, considerable interpretive uncertainty will surround questions of a firm's obligations in particular cases. The intractable complexity of ethical issues leads to the question of whether codes of conduct are an appropriate means for dealing with such problems. Thus, LaRue Hosner writes of codes of conduct in general that they

> are applicable only to the precise form of the ethical problem, with bilateral choices, deterministic outcomes, and clearly separated financial benefits and social costs. [The statement] '[S]earch for

qualified minorities . . .' cannot provide standard or approved responses for . . . complex issues . . . where there are multiple alternative, stochasic outcomes, and a jumbled mass of financial, social, and personal benefits and damages. . . . We probably will have to abandon codes of conduct as a guide to reaching complex ethical decisions.[85]

One response to this sort of skepticism about codes of conduct is that it may be demanding too much from them while, at the same time, ignoring their potential for improvement in providing more ethically sensitive and analytically rigorous decision-making methods. Given the complexity of ethical decisionmaking in domestic contexts, which is even more aggravated in international settings, MNCs and governments may need to change prevailing methods of information acquisition and processing in order to assimilate the ethically relevant data that serious and well-intentioned compliance with basic human rights standards requires.

Enforceability

Another limitation that should be considered is that of enforceability. There is considerable controversy surrounding the issue of whether international standards in general are sufficiently enforceable. In the absence of effective sanctions, it may be difficult to achieve the desired compliance from corporate signatories. One notable example from the previous decade was the U.S. reaction to the World Court's authority over the Nicaragua case.

A related issue concerns whether human rights guidelines addressed to multinational corporations would institute genuine legal obligations or simply moral obligations. To reiterate a couple of important points brought out previously in Chapter Two, effective compliance with international norms need not be the result of a fear of a sanction or out of respect for a centralized authority. Moreover, much of what we commonly term "law" in everyday domestic contexts is obeyed because it is seen to impose genuine obligations, not entirely out of a sense of being obliged to a superior authority with a capacity for imposing sanctions.

---

[85]. LaRue Tone Hosmer, "A Focus for Ethical Responsibility," in W. Michael Hoffman *et al*, (eds.) *Corporate Governance and Institutionalizing Ethics* (Lexington, MA: D.C. Heath, 1984) at 234.

CHAPTER SIX

INTERPRETING HUMAN RIGHTS TEXTS

Human Rights Texts

As demonstrated in Chapter Five, human rights texts form a cornerstone of human rights law by providing a rudimentary empirical criterion for identifying human rights as a prelude to their interpretation and application to particular cases. Further, as I have shown, this holds both in adjudicative contexts (involving court decisions) and nonadjudicative contexts (involving domestic legislation and globally-based initiatives).

This is not to say that every publication of a human right in an international document is *prima facie* a valid legal right. Rather, my argument is that conjectures about the validity of human rights are the most cogent when addressed at the level of authoritative interpretations predicated on justifying theories. In many circumstances, a strong case can be made that a textual expression of a human rights standard is a *prima facie* valid legal right. The most common method for nations to establish human rights standards *inter se* is through the formation of international documents such as treaties and conventions. These agreements sometimes create highly specific and well-defined rights and obligations between the ratifying members.

The bulk of international declarations, treaties, and conventions also contain generalizable provisions which require, in many cases, elaborate interpretation to determine their applicability to nonsignatory nations and to factual circumstances not specified in the language of the documents.

A significant degree of interpretation is also involved in deciding which, and to what extent, human rights legitimately impose obligations on nonstandard addressees of the rights, such as corporations and individuals. For example, although the United Nations Charter states that all member nations shall promote basic freedoms without discrimination as to race, sex, language, or religion, it is plausible to view the human right to freedom from discrimination --- particularly in employment --- as properly addressed to corporations doing business in the member states.[1]

Human rights texts often appeal to the abstract ideal of global moral progress. The Universal Declaration of Human Rights, for instance, proposes "a common standard of achievement for all peoples and all nations" and states that "all human beings are born free and equal in dignity and rights." In addition, many specific, and sometimes highly refined rights are listed throughout such documents. The following civil and political rights are illustrative: freedom from discrimination, torture, cruel and unusual punishment, arbitrary arrest; freedom of thought, assembly, religion, association, privacy, movement.[2]

Levels of Human Rights Texts

One might conceptualize levels of abstractness and generality of human rights provisions as arrayed on a vertical line. The top represents

---

[1]. Of course, some international texts explicitly reference corporations as bearing obligations in regard to human rights. The International Labor Organization, for instance, in an effort to promote the right to freedom from apartheid, recommends that transnational employers, together with nations, "cease all co-operation with South African authorities in the implementation of apartheid legislation" having an effect on the employment of Black South Africans. United Nations International Labor Organization, World Labor Report, vol. 2 (1985). *See also,* "ILO Conference Invites Governments, Employers & Workers to Strengthen Action Against Apartheid," Press Release, June 20, 1985.

[2]. *See, International Covenant on Civil and Political Rights,* U.N.G.A. Res. 2200 (XXI), 21 U.N. GAOR, Supp. (No. 16) 52, U.N. Doc A/6316 (1967), reprinted in 6 I.L.M. 368 (1967). Indeed, there is a sense in which the Universal Declaration and the Covenant on Civil and Political Rights are superior to, e.g., the United States Constitution as rights-granting textual instruments, since the Constitution itself has comparatively little "rights language" explicitly in it. For example, there is not statement of the right to be free from torture in the Constitution. Nor does the Constitution explicitly mention (as does the International Covenant) the right to travel, the presumption of innocence, the right to marry a person of one's choice.

the most abstract and general level of human rights terminology and extends down to more concrete and specific levels. On the highest level, a human right might be formulated as the right to dignity. Moving down the line the right to freedom from cruel and unusual punishment may be formulated as a more specific right which is "entailed" by the more abstract right to dignity in the sense that the prohibition of cruel and unusual punishment presupposes the right of dignity; further down the right to freedom from torture (*i.e.*, taken for purposes of this example as one specific form of "cruel and unusual punishment") is formulated, and so on. Such textual formulations of human rights, considered apart from juridic interpretations in accordance with justifying theories, do not contain on their face detailed specifications of their weighing, scope, applicability, exceptions and restrictions, and so on. Nor do they come equipped with recipes for implementation in specific cases. Thus, we may distinguish the "pre-theoretical" formulation of a human right in a declaration or convention from the "theoretical" statement of a human right in a juridic interpretation.

It should be noticed, however, that the terms "pre-theoretical" and "theoretical" as I am using them are only distinguishable by degree. A substantial amount of background legal and moral theory permeates the vocabulary of even the simplest formulations of human rights. Similarly, discriminating between international human rights texts and other international legal documents, such as conventions pertaining to navigable waterways, obviously is a theory-laden enterprise. Such a task is learned by the "theory" taught in law schools. Even a dyed-in-the-wool legal positivist would admit to this, however. What then, is the basis for making such an analytical distinction? A look at the enterprise of interpreting human rights in actual cases best illustrates the grounds for distinguishing these two aspects of human rights.

Juridic Interpretation

Human rights texts attempt to formulate in an abstract and general way the incipient content of important international legal rights. But the lists of human rights in texts do not, on their own, provide sufficient guidance as to their precise scope, weighing, and applicability in specific contexts. Juridic interpretations of specified rights by national and international organizations, administrative authorities, and arbitral and judicial bodies in contested contexts of application and implementation are required to keep these rights from remaining simply "on paper."

Although a paradigm case of juridic interpretation might be the application of legal rules by domestic law courts, the complexity of decisionmaking procedures and wide variety of decisionmaking bodies for international human rights suggests that a broader sense be ascribed to this phrase. It is not obviously necessary to suppose that the validity of human rights interpretations requires the presence of centralized adjudicative bodies of the kind found in most municipal legal systems. International human rights law is interpreted and applied by both national and international courts as well as by administrative institutions. Thus, institutions such as the Human Rights Court, the Committee of Ministers of the Council of Europe, the Inter-American Commission on Human Rights, and United States Federal District Courts all render juridic interpretations of international human rights. Although there may be important distinctions to be made among these decisionmaking authorities in terms of their importance and political impact, it is not essential, as a matter of principle, to exclude their construals of human rights law ab initio from the concept of juridic interpretation.

What does it mean to say that a human rights text is interpreted? In the broadest sense, juridical interpretations of human rights may be distinguished from their application in particular situations. Applying human rights requires that they first be interpreted. The meaning and scope of a right needs to be established before it can be applied to the facts of an individual dispute. However, all juridic interpretations of rights need not result in application. Two examples of unapplied interpretations are advisory opinions and declaratory judgments of human rights standards.

But it would be misleading to equate an unenforced or unenforceable judgment with an unapplied interpretation. For example, although a skeptic might point out the unlikelihood that the multimillion dollar judgment rendered by the *Filartiga* court will ever be complied with, its validity as an authoritative legal determination applicable to a particular case is not vitiated as a consequence.

As with the terminology of human rights texts, juridic interpretations of human rights may be represented vertically with respect to their levels of abstraction and generality. At the highest level, interpretations of human rights, say the right to equal respect, might be tied to abstract conceptions of justice or fairness mandated by the original position, categorical, imperative, or similar counterfactual situation of normative deliberation.

Issues concerning the scope, applicability, and meaning of rights in given circumstances require modifications at lower levels of interpretation. At some stage for example, the scope of a due process right will be tied to specific institutional constraints within a nation's domestic legal system. Similarly, the applicability of equal suffrage rights will be modified at other levels to accommodate exceptions for insane or juvenile persons and felons. The meanings and specific weighing of rights will typically be contingent on controversial issues of political morality presented at successive stages of factual states of affairs. Does the right to be free from racial discrimination recognized in the International Covenant on Civil and Political Rights encompass a plaintiff's allegation of reverse discrimination from a foreign government's affirmative action policies which affect her employment? Resolving specific issues such as this implicates multiple levels within both the text line and the interpretation line.

It is important not to overlook these different levels and deny the legality of human rights *ab initio* at one or more levels by flatly alleging, as many rights skeptics do, that strong claims to universality cannot hold up given discrepancies between the requirements of such rights and various resources and institutions in different countries.

Claims that human rights are inapplicable in given circumstances are more appropriate as specific arguments in actual cases than as an *a priori* proposition made in advance of particular disputes. This model of interpretation gives disputes about the legal status of human rights a new locus. Disagreements are centered around which interpretations give the most defensible accounts of human rights law, letting us abandon sweeping generalizations about whether international human rights law is "really" law.

Given these initial considerations, one might now ask in what specific sense or senses of interpretation are human rights interpreted? In characterizing human rights interpretation later in this chapter I will capitalize on Dworkin's idea of "constructive interpretation," which he attributes to judicial decisionmaking in American law.

Regardless of which level of linguistic generality human rights are couched in, the bold claim that they are universal rights needs some preliminary scrutiny. In what sense are human rights "universal"? Claims of universality seem to be most plausible at more abstract and general levels of discourse. This is not to say that rights at this level are "watered down," unimportant norms, however. The rights to equal protection and due process in the United States Constitution, for instance, are general and abstract yet are of extreme importance in American law. Indeed, universalized language is used in the Fourteenth Amendment's proclamation that "no state shall deny to any citizen within its jurisdiction the equal protection of the law."

Interpreting "Universality"

Although the text of the Universal Declaration of Human Rights explicitly labels human rights as "universal," a number of "realist" skeptics (discussed in Chapter 2) feel that human rights proclamations such as this are patently preposterous since the notion of universality which underpins them is hopelessly relativized in different cultures and societies. If this claim were true, then it would follow that any attempted interpretation or application of such rights would be subject to the charge of being biased by the particular moral or cultural perspective of the adjudicator. We may consider this relativist claim a threshold objection, then, which must be dealt with before any further accounts of human rights interpretations may be taken seriously. I will term the view which flatly denies the possibility of making sense of universality in human rights documents "coarse relativism."

In this section, I will show how such threshold skepticism does not, *per se*, pose a significant enough danger to the concept of universality to inhibit the rigorous conception of human rights law that the integrity model presupposes.

On a general philosophical level, the question of universality can be stated as follows: "How can the seemingly particularized views of political morality reflected in the text of the Universal Declaration be construed as universally legitimate?" On this level of inquiry, coarse relativist skeptics of universality typically hold that there is an irreducible subjectivity to all moral values. Closely akin to this doctrine of ethical subjectivism is the view that discrete moral values are the product of particular societies and cultures. This cultural relativism denies that universal norms can be identified across disparate cultural milieus. The coarse relativist argues like this: "What one society calls a human right is viewed with horror by another. Except for minimal human rights, all other rights are relative to society and considered valid only in very specific cultures." How might one respond to such a skeptical assertion?

First, it should be pointed out that both ethical and cultural relativists often exaggerate the extent to which the existence of different cultures *per se* entails incommensurability in the area of interpreting the texts of human rights norms. However, the generality and flexibility of legal language contained in, *e.g.*, the Universal Declaration of Human Rights overcomes relativist fears that this document is supposed to magically capture a "common denominator" of all moral, religious, and cultural traditions in the world. Thus, the coarse relativist attack typically sets up too strong a claim of universality as a straw person that does not fairly represent the United Nations' approach to human rights.[3]

Second, it is crucial to point out an analytical distinction frequently overlooked on this issue. A good sample of another form of the coarse relativist charge is the assertion that the San Francisco, California

---

[3]. *See*, P. Alston, "The United Nations and the Elliptical Notion of the Universality of Human Rights," in *Is Universality in Jeopardy?* (1987).

meeting which founded the United Nations in 1945 "was dominated by the West and the Universal Declaration . . . was adopted at a time when most third world countries were still under colonial rule."[4] However, issues of institutional parentage and pedigree such as those expressed in this quote are logically separate from matters of normative content.

Nevertheless, as human rights become increasingly integrated into international juridic discourse, and as nations are called on to implement human rights standards into actual policies, there will no doubt be a need for greater nuances in the interpretation of those standards. But that is not to say that one should give up the attempt before it has been launched.

Methods of Legal Interpretation of Texts

To a significant degree, the future of human rights law lies in the hands of authoritative interpreters of texts such as the Universal Declaration of Human Rights, treaties, conventions, and case precedents. The law-as-integrity approach to adjudication suggests that keen attention must be paid to problems in the interpretation of such texts. As I will illustrate, the integrity model of adjudication proposes a model of textual interpretation which is fundamentally at odds with a dominant paradigm of textual legal interpretation that originated with classical Roman jurisprudence and extended into twentieth century legal positivism.

The Received View

A root assumption under the traditional model is that the paramount goal of interpreting a legal text is to effectuate discrete and concrete intentions of the author. Whether explicit textual language or a background "speaker's intent" is controlling, one idea remains constant: the law's authoritative message propels in a one-way direction. The meaning of legal statements extend from an historical author (or an aggregate of authors) to the interpreting subject of the present.

The integrity model of interpretation, on the other hand, advances a "constructive" dimension to the tradition author-interpreter relation. Under Dworkin's account, the old assumption that the interpreter simply learns from and obeys the author's directives is supplanted by the controversial notion that the author could, ideally, learn pertinent

---

[4]. Pollis & Schwab, *Human Rights: Cultural and Ideological Perspectives* (1979) at 14.

information from the interpreter.[5] Under this fresh hermeneutic conception, the jurist stands in a symmetrical relation to the text of the law. Legal interpretation is grounded in juridical "communicative action" that travels on a two-way street. This modified conception suggests that the author and interpreter engage in a hypothetical or idealized "dialogue" with one another. Meanings are, of course, imparted by the author directly to the interpreter. Yet, at the same time, the interpreter reciprocates, contributing a variety of meanings which fill out what was either absent or in some may misrepresented by the author.

The received view has its origins in Roman Law, as it was understood by early Italian Renaissance legal scholars, the glossators. Interestingly, this traditional model persists even into much of the modern jurisprudential literature. Thus, an idea stressed by Julian --- that the incompleteness of written law means there will always be cases of uncertain application --- occupies a central place in the work of Roscoe Pound[6] and H.L.A. Hart.[7]

According to Julian, textual incompleteness stems from a number of factors: the lack of human invention, the flux of human affairs, the plethora of ways people commit malfeasances.[8] Julian also discusses the interpretive problem of extending old rules to new cases. Reasons cannot be provided for everything that predecessors have decreed. If a rule sets the period for adverse possession (*usucaption*) at three years, why not expand it to four years, or reduce it to two? In Julian's words,

> A reason should be such as to be general and necessary and wherever the reason applies, so should the law . . . but such a reason cannot always be given, as this text says, because sometimes the reason

---

[5]. *See*, R. Dworkin, *Law's Empire* (1986) at 420. Dworkin is referring (though he omits from his references the exact citation) to Habermas' discussion at page 134 of I The Theory of Communicative Action (T. McCarthy trans., 1984). In Dworkin's words: "Habermas makes the crucial observation (which points in the direction of constructive interpretation) that interpretation supposes that the author could learn from the interpreter." *Id.*

[6]. *See*, R. Pound, *Introduction to the Philosophy of Law* (1922).

[7]. *See*, H.L.A. Hart, *The Concept of Law* (1961).

[8]. *See*, R. Simonds, *Reflections on the Jurisprudence of the Glossators* (1973).

applies and not the law . . and [sometimes] on the other hand the law applies and not the reason.[9]

In sum, reasons explicitly stated in the text may not always apply. Nevertheless, some sort of reason will always apply, albeit in the form of custom or convention. But if a rule lacks an explicit reason, or if the requisite general and necessary reasons cannot be given, Julian counsels against speculating about the law. As he warns, "otherwise, many things in these laws which are certain will be subverted."[10] When meanings expressed in the text have always been comprehended in a particular way, the shared understanding establishes a convention which has the force of law itself. That is, customary meaning carries interpretive priority. As the jurist Paul writes in a gloss, "what has always had a certain interpretation is to be changed as little as possible."[11]

On the topic of textual vagueness or ambiguity, the glossators speak of looking to the intent of the writer, which would otherwise be irrelevant to interpretation. A question arises whether customary meanings, normally dispositive when the language is clear, are validated by the fact that they manifest the best evidence of the writer's intent. Some glossators suggest that conventional meanings are legitimated in this way, and in addition, that such meanings are to be jettisoned only if it is clear that the author so intended.[12] It should be added that the *Corpus Juris* Civilis of Justinian repeatedly prefers intent to strictly literal meaning in cases where these conflict.

Dworkin's "Constructive" Interpretation

Dworkin's idea of "constructive" legal interpretation is useful in explaining, *inter alia* how theoretical (that is, "constructive") justifications of statutory intent supplant actual empirical (that is, "original" or "historical") legislative intent in adjudication of hard cases where intent is a dispositive issue. This idea of constructive interpretation is generally relevant to the human rights context in illustrating how interpretations of international law, *contra* the view suggested by positivist accounts, need not be limited to actual empirical

---

[9] *Id.* at 7.

[10] *Id.*

[11] *Id.* at 8.

[12] *Id.* at 9.

phenomena such as international custom and the language of human rights texts, but are predicated on justifying theories which ultimately derive from abstract concepts originating in non-empirical loci such as hypothetical models of philosophical deliberation (Rawl's original position, and Dworkin's Judge Hercules to name only two).

Senses of "Interpretation"

In depicting American law as an interpretive enterprise, Dworkin argues that judges aim to give the best possible interpretation of "empirical" sources of law. Thus, in its most rudimentary empirical aspect "the law" is embodied in textual sources like statutes, case precedents, and the United States Constitution. Such textual sources may be seen as a kind of official communication to a judge. A central tenet of Dworkin's recent work is that judges interpret this communication constructively. To make this assertion, Dworkin segregates several senses of interpretation --- conversational, scientific, and artistic --- and concludes that judicial interpretation is most akin to the latter of these. It will be instructive to examine each of these senses that Dworkin distinguishes.

As Dworkin points out, each of us uses conversational interpretation everyday. Talking to other people requires us to determine what they mean by what they say. We assume that those to whom we give an ear have definite intentions which we need only come to know. This kind of interpretation "assigns meaning in the light of motives and purposes and concerns it supposes the speaker to have, and it reports its conclusions as statements about his 'intentions' in saying what he did."[13] Obviously, legal interpretation is not so simple, however.

Scientific interpretation, on the other hand, is used to decipher what empirical data mean. Unlike conversational interpretation, it does not involve unearthing human intentions at all. Nature does not, strictly speaking, "talk to" microbiologists and astronomers.[14]

It should be pointed out that it is slightly misleading for Dworkin to single out scientific interpretation as a kind of interpretation distinct from artistic (read as: "constructive") interpretation. In the philosophy of science, there is considerable controversy over the nature of scientific interpretation. Though obviously beyond the scope of the present work, suffice it to say that the debate between scientific realists (who maintain that scientific theories --- and consequently any interpretations thereunder

---

[13]. R. Dworkin, *Law's Empire* (1986) at 50.

[14]. *Id.* at 51.

--- are held out as true) and antirealists (who maintain that scientific theories are at best merely empirically correct) calls into doubt any facile appeal to a univocal sense of "scientific interpretation."

In the case of literary works --- and, as it turns out, the texts of the law --- a unique problem of interpretation arises. Literature typically has meanings which surpass the specific intentions of its creator. Accordingly, artistic interpretation normally tries to construe the meaning of the work as a whole. The meaning of a poem, for instance, is not equivalent to any specific mental content of the poet expressed in the verse. In this sense, artistic interpretation implicates a creative act. Meaning is imposed from outside, not simply discovered from within the work itself.

Dworkin asks how a modern director of *The Merchant of Venice* might cast Shylock to best accord with Shakespeare's intentions about the play. Bowing to Shakespeare's actual notions about the character of Shylock might frustrate a more general artistic intent pertaining to the work as a whole. If a Shylock different from Shakespeare's specific conception is played, it is evident that a creative use of the director's own ideas is involved. This type of interpretation, Dworkin says

> is far from a neutral, historical exercise in reconstructing a past mental state. It inevitably engages the interpreter's own artistic opinions . . . because it seeks to find the best means to express, given the text in hand, large artistic ambitions that Shakespeare never stated or perhaps even consciously defined but that are produced for us by our asking how the play he wrote would have been most illuminating or powerful to his age.[15]

Dworkin identifies this sense of creative interpretation with judicial interpretation. The judge who interprets the meaning of, *e.g.*, a statute or constitutional provision engages in a hybrid task of discovery and creation. Initially, empirical questions as to what the relevant text of a law is might have to be resolved. For instance, determining which specific provisions of the Internal Revenue Code apply to the facts involved in an intricate tax case involves such an inquiry. In this sense the judge is discovering what the law is. But in cases involving deeper theoretical disagreement about the law the judge must turn to more general principles which might serve to justify one interpretation over another.

---

[15]. *Id.* at 56.

Clearly, Dworkin opposes the "speaker's intent" conception of legal interpretation. The speaker's intent school takes judicial interpretation to be of the conversational, rather than the constructive sort. Dworkin cites a number of court cases in which problems plague the conversational model. His discussion of legislative intent in statutory interpretation deals directly with this point. Since issues of intent are central to interpretations of human rights in domestic courts, it warrants discussion here.

The Problem of Intent

According to Dworkin, in hard cases of statutory interpretation it is unclear whose intentions --- the overall average, the majority, or a plurality --- of those voting for a bill must be consulted to determine the appropriate legislative intent. Moreover, if the issue at bar is not covered by the text of the bill, the judge must ask hypothetically how the "author" (as established by one of the above formulas) *would have* resolved the issue if he or she had actually been confronted with the facts of the case and thought about it. But the requisite information will usually be unavailable or incomplete. So in the end, interpreting how to apply the statute requires weighing different possible legislative votes and sorting out resultant conflicting legislative convictions expressed by them. The judge must ultimately decide "which combination of which principles and policies, with which assignments of relative importance when these compete, provides the best case for what the plain words of the statute require."[16]

At this point, it should be observed that the integrity model assumes that recourse to counterfactual acceptance of a proposed construction of statutory intent is in order. The adjudicator is giving an answer to the question of how the framers of a statute would have voted, given access to some presumed set of information (the present facts of the case), which they lacked at the time they passed the law. Moreover, the goal of the interpretation is to give the best possible reading of the text of the statute. This situation represents one among many junctures at which a justifying theory appeals to the device of a proposed counterfactual acceptance of a theoretical claim.

Dworkin's examples of literary and artistic interpretation are well-suited for situations in which there exists general agreement about the empirical sources of domestic law, but disagreement about how that law is to be applied in particular cases. Thus, in his discussion of the "snail darter" case, it is clear what the relevant statute is that must be applied. There is no disputing that the authors of the statute intended that it be

---

[16]. *Id.* at 338.

law. The controversy over intent instead ranges over what sorts of cases the authors intended the statute to cover. In other words, the inquiry for the adjudicator is how to interpret what is conceded to be a legal directive. This is an instance of constructive interpretation in a "weak" sense. It fits Dworkin's example of asking how Shakespeare would want the character of Shylock to be played in a contemporary performance.

It is not clear that such examples work effectively in situations in which there is seemingly interminable disagreement about the sources of law itself --- as is the case with international human rights law --- even when that law is taken as a genre of domestic law. Thus, as was seen in Chapter 5, it is not clear that the authors of the United Nations Charter intended its provisions to be full-blown legal rights applied by domestic courts. The root inquiry, therefore, is whether such human rights texts are to be interpreted as law, or simply as aspirational language. This situation is analogous to asking not how Shakespeare would have wanted Shylock to be played but whether Shakespeare would have intended *The Merchant of Venice* to be performed as, say, a motion picture or rock video. This kind of inquiry implicates constructive interpretation in a "strong" sense.

The peculiarly strong dimension of constructive interpretation which is involved in contemporary domestic interpretations of human rights law involves the interpreter in ascribing the property of legality to texts which may not have been intended (even in a general sense) by their authors to possess that attribute. This "strong" aspect of constructive interpretation must be accounted for by looking beyond Dworkin's set of examples to instances involving more pronounced hermeneutic effort.

Girard's "Structural" Interpretation

In work, *The Scapegoat*, Rene Girard ponders problems regarding the interpretation of a genre of literature he terms "texts of persecution." Girard sees Guillaume de Machaut's *Judgment of the King of Navarre* as a paragon persecution text. In this fourteenth century poem, Guillaume de Machaut writes that Jews were massacred because they poisoned rivers, which action, it was thought, was responsible for making the population in the surrounding area ill. We now know, however, that the Black Plague was the real culprit. Consequently, says Girard, we conclude that the Jews were scapegoats --- victims of a persecution effectuated by a lie. Despite out modern conviction that the text of the poem embodies this falsehood, however, Girard observes that we do not revert to complete skepticism as regards the text and reject it *in toto*. Instead, we find within the erroneous text persuasive evidence of the fact that the Jews were scapegoats. In effect, the text documents false stereotypes of Jews. For Girard, moreover, the greater the falsehood expressed by the text, the greater our conviction becomes that the persecution actually occurred.

An interpretation of the text entails the recognition of a partly accurate and a partly false perspective of the author-"persecutor." The task for the interpreter, then, is to give the best reading of the text possible. This requires an appeal to structural principles not found explicitly in the text. In Girard's example, the "scapegoat" theme --- the principle that the Jews were scapegoats for the Black Plague, and consequently massacred --- actually contradicts the sense that Guillaume de Machaut apparently intended.

Girard explains this style of interpretation by distinguishing between thematic criticism and structural criticism. In thematic reading, a theme is identified explicitly *in* the text. This is the method employed by literary positivists, such as Frazer, who Girard accuses of being myopic in their preoccupation with explicit themes only.

For structural literary critics, however, themes need not be explicit. A theme may be uncovered as a hidden principle *of*, though not *in*, the text. On the basis of this distinction, Girard regrets that, for the positivists, "the concept of a structural principle that is *absent* from the text it structures would have seemed epistemologically incomprehensible . . . ."[17]

I have included the foregoing discussion of Girard to highlight in a provisional way some important differences between what I have identified as the weak sense of constructive legal interpretation Dworkin offers and a stronger sense that is sometimes involved in contemporary interpretations of human rights as legal rights. When the strong sense of interpretation is involved, the actual intent of the author --- even if manifestly clear and indisputable --- need not dominate in ascriptions of textual meanings by the interpreter. In fact, a clear finding of actual intent may in some instances be supplanted with a contrary meaning. In the particular examples of legal interpretation Dworkin supplies only two scenarios of interpretive impasse arise in connection with determinations of authorial intent. Either (1) it is problematic to determine what the author's (or authors') intent really was (as in ascertaining a unified legislative intent on the basis of multiple, and/or conflicting votes), or (2) the actual intent of the author is insufficient (*e.g.*, because its scope is too narrow) to form an acceptable basis for a judgment concerning a particular set of facts. The latter situation exists in cases where the facts

---

[17]. R. Girard, *The Scapegoat*, Y. Freccero, trans. (1986) at 121.

of the present controversy were simply not anticipated by the author at the time of enactment.[18]

But as Girard's example illustrates, the epistemological limitations of the author must be taken seriously, to the extent that should the author be found to be wrong about some feature that forms the basis for a reasonable interpretation of the text, it may be appropriate to disregard, or substantially modify, the specific intent of the author altogether. Thus, the best interpretation of Machaut's text requires that a prominent feature of its specific (and explicitly expressed) intent --- that of ascribing blame to Jews for poisoning the river --- be identified as erroneous, and substituted with a contrary theory --- that the Black Plague was the responsible agent.

Habermas' "Psychoanalytic" Interpretation

Jurgen Habermas' models of interpretative critique pertaining to problems of *parapraxes*, or errors in textual exegesis, are especially germane to human rights interpretation. Habermas wants a method of interpretation that will engender a correct understanding of faulty texts which simultaneously express and conceal self-deception on behalf of their author.[19] How does this relate to human rights interpretation by U.S. courts? Many examples could be given, but the following will be illustrative. In *Sanchez-Espinoza v. Reagan*, which involved claims brought against President Reagan and other defendants for United States actions against the government of Nicaragua, Judge Scalia expressed the following view about the intent of 28 U.S.C. 1350, the Alien Tort Claims Act:

> This obscure section of the Judiciary Act of 1789, ch.20, s 9, 1 Stat. 73, 77 (Judge Friendly has called it "a kind of legal Lohengrin; . . . no one seems to know whence it came," ITT v. Vencap, Ltd, 519 F.2d 1001, 1015 (2d Cir. 1975)) may conceivably have been meant to cover only private, nongovernmental acts that are contrary to treaty or the law of nations - - - the most prominent examples being piracy and assaults upon ambassadors.[20]

---

[18]. *See*, Dworkin, *Law's Empire*, at 313-54.

[19]. *See*, J. Habermas, *Knowledge and Human Interests*, J Shapiro, trans. (1971) at 219.

[20]. 770 F.2d 202 (D.C. Cir., 1985) at 206.

Another example can be given in the context of civil rights in the United States. The framers of the Constitution were, for the most part, coinstantaneously disciples of equality and of slavery. Consequently, historical exegesis of the actual intentions of those who authored the Constitution reveals a "self-deception" on their part. We do not for that reason, however, seriously consider abandoning the entire text of the document. The integrity of the Constitution as a whole is sought to be preserved, despite the fact that some of its authors harbored misguided assumptions about political morality which conflict with contemporary views about what the Constitution allows and forbids.

Consider also the problem of open texture which H.L.A. Hart describes in *The Concept of Law*. As applied to domestic adjudications of human rights, the problem may be posed as follows. The nations which draft, say, a human rights provision in a United Nations Resolution cannot possibly foresee all possible cases in which their law will be applied. They may have a fairly clear conception of how the law might apply to obvious, clear-cut cases. But they will need to use general language which is vague, or "open textured," so that the provisions will be extendable to other as yet uncertain states of affairs.[21] Hence there is an important sense in which the authors of the law are "deceived" about the meaning of their prescriptions vis a vis the future. Their present grasp of its legal meaning and applicability are distorted since they lack a complete awareness of exactly how the law will be interpreted in circumstances which are temporally and conceptually inaccessible.

The rather unusual claim I have made --- that there is a similarity between the "distorted" conceptual framework of the author of certain human rights texts and the psychological delusions of a patient who undergoes psychoanalysis --- must now be supported. I will begin by showing how Habermas exposits his model of psychoanalytic interpretation as an improvement over preexisting methods.

The Dilthey-Gadamer Debate

Habermas builds much of his analysis of interpretation around critiques of Dilthey and Gadamer (as well as Freud, discussed *infra*). Dilthey introduced, in the context of social science, the problem of *verstehen*. The type of understanding captured by *verstehen* is when one comprehends *alongside* the subject of study (say, the members of a foreign culture). One thereby understands traditions and social norms

---

[21]. H.L.A. Hart, *The Concept of Law* at 120-32.

from the "inside," rather than as a detached external observer who describes the behavior of objects. Dilthey extended this notion to the problem of historical interpretation, and claimed that a type of transcultural *verstehen* was attainable in the form of an historical consciousness. Certain superior scholars are in principle capable of achieving an epi-temporal historical interpretation.[22]

This view was attacked by Gadamer, who doubted whether such a non-contextualized, or non-prejudicial historical consciousness was possible. For Gadamer, the goal of interpretation is to comprehend how one's vantage point might be affected by the very phenomena one seeks to interpret.[23]

In *The Theory of Communicative Action Habermas* takes issue with Gadamer's model of *verstehen* on the grounds that it has a uni-directional bias. The interpreter is not, as Gadamer's view suggests, held hostage by the author's specific intentions. Rather, the nature of the communicative channel between author and interpreter is such that the author *could*, ideally, be thought to learn something from the interpreting agent. Habermas' position on this point is expressed in the following passage:

> . . . Gadamer gives the interpretive model of *Verstehen* a peculiarly *one-sided* twist. If in the performative attitude of virtual participants in conversation we start with the idea that an author's utterance has the presumption of rationality, we not only admit the possibility that we may learn something from it, we *also* take into account the possibility that the author could learn *from us*. Gadamer remains bound to the experience of the philologist who deals with classical tests: 'The classic is that which stands up in the face of historical criticism.' The knowledge embodied in the text is, Gadamer believes, fundamentally superior to the interpreter's.[24]

The interpretive situation of the philologist referred to in this passage is treated separately by Habermas in *Knowledge and Human Interests*. In that book he develops his model of psychoanalytic

---

[22]. *See*, H.P. Rickman, *Meaning in History: Dilthey's Thought on History and Society* (1961).

[23]. *See*, H.G. Gadamer, *Truth and Method* (1979); *see also*, Dworkin, *Law's Empire* at 420.

[24]. J. Habermas, *The Theory of Communicative Action*, T. McCarthy, trans. (1984) at 134.

interpretation. It is in this connection that the notion of parapraxes becomes most crucial.

Habermas begins by distinguishing Dilthey's philological approach to interpretation from Freud's psychoanalytical methods. For Dilthey, critical methodological interpretation is restricted to a language in which conscious intentions are expressed. The pertinent meaning structures are "objectiviated," embodied in the text itself. The historical science of philology seeks a formal study of languages in which tradition has been crystallized linguistically. For Dilthey, moreover, the autobiography represents a "life history" --- a story held together by an ego identify understood in terms of symbolic structures.

This ego identity may be represented as a "vertical" structure, composed of cumulative experiences of the individual. The big question, of course, is how these experiences are to be interpreted. Dilthey's answer is that "[i]n every moment all past events of a life history are subjected to the force of retrospective interpretation. The interpretive framework of each present retrospection is determined by an anticipated future."[25]

Further, Dilthey contends that the individual memory itself is selective as to what is deemed significant in terms of the overall unity of one's life. Does this mean that the true significance of a person's life history becomes hopelessly locked away in his or her own subjective interpretations? Not necessarily, since, as Habermas says, the meanings have an additional *intersubjective* dimension, which may be represented as a "horizontal" structure. The intersubjective validity of symbolic meanings are a precondition of communication itself. As Habermas states it,

> Language is the ground of intersubjectivity, and every person must already have set foot on it before he can objectivate himself in his first expression of life, whether in words, attitudes, or actions.[26]

Thus, in the interpretive realm, the vertically represented dimension of ego identity and the horizontally represented communicative dimension of public expression among different individuals become complementary concepts.[27]

---

[25]. J. Habermas, *Knowledge and Human Interests*, at 152.

[26]. *Id.* at 157.

[27]. *Id.* at 158.

When the philological approach is abandoned in favor of the psychoanalytical model a new consideration crops up. Since individual memory is prone to error, it is not always the most reliable index for a hermeneutical method. Since a patient's memory is often unreliable and/or confused, it is necessary sometimes to critically "reconstruct" what he or she is reporting to the psychotherapist. As Dilthey observes, "[t]he first condition of the construction of the historical world is thus the representation of mankind's confused and in many ways corrupted memories of itself through critique correlated with interpretation."[28]

Psychoanalytic Interpretation

Habermas finds Freudian psychoanalysis "concerned with those connections of symbols in which a subject deceives itself about itself."[29] It is the psychoanalytic model of interpretation, therefore, which holds promise for interpretations of texts which reflect "self-deceptions" of the author. Freud dubbed this unknown region the "internal foreign territory" of the self. There is a form of alienation present, obviously, in this situation, since a meaning "belongs to" the subject but remains inaccessible nonetheless.[30] The key which psychoanalysis provides is a method for self-reflection which transcends a brute understanding of symbolic structures *per se*. Self-reflective understanding, or "depth hermeneutics," breaks into the "foreign territory" that is concealed by self-deception, and corrects distorted meanings embedded in symbolic structures.

Since there is, as we have seen, a "horizontal" aspect to this interpretive framework, Habermas seeks to demonstrate the possibility of "pure communicative action" in which "all habitual interactions and all interpretations relevant to life conduct are accessible at all times."[31] In the world of intersubjective communication, the self-reflective method yields hope for an "unrestricted ordinary language of uncompelled and public communication."[32]

---

[28]. *Id*. at 215.

[29]. *Id*. at 218.

[30]. *Id*. at 217.

[31]. *Id*. at 232.

[32]. *Id*.

The subjective "censorship" reflected in the patient's self-deceptions have their counterpart in the repressive official censorship of the state. Thus, both individual and social pathologies are corrigible by releasing language and communication from their structural deformations. For the case of the individual, of course, the distortions of repressed communication manifest themselves as delusions or neuroses. On the social and cultural level, however, the pathology of distorted communication is reflected in what Freud terms "illusions." It is in this connection that Habermas finds in Freud's *The Future of an Illusion* a challenge to achieve "an organization of social relations according to the principle that the validity of every norm of political consequence be made dependent on a consensus arrived at in communication free from domination."[33]

The desire to resolve problems of authorial deception and textual distortion is thus present in Habermas' analysis of interpretation, which I have argued, constitutes a fourth important sense of "constructive" legal interpretation. It is now time to see how these problems are related to jurisprudence in the area of human rights interpretation.

Constructive Interpretation and the Texts of Human Rights Law

In order to demonstrate the relevance of Habermas' views on psychoanalytic interpretation to the special sense of interpretation that the integrity model advocates, I propose that the relation between the author and the interpreter be viewed as a "dialogue" in which the interpreter seeks to reach an understanding of the author's intentions. The dialogic (two-way) aspect of the relationship thus established inheres in the idealized possibility that the author could learn from the interpreter.[34] This procedure, then, may be portrayed as a dialogue between the interpreter (I) offering a contemporary justification of the legal text to the author (A) who in turn assesses the validity of that justification from the perspective of that law's intent. What might the author stand to learn from such a dialogue? Presumably, the author, who was most intimately acquainted with the intention of the law in the first place, would come to understand how the law could, in accordance with its general intent, be applied to factual situations which were not foreseeable at the time of the enactment of the law. In addition, the author would learn how the

---

[33]. *Id.* at 284.

[34]. R. Dworkin, *Law's Empire* at 420; J. Habermas, I *The Theory of Communicative Action* at 134.

meaning of the law relative to the entire fabric of other laws in the system at the time of enactment is perhaps fundamentally different from its meaning relative to the evolved legal system extant at the time of its application by the interpreter. Thus, for the interpreter to release the conceptual tethering of the law from its original intentions and establish its present justification, amounts to the analogical counterpart of the author being "convinced" by the interpreter's proffered justification in the dialogue.

How "Constructive" Should a Legal Interpretation Be?

In applying the analyses of the hermeneutics of psychoanalytic dialogue to problems in human rights interpretation the thematic-structural distinction, discussed by Girard, is central here. If human rights principles are comprehended as arising from a "structured" interpretation of international law, then those rights will *in some respects* have to be consistent with the intent of their "authors." However, it is not clear that this need always be the case. Furthermore, the consistency need not hold in a strong sense. Dworkin has considered --- and rejected --- theories of interpretation based on what he terms the "conversational" model of legal interpretation which, as shown previously, aim at determining specific intentions of the author. Dworkin adheres to the idea that a judge committed to "law as integrity" must take the law, and also rights, seriously. Sometimes judges must recognize rights, such as the constitutional right of privacy (*Griswold v. Connecticut*,[35] *Roe v. Wade*,[36]) which do not appear explicitly in the text of the Constitution at all. The same may be said for the international human right not to be a victim of acts that are *hostis humani generis*, as argued in *Filartiga v. Pena-Irala*.[37] Such a general right is not explicitly stated in any international declaration, charter, or convention, though the specific right to freedom from torture is at issue in Filartiga.

A hard question therefore arises: to what extent is a judge at liberty to identify explicit and relevant precedents and statutes as "mistakes" to be corrected in the interest of getting a superior interpretation? Further, if a judge is *imposing* a normative meaning on human rights law, what legitimates one interpretation in favor of another?

---

[35]. 381 U.S. 479 (1965).

[36]. 410 U.S. 113 (1973).

[37]. 630 F.2d 876 (2d Cir. 1980), *remanded*, 577 F. Supp. 860.

Girard's structural interpretation, as well as Dworkin's constructive interpretation, deploys the device of reasoned selection of textual distortions. Imperfect texts are not burned. Extreme skepticism is avoided. On the other hand, everything explicitly said in a text may, in light of future knowledge and circumstances, be subjected to a revised reading.

Dworkin discusses what may be termed a chain of "distorted" judicial interpretations of the principle of equal protection stretching from *Plessy v. Ferguson*[38] ("separate but equal") to *Brown v. Board of Education*[39] ("banned categories") to *Regents of the University of California v. Bakke*[40] ("banned sources"). Although the general human rights principle of equal protection is affirmed throughout American constitutional law as interpreted in different historical epochs, specific Supreme Court decisions are reconceptualized, revised, and in some instances completely overturned.[41]

Controversy is a hallmark of human rights interpretation. Consider the deep and seemingly intractable controversy, waged in both domestic and international law, on the issue of whether the death penalty constitutes "cruel and unusual" punishment.[42]

Dworkin concedes that judicial interpretation, even the ideal kind given by Judge Hercules, may be highly controversial. His position is that through reasoned arguments, which center around competing conceptions of political morality, any given interpretation may always be subjected to rational scrutiny. Nevertheless, even granting with Dworkin that such controversy is "objective" and "rational" in a strong sense, it does not follow that there must always be only one right answer, as Dworkin repeatedly insists there is. One can accept that at some level there are a plurality of competing, perhaps even conflicting, objective

---

[38]. 163 U.S. 537, 16 S.Ct. 1138 (1896).

[39]. 347 U.S. 483, 74 S.Ct. 686 (1954).

[40]. 438 U.S. 265, 98 S.Ct. 2733 (1978).

[41]. *See*, R. Dworkin, *Law's Empire*, *supra*, at 381-99.

[42]. The International Covenant on Civil and Political Rights provides, in relevant part, that "No one shall be subjected to torture or to cruel, inhuman or degrading treatment or punishment." Part III, Article 7, *U.N.G.A.* Res. 2200 (XXI), 21 U.N. GAOR, Supp. (No. 16) 52, U.N. Doc. A/6316 (1967). *See also*, *Gregg v. Georgia*, 428 U.S. 153 (1976).

norms, while at the same time admit that there may not be a unique resolution possible for the tensions between them.

However, it seems that any adequate model of human rights interpretation that leads to controversy concerning the grounds for one possible reading versus another requires some mode of legitimation. A reasoned basis for preferring one interpretation to another when they conflict is essential. A means of dealing with such conflicts in interpretation is afforded by expanding upon the dialogue analogy between the author and interpreter. The notion of a rhetorical audience, in Perelman's sense, may be added as a party to the (I)-(A) dialogue. The audience determines the rational acceptability of the justification constructed by the interpreter. In this more complex arrangement, the interpreter (judge) is faced with constructing interpretations which will be acceptable not only to the author (legislator), but in addition, to an appropriate audience.

As regards the justification of interpretations of universal human rights norms, such an audience may be thought of as either an empirically real, concrete one that is relevant to the assessment of the justification in question (say, all members of the international community) or as some idealized version thereof, constituted with certain characteristics (*e.g.*, Perelman's "universal audience"). In Dworkin's presentation of the integrity model, the notion of the "true" community is arguably advanced as a kind of particular ideal audience (in Aarnio's sense),[43] but with a somewhat different end in mind. Dworkin does not suppose that the interpreting Judge Hercules directly "presents" his theories of law to the community. Rather Dworkin confers on Hercules himself --- since this mythical jurist is postulated as an ideally maximally rational agent --- the ultimate task of assessing how any proposed interpretation comports with the principles that are given allegiance to by the community personified.

---

[43]. *See* A. Aarnio, *The Rational as Reasonable* (1987) at 222-25, and my discussion of his critique in Chapter 5, *infra*.

CHAPTER SEVEN

THE INTERNATIONAL COMMUNITY AS THE "AUDIENCE" OF HUMAN RIGHTS

Introduction

Ronald Dworkin offers his notion of the community of principle as the key to the interpretive integrity of a community's laws. Since the present study seeks to *inter alia* assess the integrity model in light of the enterprise of human rights interpretation and implementation, I will center this chapter around a critical treatment of Dworkin's conception of the "community personified." I will relate my analysis of Dworkin's notion of the community to two other insightful theories of interpretive normative communities --- those of A.J.M. Milne and Chaim Perelman. As applied specifically to interpretations of international human rights, each of these three accounts harbor, I will argue, appreciable defects. However, when studied together critically --- yet at the same time charitably (as I will attempt to do) --- their more positive salient features work synergetically to provide some regulative concepts that will facilitate an understanding of the complex relationships between theoretical justifications of human rights norms and the world community.

Because Dworkin's conception of the community is advanced as an idealized model to support his theories about domestic interpretations of (principally) constitutional rights, that conception poses a special problem for international human rights law. Human rights adjudications in the United States routinely pertain to addressees and claimants who are outside the scope of the true community as Dworkin defines it (*i.e.* a community of citizens only). The parties in the *Filartiga and Trajano* decisions, for instance, were aliens relative to the courts which pronounced judgment on their human rights claims. So there is an apparent deficiency in Dworkin's model: as it stands, it cannot account for why United States courts must follow integrity in human rights adjudication (which, arguably at least, they in fact do, as was seen in Chapter Five).

Since Dworkin's view of the community is restricted to citizens alone, it is not clear how human rights which impose obligations on non-citizens are justified under the integrity conception. After critically examining the relevant aspects of Dworkin's position on the community, I will give a critical treatment of the "modified realism" of Professor Milne. I have singled out his theory because it would appear, at least initially, to offer an enhanced framework for human rights interpretation consistent with at least the broad outlines of the "integrity" conception of adjudication, while also respecting the existence of cultural and ethical diversity of the world community. That is, Milne stresses the need for developing an interpretive context for human rights discussion while remaining sensitive to the impact of different societies (their moral and cultural values) on rights. Milne recognizes, whereas Dworkin effectively declines to address due to constraints built into his theory, the ramifications of pervasive cultural and moral diversity of the world community on human rights interpretations.

Later on in the chapter I will present the notion of the universal audience from the "new rhetoric" of Chaim Perelman. This notion, if appropriately qualified along the lines recently taken by Aulis Aarnio, offers some promising insights for the establishment of an objective norm of justification for human rights interpretations in the face of the challenges to objectivity Milne associates with the ethical and cultural diversity of the world community.

After having presented critical analyses of Dworkin, Milne, and Perelman, I will abstract a number of regulatory concepts from their views which will help highlight the synergetic relationships between them. Although none of the views on their own provide a sufficient account of the connection between human rights interpretation and the world community, a selective use of their ideas yields a powerful framework for making sense of community consensus as an "interpretive" concept.

Dworkin's "Community Personified"

Dworkin's concept of the "community personified" is expressed in the following passage:

My account of political integrity takes the personification much more seriously, as if a political community really were some special kind of entity distinct from the actual people who are its citizens. Worse, it attributes moral agency and responsibility to this distinct entity. For when I speak of the community being faithful to its own principles I do not mean its conventional or popular morality, the beliefs and convictions of most citizens. I mean that the community has its own principles it can itself honor or dishonor, that it can act in good or bad faith, with integrity or hypocritically, just as people can.[1]

Dworkin sees the personification referred to in the above passage as intimately tied to the integrity model of a political community. The integrity model of a community is distinguished by Dworkin from two other competing models of community: the "community of circumstance" and the "rulebook" models. In the community of circumstance there is only a de facto association of individuals due to historical or geographical accident. For Dworkin, this rudimentary form of association does not suffice to constitute a true "associative" community. The rulebook community, on the other hand, is one which sees rules as exhaustive of obligation. As such, the rulebook model is consistent with conventionalism, which, of course, Dworkin rejects as a theory of law. The integrity model of community, on the other hand, is bound not by the pragmatist's "rules hammered out in political compromise," but by principles of justice, fairness, and due process which are both endorsed and presupposed by the decisions of its political institutions.[2] The integrity model of community, then, in Dworkin's view, satisfies the conditions of a true community better than the other two models.

Dworkin attributes a metaphysical status to the community by describing it as a "personification." Thus, for Dworkin, a community such as that constituted by United States citizens has an allegiance to principles of due process, fairness, and justice. Dworkin distinguishes a "bare" community from a "true" community in the following way. The former is merely "a community that meets the genetic or geographical or other historical conditions identified by social practice as capable of constituting a fraternal community." The latter, however, is a bare

---

[1]. R. Dworkin, *Law's Empire* (1986) at 168.

[2]. R. Dworkin, *Law's Empire*, at 211.

community in which the following four conditions[3] are present which establish its identify as a "fraternal" community: (i) the members of the community regard the group's obligations as special (obtaining distinctly within the group); (ii) the group accepts responsibilities as personal (running from individual to individual, not to group as a whole); (iii) responsibilities are seen as coming from general concern for well-being of other group members; (iv) the members of the community "must suppose that the group's practices show not only concern but an *equal* concern for all members."[4]

Criticism of the Community Personified

An important question arises when one considers that the human rights which United States courts are coming to interpret as legal rights are addressed to individuals outside of the scope of the United States community. Is the heterogeneity of world cultures inconsistent with integrity's notion of a ("true") legal community whose associational obligations would serve as the foundation for the moral and political integrity of human rights law?

As a preliminary consideration, it is worth noting that substantial cultural and ethical relativity exists even within the context of the United States community itself. On this basis, one might argue that Dworkin's "true" community mistakenly presupposes the presence of much more homogeneity (of cultural and moral values) than actually exists within the United States. As such, a critic might contend that, as far as ethical and cultural diversity is concerned, the United States is a sort of axiological microcosm of the global community. A sentiment of this kind is expressed by Wyndham Lewis, who indicates that in drawing citizens from throughout the world, the United States has a spirit of "revolutionary universalism" akin to a global society:

> U.S. citizenship is something as unique as it is extraordinary; it differs radically from what is understood in Europe as 'nationality.' The United States is a fragmentary, most imperfect, and in some respects grotesque advance-copy of a future world-order.[5]

---

[3]. Dworkin does not state whether he takes them to be necessary and sufficient conditions.

[4]. Dworkin at 199-202.

[5]. W. Lewis, *America and Cosmic Man* (1948).

If this sort of assertion were to be roughly correct, it would indicate, I think, two important consequences for Dworkin's model of the community, relative to the interpretive context of the present study. First, it would reveal a defect in the model, albeit of a different sort from the one I am addressing in this chapter. The defect would stem from an incorrect representation of uniformity of values that Dworkin associates with "fraternal" citizenship. Second, it would imply a direct correspondence between the (culturally and ethically diverse) nature of the domestic community and the (culturally and ethically diverse) nature of the world community. As such, the problem of establishing a community of principle for interpretive integrity in the domestic context would parallel the search for such a community in the international context.

Dworkin himself, however, has a response at his disposal to criticism along these lines. Since he insists that his model of the community is not purely a sociological description, but rather an ideal construct, it would be possible for him to disassociate the model from any empirical thesis about the extensive diversity of the domestic community. An alternative response to the diversity challenge would be to deny that the existence of ethical and cultural diversity *per se* rules out the possibility of the four conditions of a true community obtaining. Thus, although a high degree of diversity of ethical values might make a consensus on highly specific substantive conception of rights difficult to achieve, Dworkin's ideal version of the community is set up so that all that is needed as a prerequisite for integrity is a general consensus of acceptance of the abstract principles of justice, fairness, and due process. Nevertheless, as applied to the international context at least, Dworkin has effectively ruled out any possibility of construing the world community as a true community by making citizenship a condition for a bare community. Thus, since the existence of a bare community is a necessary condition for the existence of a true community,[6] it would follow, under Dworkin's theory, that non-citizens cannot comprise a true community.

But if all that is ultimately to be expected from a true community is a shared commitment to the principles of justice, fairness, and due process, then it seems arbitrary to posit the criterion of citizenship as a

---

[6] *See*, Dworkin at 201-02. "It is therefore essential to insist that true communities must be bare communities as well. People cannot be made involuntary 'honorary' members of a community to which they do not even 'barely' belong just because other members are disposed to treat them as such. I would not become a citizen of Fiji if people there decided for some reason to treat me as one of them."

necessary condition for genuine participation in such a general and abstractly stated interpretive attitude towards normative standards. Even the members of Dworkin's true community, despite their common citizenship, will disagree about specific substantive conceptions of legal rights in hard cases. This is so because hard cases, by definition, involve controversy about the specific rights of litigants.

Construing the Consensus of the International Community as an "Interpretive" Concept

As has been seen, the law-as-integrity conception of domestic law advances a strong claim about the role of the domestic community in adjudications of legal rights. The question naturally arises, therefore, as to what the role of the international political community is in regard to domestic adjudications of international human rights. Dworkin sees the domestic political community of, *e.g.*, the United States, which he terms a "true" community, as the key to maintaining integrity in rights adjudication. As I have pointed out, a problem with grounding integrity in such a community, however, is that as regards adjudications of human rights norms, it is too parochial and underinclusive. This is so because the addressees and claimants of human rights norms in the adjudicative interpretive context under consideration in the present study are not citizens of the United States. Hence, they are outside of the "true" community which Dworkin postulates as being a precondition of interpretive integrity.

One might attempt to avoid the objection of underinclusiveness by arguing that, though not citizens, resident aliens in the United States may be considered as part of the "true" community. Perhaps one might argue that aliens are, for purposes of human rights adjudication, a kind of "surrogate" citizenry, since they have chosen to avail themselves of the machinery of justice of the United States federal courts, and that fact indicates a significant connection to the "true" community Dworkin has in mind. But this is not a plausible argument. The aliens who sue under such instruments as the Alien Tort Claims Act need have no significant political or moral connections with the United States whatsoever. Indeed, technically speaking, they may be outright hostile toward the United States government and its people. Moreover, as I have already shown, Dworkin himself explicitly inscribes the boundaries of "bare" communities around existing national borders.

Even if it were granted that aliens suing in United States courts as claimants of human rights had in some sense become "surrogate" citizens, the fact remains that the addressees of the rights at issue (*e.g.*, officials from foreign governments who violate the human rights of aliens) are still not a part of the "true" community.

All of this raises a significant problem for the integrity model because Dworkin sees legal and political obligation as arising from membership in the true community. So the question becomes as follows. By what authority can United States courts adjudicate human rights whose addressees (*i.e.*, those who are being held under a legal obligation) are outside of the true community? This situation appears to expose a serious shortcoming of Dworkin's model, given the increasing tendency of the United States judiciary to decide international human rights violations.

It is therefore appropriate to look to a different model of the interpretive community for international human rights. Such an alternative perspective is provided by A.J.M. Milne, who advances a theory about the relationship between what he takes to be the objectivity of fundamental human rights on the one hand, and what he considers the ethical relativism associated with the diversity of the world community, on the other.

Milne's "Qualified" Realism

According to Milne, there are two ways of understanding human rights: (a) as ideal Western-democratic-industrial-liberal standards; or, (b) as minimal moral standards. Milne prefers the latter conception on the grounds that it is "compatible with much moral and cultural diversity."

Milne finds cultural and ethical diversity to act as a constraint on human rights interpretations. In support of the "minimal moral standards" conception of human rights, Milne states the following:

> A minimum moral standard which is applicable to all cultures and societies does not deny that every human being is largely made what he [sic] is by his particular cultural and social experience. It does not presuppose homogeneous desocialized and deculturalized human beings. Rather it presupposes social and cultural diversity and sets minimum moral requirements to be met by all societies and cultures. Such requirements set moral limits to the scope of diversity but in no way deny its existence. The universal applicability of the minimum moral standard entails that the rights for which it requires respect should be universally recognized. In an intelligible sense, they are the

moral rights of all human beings at all times and in all places: that is, universal moral rights.[7]

Milne's theory is relevant to the present chapter because the theory holds that the ethical and cultural diversity of the international community as such is a sufficient reason for restricting the set of universal human rights to a total of seven fundamental rights which are "necessary for social existence as such."

Criticism of Milne

A preliminary objection to Milne's approach to human rights interpretation is that he is overly general. He assumes that the law of international human rights is somehow completely spelled out in the generalized textual sources of those rights. This is, to say the least, an extraordinarily naive perspective. In addition, his facile division of the concept of human rights into only two classifications misrepresents the multitude of subtle gradations between these two extremes. Moreover, the association of his first category of human rights with "Western-democratic-industrial-liberal" standards is itself suspect. It wrongly equates the conceptual substance of human rights --- *i.e.*, that conception which he is distinguishing from a "minimal moral standards" conception --- with the pedigree, or institutional parentage of that conception.

The more significant problem with Milne's theory, however, is that he subscribes to a form of "prescriptive relativism," though without adequate support for such a position. That is, Milne does not show why considerations of cultural and moral diversity should prevail in all instances over preservation of all but the most minimal human rights. In fact, Milne moves from a factual claim about the existence of substantial ethical and cultural diversity in the world to a normative claim, which is never supported, that such diversity is worth preserving at the cost of sacrificing all but the most fundamental human rights whose recognition does not jeopardize the diversity.

Thus, what Milne fails to distinguish is the factual claim --- that there are differences in moral standards and values among different cultures --- from the normative hypothesis (which he fails to support with argumentation) that it is desirable to preserve differences in moral standards, that tolerance for the peculiar moral practices of other cultures is good and weighty enough to act as a constraint on one's assertions of universal rights.

---

[7]. A.J.M. Milne, *Human Rights and Human Diversity* (1986) at 6.

Even granting that the preservation of cultural and ethical diversity may be one reason counting against a given claim that a right is universal, it does not follow that it is always a sufficient reason.

There is an additional difficulty for Milne's theory which arises from his predicating different aspects of his argument on two conflicting meta-ethical theories: ethical objectivism and ethical relativism. Thus, Milne argues along the lines of ethical objectivism in asserting that there are seven basic human rights --- those which he terms "minimal moral rights" --- which are necessary to social existence. Along the line of ethical relativism, however, Milne also argues (i) that assertions of human rights beyond these most basic rights are invalidated because ethical standards are relative to different societies (the "relativity" hypothesis);[8] and (ii) that it is desirable to preserve global normative diversity by rejecting claims to other than the minimal human rights (the "prescriptive relativism" hypothesis).[9]

Unfortunately, once Milne advances the thesis that ethical standards are relative to different societies, he undermines the effectiveness of his own normative assertions about the high priority of the seven minimal rights he advocates since, by his own thesis, such assertions, too, are relative to his societal perspective.

The "Universal Audience"

Chaim Perelman's notion of the Universal Audience is simply that of "the whole of mankind, or at least, of all normal, adults"[10] may be distinguished from, say, a single interlocutor --- a person who is addressed in a dialogue, and from a single deliberating subject --- a person who engages in self-reflection and gives reasons for certain actions. For Perelman, the latter two cases are particular incarnations of the universal audience. The universal audience has "primordial importance;" it provides a basic norm for objective argumentation.[11]

In his essays on legal argumentation, Perelman stresses that the aim of a legal theory is to convince and persuade those toward which it is addressed. The following passage is illustrative:

---

[8]. *See*, J. Nickel, *Making Sense of Human Rights* (1987) at 71 for an explanation of such a moral position.

[9]. *See*, *id.* for a discussion of prescriptive relativism.

[10]. C. Perelman & Olbrechts-Tyteca, *The New Rhetoric* at 30.

[11]. *Id.* at 31.

The jurist who elaborates legal theories, who furnishes a justified interpretation of a text or who proposes new legislation will measure the success of his enterprise by the approval of the courts or that of the legislator. From this perspective, legal theories do not have the task of stating the truth but of preparing and justifying decisions.[12]

Perelman believes that both philosophy and law, as enterprises that employ rational argumentation which is valid for the entire human community, are committed to making arguments addressed to the universal audience. Thus, he writes:

A reflection on law, its problems and its methods can reveal a philosophy of the reasonable which . . . seeks to elaborate perspectives which can be proposed to the universality of men.[13]

So, the universal audience is a rhetorical embodiment of the conviction that "[t]he characteristic of rational argumentation is the aim to universality."[14]

Aarnio's Critique of Perelman

Aulis Aarnio has observed that Perelman's concept of the universal audience is ambiguous. On the one hand, Perelman asserts that the audience is ideal and universal, on the other hand, however, he maintains that it is culturally and socially bound. In other words, the constituency of the universal audience seems to depend, in part, on contingent facts. Thus the question arises for Aarnio whether Perelman's audience can be sensibly thought of as both universal and dependent on contingent facts.

Aarnio proposes making several analytical distinctions to clarify how the notion of a universal audience might be interpreted. The first set of distinctions is that of a concrete versus an ideal audience. The second set of distinctions breaks down the concrete audience into a universal concrete audience and a particular concrete audience. Similarly, the ideal audience is broken down into a universal ideal

---

[12]. C. Perelman, "Legal Reasoning," in *Justice, Law, and Argument* at 129.

[13]. C. Perelman, "Law, Philosophy and Argumentation," in *id*. at 161.

[14]. C. Perelman, "Justice and Reason," in *id*. at 73.

audience on the one hand, and a particular ideal audience, on the other.[15]

A concrete audience is comprised of real, extant individuals whose membership is limited to a finite number. The composition of a concrete audience in its universal aspect would be all the living humans in the world at a given time, without regard for their possession of other particular properties. With regard to the present study, it is important to notice that such a concept of an audience directly corresponds to the pre-interpretive referent supplied by the standard view of human rights claimants, namely, that of "all people at all times and places." Such a construal of human rights claimants was rejected as implausible earlier in this study, however. The problem with such a concept for an audience, however, is that it would not ensure that arguments presented to it for acceptance would even be received by all of its members. Perhaps some of the members of the audience do not have sufficient mental capacity to understand the nature of the arguments advanced. Clearly, this is not Perelman's idea of the universal audience since he restricts its membership to, roughly, that of all rational adults.

As for a particular concrete audience, there would be some restriction in its scope of membership based on the possession of certain characteristics, such as similarity in professional legal training, or a shared interest (as in the audience of a lecture). But there is no guarantee that the acceptability of arguments addressed to such an audience will be rationally based, since non-rational elements (such as an acceptance of the authority of the speaker, *per se*, or a coercive element) may influence the audience's acceptance of a given interpretive position. So a particular concrete audience as such does not provide an adequate foundation for the rational acceptability of an interpretive standpoint.

An ideal audience, as Perelman presents it, consists of rational persons only. As such, the individuals in an ideal audience would be capable of engaging in rational discourse with an eye toward ultimately reaching an agreement. Under Perelman's account, the members of a universal audience, in its ideal aspect, would be able to come together in their views even though, antecedent to their discourse, they might have had divergent views. Aarnio dislikes the assumption of an objective "cognitive value theory" which lies behind Perelman's notion of the universal audience, taken in this ideal sense. Accordingly, Aarnio proposes that Perelman's universal audience be comprehended as a kind of particular ideal audience. In this interpretation of the universal audience, the members of the audience share common values. As such,

---

[15]. A. Aarnio, *The Rational as Reasonable: A Treatise on Legal Justification, 1987*, at 222.

there is no need to postulate the presence of objective, universal values as a precondition for consensus being reached within the audience.

There is a connection between the notion of the ideal particular audience as Aarnio has framed it and Dworkin's notion of the "true" community. That is, Dworkin's community is constituted with particular characteristics, such as a common citizenship and a shared commitment to the general principles of justice, fairness, and due process. Further, they may be assumed to be ideally rational (at least in Rawl's sense) given the postulation that they would accept such moral principles as priorities for their political institutions.[16] This ideal component of the audience further corresponds to Habermas' "Ideal Speech Situation" in the sense that the participants therein are supposed to share a hypothetical position of engagement in rational discourse that is free of any influence of manipulation or persuasion.

One of the principal difficulties with Dworkin's particular ideal audience, however, is that the common values which he attributes to it --- the "associative" obligations of citizenship on the one hand, and allegiance to justice, fairness, and due process for citizens only, on the other --- are too parochial to provide a basis for a commitment to interpretive integrity with regard to human rights norms.

Thus, the remedy for this defect of the integrity conception is to expand the assumption of common values of the interpretive community

---

[16]. Rawls himself gives the following reconstruction of the original position for purposes of arriving at principles of justice applicable to international contexts:

. . . [O]ne may extend the interpretation of the original position and think of the parties as representatives of different nations who must choose together the fundamental principles to adjudicate conflicting claims among states. Following out the conception of the initial situation, I assume that these representatives are deprived of various kinds of information. While they know that they represent different nations each living under the normal circumstances of human life, they know nothing about the particular circumstances of their own society, its power and strength in comparison with other nations, nor do they know their place in their own society. Once again the contracting parties, in this case representatives of states, are allowed only enough knowledge to make a rational choice to protect their interests but not so much that the more fortunate among them can take advantage of their special situation. This original position is fair between nations; it nullifies the contingencies and biases of historical fate. Justice between states is determined by the principles that would be chosen in the original position so interpreted.

A Theory of Justice (1971) at 378.

to include at least the possibility of non-citizenship membership for certain human rights norms, especially fundamental norms like freedom from torture.

Consensus as a Multilayered Concept

Issues as to the existence of consensus within a community with respect to normative standards arise chiefly at three distinct levels in human rights interpretations. To facilitate a concrete understanding of my analysis, I will give an account of each of these three levels within the context of the cases of *Filartiga v. Pena-Irala* (discussed previously in Chapter Five) and *Gregg v. Georgia*. I will also relate the analysis at the appropriate times to the various models of interpretive legal communities that have been presented in this chapter so far.

Briefly, the three levels may be distinguished as follows. The first level involves determining whether there is a consensus within the community morality as to a fairly substantive conception of a given right. The second level involves determining whether there is a consensus within the community as to abstract and general principles, such as those of justice and fairness, or as to abstract and general human rights standards. The third level involves determining whether there is a consensus within the community as regards the acceptability of the particular justifying theory for the right in question. I will elaborate on each of these levels below.

First-Level Consensus

Courts frequently rely on interpretations of international consensus as a basis for finding human rights norms to be universal. For example, the *Filartiga* court found that "torture is viewed with universal abhorrence; the prohibition of torture by international consensus and express international accords is clear and unambiguous. . . ."[17] But the assertion that international consensus as such is an appropriate criterion (it need not be the sole criterion) must be a consequence of some theory about how the scope of human rights is determined. Such a theory would have to show why reliance on a consensus rather than some other procedure (say, the opinions of randomly-selected individuals) is the best means of interpreting human rights law. Moreover, a theory would have to account for how claims about consensus themselves are to be understood. Is a consensus to be understood as an actual consensus among nations (or individuals) or is it a counterfactual consensus --- an

---

[17]. 577 F.Supp. 860 at 863 (1984).

agreement that would be reached under certain conditions? Are all opinions to be counted as relevant in ascertaining the consensus, or only those of rational persons? The pressing questions in this respect, then, are these: how are the international community, and the consensus (or lack of consensus) within that community to be interpreted? Is a claim that a consensus exists about human rights inconsistent with the fact that there exists great cultural and moral diversity in the world? It is important to recognize that the interpretation of consensus called for on this level is an issue internal to a justifying theory for the human right in question.[18] Conflicting positions on how to interpret first-level consensus were taken in the case of *Gregg v. Georgia*. The majority opinion maintained that an actual consensus could be found within the United States concerning the acceptability of capital punishment. Specifically, the majority found that the fact that thirty-five state legislatures had enacted new statutes providing for the death penalty since the Furman decision evidenced "society's endorsement" of the penalty.[19]

The minority opinion, on the other hand, argued that the dispositive issue was whether *if fully informed* a majority of citizens would approve of capital punishment. Thus, the minority opinion represents a counterfactual approach to interpreting first-level consensus within a community. The different interpretations of first-level consensus in *Gregg* reflect opposing substantive conceptions of the constitutional right (which is also stated as a human right in Article 5 of the Universal Declaration) to be free from "cruel and unusual" punishment.

Employing the analysis given by Aarnio, it becomes clear that the Gregg majority approach is to assume that a particular concrete audience is the appropriate regulatory conceptual device for inquiring into the issue of consensus surrounding capital punishment. On the other hand, the minority opinion assumes that a particular ideal audience is appropriate. The ideal component here derives from the supposition that the citizens of the United States are *fully informed* about relevant facts concerning capital punishment.

As for the *Filartiga* interpretation of first-level consensus, it may be assumed that the same variety of construals of audiences are available. However, given that the right under consideration in that decision is a

---

[18]. I will explain the concept of a justifying theory for human rights in detail in Chapter 6. At this point in the discussion it is only necessary to explain that a justifying theory may be roughly equated with the judicial opinion (and its presupposed philosophical underpinnings) that is interpreting the right in question.

[19]. *Gregg v. Georgia*, 428 U.S. 153 (1976).

purportedly universal standard, it would seem that some form of a universal audience would be appropriate. However, Milne's perspective would suggest that, in light of considerations of value-relativity in the global context, a universal audience is susceptible to being dissolved into a plurality of particular audiences corresponding to different ethical traditions. However, even a plurality of particular audiences might still converge in their acceptance of a given normative standard (just as they might diverge), depending on the circumstances.

Second-Level Consensus

When assertions of human rights are more broadly and abstractly formulated, consensus at the second level is generally to be expected, unless there is significant value diversity within the community which would inhibit such a finding. Dworkin's notion of the community personified may be thought of as a useful heuristic device for getting at the concept of community consensus in this sense. In Dworkin's ideal community there is a shared commitment to integrity in legal interpretation, enshrined in a general acceptance of the abstract principles of justice, fairness, and due process. In Aarnio's terminology, this model of the community may termed a "particular ideal audience."[20] The ideal aspect inheres in the fact that the members are all bound to the ideal of "fraternal" association.[21] The particularity of the model inheres in the fact that the members of Dworkin's particular community, as United States citizens, are assumed to share common values, a certain "form of life" (*lebensform*) or "picture of the world" (*weltbild*) to appropriate a phrase from Wittenstein.[22] The make-up of the community qua normative audience is thus in part culturally and socially determined, as envisioned by Perelman.

Third-Level Consensus

Inquiry into consensus at the third level is represented conceptually in Perelman's notion of the acceptability of justifying legal theories by the universal audience. Perelman supposes that real judges address their judicial opinions to a universal audience with the ideal of attaining a

---

[20]. Aarnio at 225.

[21]. Dworkin at 214.

[22]. *See*, L. Wittgenstein, *On Certainty* (G.E.M. Anscombe & G.H. von Wright, eds., 1969) at 34.

consensus from that audience. In searching for a consensus from an audience of rational individuals, a commitment to attaining rational acceptability in judicial decisionmaking is instituted. The acceptance of the judge's theory of law by the audience serves as a criterion of rational, objective legal argumentation.

From the point of view of the integrity model, however, a different situation is proposed concerning the acceptability of a judge's theory of law. Dworkin's hypothetical Judge Hercules is the final arbiter of the reasonableness of the justifying theories he constructs. Although Hercules does deliberate about interpretations of first-level and second-level consensus within the community, Dworkin does not suggest that Hercules addresses his theories, in their final formulations, to an idealized audience.

As regards justifying theories for international human rights, it seems plausible to give preference to a model in which the rational acceptance of the theories is affiliated with a plurality of particular ideal audiences, each patterned after the particular "forms of life" existing in the global community. On such a model it is conceivable that there would be overlap as between two audiences, according to their shared moral values. An advantage of this representation is that it reflects the possibility of both convergence and divergence among the audiences to whom justifying theories of human rights are proposed.

Summary of Arguments

In this chapter I argued that the community-related theses of integrity are underinclusive *vis a vis* human rights interpretations since they exclude from the "true" community many of the claimants and addressees of the rights in question. I also advanced arguments against the "qualified" legal realism of Professor Milne, while also indicating the extent to which I am in agreement with his general methodology which emphasizes the importance of contextual interpretation of human rights.

Briefly, my arguments against Milne were that (i) he takes an overly general context for human rights interpretation. The textual provisions he uses as examples are in a "pre-interpretive" state -- before having been interpreted by adjudicative tribunals in particular cases. (I demonstrated in Chapter Five how a more specific context for human rights now exists. Milne would have done well to appreciate that context.) (ii) Milne's claim that there are only two possible conceptions of human rights --- as Western industrialized liberal democratic ideals or as his own "minimal moral standards" is false. There are innumerable gradations between these extremes. (iii) Milne's claim that many human rights are simply the product of Western ideology is confused. He mistakes the issue of pedigree with the issue of substantive content. (iv) Milne commits a logical error by moving from premises based on a factual thesis about the existence of cultural and ethical diversity in the world community, to a concluding normative thesis that the diversity ought to be preserved as against all but the most minimal human rights standards; (v) Milne's attempt to hold that all moral judgments are relative to culture *and* that there is nevertheless an objective perspective for moral judgments is inconsistent. He leaves himself open to the criticism that his own particular perspective (that of an English liberal academic) is biased.

I presented Aarnio's criticism of the notion of the universal audience as it was originally conceived by Perelman. This analysis afforded a useful distinction between different senses of audience that may be employed when speaking about the world community in connection with human rights interpretations.

Following the critiques of the three views of an interpretive legal community, I provided a provisional framework of analysis that employed a distinction between three levels at which the consensus of the community might be sought in connection with interpretations of specific human rights.

I argued that the concept of community consensus is best understood as an "interpretive" notion. Construals of community consensus are likely to be controversial due in part to the variety of types of audiences a given community may be taken to be (ideal or concrete, particular or universal), and in part to the different senses of consensus (actual or counterfactual) that may be employed in one's interpretation. Moreover, I demonstrated how issues of consensus within the legal audience arise at three different levels of interpretation in the formulation of justifying theories. The role of justifying theories in establishing the rational acceptability of human rights claims will be investigated in the next chapter.

CHAPTER EIGHT

JUSTIFYING INSTITUTIONAL THEORIES OF HUMAN RIGHTS

Introduction

In the previous chapters it has been seen how, with appropriate modifications, the integrity model has facilitated making philosophical sense of the emerging international human rights obligations as interpreted by United States courts and other authoritative institutions. Briefly, the modifications which the integrity model required in order to accommodate this body of law were as follows. Although it was observed that contemporary human rights disputes posed "hard cases" in the general sense (employed by Dworkin) that reasonable and competent lawyers might disagree as to how such cases should be resolved on the basis of relevant domestic statutes, constitutional provisions, and case precedents, there was an important difference identified between the relative degree of "hardness" implicated in international human rights issues and strictly domestic rights issues (*e.g.*, the constitutional and civil rights cases Dworkin discusses to illustrate his theory). The difference consisted in the fact that the appropriate empirical sources of law for human rights adjudication were themselves in question in a way that the sources of strictly domestic law were not.

Nevertheless, the judicial methodology (explored in Chapter Five: "Adjudicative Contexts") of interpreting legislative intent within the confines of the doctrine of self-execution of treaties provided a close parallel between the actual process of deciding several key human rights decisions and the process recommended by the integrity model. As was seen, that process involved taking the question of legislative intent as a special interpretive question rather than as a narrow empirical question of historical fact about actual intent.

Moreover, in examining the peculiar relationship between the "author" and "interpreter" involved in integrity's "constructive" conception of legal interpretation, it was seen (in Chapter Six) how integrity, modified so as to license the deployment of "strong" (or "structural") interpretive procedures when necessary, could be understood as being committed to an ideal "dialogic" model of legal heuristics. Such a model, which was consistent with the idea that legal interpretation sometimes seeks to emancipate the limited and occasionally distorted epistemological perspective of the "author," proved to be a suitable vehicle for making sense of the apparently "revisionist" approach taken by United States courts in selectively interpreting various human rights standards from international texts (many of which were not explicitly intended to be "legal" standards) as legal norms.

Finally, integrity's account of the "true" community was found to be defective *vis a vis* human rights adjudication in that it arbitrarily excluded from its membership non-citizens, which comprised a segment of the addressees and claimants of human rights law.

As a means of conveniently referring to the resultant modified conception of law-as-integrity, I propose to identify the enhanced framework for human rights adjudication with the concept of "justifying theories" of institutional rights.

An advantage of construing human rights law adjudication within justifying theories is that it allows one to account for human rights as enjoying an existence independent of (albeit theoretically related to) their actual recognition or implementation in specific domestic legal orders. The validity and authoritativeness of human rights law derives from justifying theories which undergird the wide variety of interpretations actually advanced by legal institutions worldwide. Granted, it is usually controversial as to precisely which interpretations of rights are justified. But this fact alone does not show that the idea of a justifying theory is spurious.

In the preceding chapters I have been speaking somewhat abstractly about justifying theories. I have argued that when a United States court is faced with interpreting the meaning of concepts like international custom and consensus in applying human rights law in particular cases, it typically will not be able to do its job by turning exclusively to empirical tests of the sort contemplated by traditional positivist doctrines. If this is so, then a court will have to "construct" its interpretation of the law with the help of the best justifying theories available to it. I use the term "justifying" as opposed to "justified" to emphasize that a legal

at the present time.

If a court is faced with a case like *Filartiga*, it will have to make sense out of and seek to justify its own conceptions of the controversial notions of a universal consensus, international custom, and the idea that the right to be free from acts of torture is a universalizable human rights standard.

Thus, justifying theories, not simply facts about existing practices in the world community alone, supply background conditions for the legal validity of human rights. Because of the important connection positivists find between the existence of a system of law E(S) and the validity of particular laws V(R),[1] it is reasonable to suppose that a justifying theory must either justify that connection or show why it is unjustified. For example, a justifying theory might show why the concept of a centralized system, otherwise appropriate for the concept of domestic law, is not appropriate for the concept of international law by explaining why a decentralized and comparatively indeterminate and unenforceable normative order is sufficient for the existence of authoritative interpretations and applications of international legal standards.[2]

Likewise, a justifying theory might show why recourse to empirical procedures specified by a secondary rule are insufficient for establishing the validity (or invalidity) of some rule R in legal system S, and accordingly provide a rationale for judgment based on principles taken to be presupposed by S as a whole.[3]

Definition of Justifying Legal Theories

By the locution "justifying legal theories" I mean philosophically-based theories which aim to legitimate, that is, provide the best possible moral and legal justifications for, interpretations and applications of specific human rights by United States courts. Justifying theories supply the philosophical ratio decidendi of contemporary human rights adjudication. Justifying theories may be thought of as ideal judicial opinions, and need not be identified with actual human rights decisions, although as I will show, such decisions are ultimately dependent on justifying theories.

---

[1]. *See*, Chapter Two, *supra*.

[2]. For an argument of this sort, *see* T. Nardin, *Law, Morality and the Relations of States* (1983), especially 133-48, 158-66.

[3]. *See generally*, R. Dworkin, *Taking Rights Seriously* (1977), 81-30.

Functions of Justifying Theories

In this section I will discuss some of the primary functions of justifying theories in the context of some critical issues involved in justifying and applying the purportedly universal right to freedom from torture that the *Filartiga* interpretation was premised upon. These key functions are: weighing, scope delimiting, "booting," and showing entailment relationships.[4] I do not mean to suggest that these four particular functions are exhaustive. Rather, they are intended to be illustrative. And although there is some overlap between these notions I take it that they are nevertheless sufficiently distinct to warrant the separate treatment I will give them here.

Weighing

Justifying theories perform weighing functions when they specify the priority or "gravity" of a particular human right relative to other considerations. Issues of weight concern how specific rights should be ranked when they conflict with other legal or moral rights or with other important considerations, such as cost or social utility.

Suppose it is argued that the cost of upholding the right against torture might, in some possible circumstances, justify suspending that right. The prohibition of torture effectively denies some governments their chosen means of police investigation. A justifying theory might seek to overcome that objection in the following way. It might assert that the cost of upholding the right against torture does not *ipso facto* disparage the justiciability of the right, while admitting that it does constitute an impediment to one means of achieving the social goal of efficient (though cruel) law enforcement. It could then show that other means to that goal are available which do not involve as extensive an intrusion into personal dignity as torture. The crucial point here is that such an argument takes the right against torture to be a weighty enough standard as to overcome the cost factor.

Or, a justifying theory might point to institutionally recognized textual sources for human rights in overcoming the objection. Article 15 of the European Convention, for instance, effectively specifies the weight

---

[4]. My use of these general categories corresponds to various parts of James Nickel's discussion in *Making Sense of Human Rights* (1987). However, my specific analysis is significantly different from his own.

of several rights, among them the right against torture,[5] by stating that it is prohibited (presumably even in emergency situations) to suspend such rights. This means that the right against torture is absolute in weight against purportedly exigent circumstances that might be cited in specific cases. Here the appeal to institutional support (the text of the Convention) backs up the assertion that the right against torture is more weighty than any cost which might be involved in suspending it in emergencies.

Scope Delimitation

This is not to say that rights with "absolute" weighing in the sense discussed above in connection with Article 15 may not contain implied exceptions. Making judgments about the existence or nonexistence of exceptions to rights is a matter of delimiting the scope of such rights. This, then, is another significant job of a justifying theory --- to specify possible exceptions (or, in some cases, indicate the nonexistence of exceptions) to a human right in certain circumstances. A paradigm case of scope delimitation might be the interpretation of the scope of a right or liberty as being justified so far as it is consistent with the capacity of others to enjoy that right. (A's right to free speech might be said to contain the exception that A may not outshout B in a debate, denying B her right to free speech.) Granted, issues of weighing and scope are often interrelated. A decision that a right is very weighty may support a further decision that it is not subject to a particular exception. A claim that the right to be free from torture would not permit an act of torture even in a national emergency might be backed up with an analysis of weighing (*i.e.*, the right is so important it cannot be overridden) or of scope (*i.e.*, the right is not qualified by the proposed exception).

"Booting"

Another basic problem which justifying legal theories must tackle

---

[5]. According to Article 3, "No one shall be subjected to torture or to inhuman or degrading treatment or punishment." Also included in the European Convention are, e.g., the rights against slavery (Article 4), retroactive criminal laws (Article 7), and life (Article 2). Article 15 states, in relevant part, that: No derogation from Article 2, except in respect of deaths resulting from lawful acts of war, or from Article 3, 4 (paragraph 1) and 7 shall be made under this provision.

is how to "boot up" or advance initial postulates for human rights.[6] Ideally, the most promising sort of initial postulates would be universally acceptable and would readily enable further inferences or derivations of specific human rights to be made.

At the most philosophical stage, abstract conceptual devices seem appropriate for supporting interpretations of human rights as universal norms --- institutional standards valid for the entire human community *qua* humans. Such devices might include a hypothetical model of rational moral choice by persons situated behind a "veil of ignorance" in the "original position" (Rawls), or the presupposition of a consensus by the "universal audience" (Perelman) construed as an abstract counterpart of the international community of individuals *qua* addressees of human rights norms.[7]

---

[6]. Alan Gewirth has identified some of the typical approaches to establishing the basis for human rights. These different approaches may be summarized as follows: (i) intuitionist (taking the existence of human rights as self-evident); (ii) institutionalist (existence of formal/informal institutional rules establishes human rights); (iii) interest-based (humans have rights because they have interests); (iv) intrinsic-based (humans have intrinsic worth/dignity); (v) Kantian (humans are ends in themselves, and therefore have rights); (vi) religious (humans have rights because they are God's children); (vii) Rawlsian (humans situated behind veil of ignorance would ensure that all have basic rights). *Human Rights: Essays on Justification and Applications* (1982) at 43-44.

[7]. An important element of Chaim Perelman's legal philosophy is his application of the concept of the "universal audience" to the problem of justifying legal argumentation. The universal audience is conceived of as "the whole of mankind, or at least, of all normal, adult persons." *The New Rhetoric* at 30. The universal audience may be distinguished from a single interlocutor --- a person who is addressed in a dialogue, and from a single deliberating subject --- a person who engages in self-reflection and gives reasons for certain actions. For Perelman, the latter two cases are particular incarnations of the universal audience. The universal audience has "primordial importance" as it provides a basic norm for objective juridical argumentation. *Id.* at 31. In his essays on legal argumentation, Perelman stresses that the aim of a legal theory is to convince and persuade those toward which it is addressed. The following passage is illustrative:

The jurist who elaborates legal theories, who furnishes a justified interpretation of a text or who proposes new legislations will measure the success of his enterprise by the approval of the courts or that of the legislator. From this perspective, legal theories do not have the task of stating the truth but of preparing and justifying decisions.

Obviously at such abstract levels all potential conflicts between human rights and regional constraints specific to individual cases can neither be fully anticipated nor definitively resolved. However, refinements in scope, applicability and weighing which appear in various interpretive stages will be supported at various levels of argumentation. Abstract presuppositions of rational objectivity are supplanted by actual reasons adduced by a jurist in support of her or his interpretation of a provision in a human rights text at some lower level. Disagreements about specific interpretations must match arguments given in favor of the interpretation. If objections do not measure up to the character of justifying argumentation they will not serve as valid counter-interpretations for the level at hand.

Suppose an argument is given in support of a reading that a *prima facie* human right is not subject to an apparent exception or qualification. An objection to this claim must not attempt to refute the portion of the argument alleging the *prima facie* validity of the right on the grounds that human rights are not absolute, but must instead contest the specific allegation of non-exception or non-qualification at issue. This requirement renders irrelevant objections that human rights are not absolute when no such strong claim has been advanced. An argument that a human right is *prima facie* valid does not entail the different argument that the human right is absolute and without qualification.

"Legal Reasoning," in *Justice, Law and Argument* at 161.

Perelman maintains that in both philosophy and law, as enterprises which employ rational argumentation which is valid for the entire human community, are committed to making arguments addressed to the universal audience. Thus, he writes:

A reflection on law, its problems and its methods can reveal a philosophy of the reasonable which . . . seeks to elaborate perspectives which can be proposed to the universality of men.

"Law, Philosophy, and Argumentation," in *id.* at 161.

So, the universal audience may be seen as a rhetorical embodiment of the thesis that "[t]he characteristic of rational argumentation is the aim to universality."

"Justice and Reason," in *id.* at 73.

Showing Entailment Relations

Justifying theories ground interpretations of human rights by accounting for the manner in which specific human rights are entailed by abstract considerations. Thus, specific human rights may be shown to follow from various abstract considerations which are conceded to be important, albeit within the context of given institutional capacities and restraints. At specific, concrete levels of interpretations, justifying theories will aim to support decisions for actual implementations and applications of human rights.

Justifying theories may therefore be employed to show how specific rights like the right to be free from torture are justified by appeals to more abstract principles like human claims to life, liberty, and dignity. Selecting and formulating specific rights cannot, of course, simply be deduced from abstract principles. For example, the transition from abstract claims to more specific human rights will usually require empirical information about modern institutions, a country's resources, its legal system, and so on. Showing the entailment of a specific human right from an abstract claim will involve some accounting of the importance of the specific right at issue. In the case of torture, it can be plausibly argued that, given the fact that the basic claim to have a life is threatened by acts of torture of the kind carried out by officials of some governments, one's interest in being free from torture is, to say the least, of critical importance.

Acceptability of Justifying Theories

The integrity model suggests that formal human rights interpretations of the kind analyzed in Chapter Five reflect hard case situations (in Dworkin's sense). As such, the adjudicator will be faced with alternative interpretations from which to choose. As has been shown, a justifying theory will attempt to provide the interpreter with the "best justified" interpretive standpoint. At a minimum, a justifying theory will have to ensure that the relevant textual legal sources have been identified and prioritized according to standard canons of legal interpretation such as those routinely followed by United States federal courts. However, since many of the standards for legal interpretation are themselves open to disagreement, a choice of preference for the appropriate sources of law assumes some reference to evaluation even at this rudimentary level. Moreover, there exists the possibility (though Dworkin would deny this) that there will be more than one well-justified interpretation in a hard case. Is it therefore cogent to speak of a *best* justified interpretation in human rights cases?

Factual vs. Counterfactual Aspects of Acceptability

As a preliminary matter, it should be acknowledged that in seeking an interpretation with the greatest degree of acceptability --- that is, the best justified one --- a question arises concerning whether the notion of acceptability is to be understood in a factual or in a counterfactual sense. A concrete version of such a question was resolved in different ways in the context of the Supreme Court's decision in *Gregg v. Georgia* concerning the acceptability of capital punishment in the United States. Thus, the majority opinion in *Gregg* found evidence for a societal endorsement of the death penalty by observing that, after the Furman decision, thirty-five states had enacted new laws providing for the penalty of death for some crimes.[8] As such, the majority was basing its interpretation of acceptance on the factual question of how state legislatures had actually acted on the matter. In the human rights setting, the analogue to such an approach would be found in an inquiry into whether, say, a majority of nations had enacted a given right into their respective legal systems, or whether a majority of nations had signed a given treaty with human rights provisions.

The dissenting opinion in Gregg took a counterfactual approach in addressing the question of acceptability of capital punishment in maintaining that a majority of United States citizens *if fully informed* about "information critical to a judgment on the morality of the death penalty" *would* consider the penalty unacceptable. Again, the counterpart for this kind of method can readily be identified in human rights settings as well.

My point in making the distinction between factual and counterfactual senses of acceptability is this. The textures of justifying theories of rights are complex and multilayered. It is consistent with the integrity model that at certain rudimentary levels of inquiry a justifying theory will employ the factual method of determining acceptability. At more abstract levels, however, the counterfactual method becomes necessary. For instance, in the "snail darter" case, the Supreme Court did not (nor would it have been appropriate for them to) claim that the Endangered Species Act had not been duly enacted because a majority vote by Congress was not dispositive of the matter. At the level of inquiry as to the passage of the law, the factual question of acceptability by majority vote is obviously not subject to being disregarded in favor of a counterfactual counterproposal. At other levels of theoretical inquiry,

---

[8]. 428 U.S. 153 (1976).

however, integrity proposes that it is appropriate for counterfactual methods of assessing acceptability to be employed. Since it is not obvious that integrity endorses such a method, however, a brief digression is needed to back up the preceding claim with a textual exegesis of the relevant passages from Dworkin's work. In discussing the problem of judicial interpretation of legislative intent, where it is in question, Dworkin recommends that a general legislative intent be constructed by the adjudicator which will "directly" justify the law in a manner consistent with the principles subscribed to by a community of principle.[9] This method (Hercules' procedure) is offered as a better alternative than (Hermes' counterfactual procedure of) trying to sort out different possible combinations of how the various legislators *would have* voted on the issue if they had thought about it. The so-called direct method avoids involvement in the immense complexity associated with sorting out the different possible combinations of legislative convictions on an issue. Granted that Hercules' method represents a more direct way of framing the issue of intent, one may wonder whether it still implicates a counterfactual methodology.

I maintain that it does. Strictly speaking, absent an explicit statement of general intent in the *travaux preparatoires*, there is no actual general intent lurking within a statute. Hercules' formulation of a general intent is therefore a hypothetical construct (just as Hercules himself is) which is designed to facilitate the application of the statute to contemporary fact situations. The counterfactual aspect of the inquiry is now seen in the operative issue, and is expressible as follows: If the legislators had written a statement of general intent into the statute, *would* the expression of that intent be justified by such and such principles?

In my view, questions surrounding the relative degree of acceptability amongst competing justifying theories of human rights, or of component features of such theories, depend upon counterfactual assumptions which the interpreter must make about the attributes and predicted responses of such idealized entities as an audience, judge, or legislative body. As such, it turns out that factual claims about the ethical and/or cultural homogeneity (or diversity) of a community are not dispositive *per se* concerning the "acceptability" of a justifying theory, nor indeed, for any of its postulates. Thus, skeptical assertions that a given human right is not in fact recognized as a high-priority norm in all or even in a majority of cultures may be countered with the claim that, assuming certain modified attributes of the community (*e.g.*, rationality of its members) the right in question *would be* so recognized.

---

[9]. R. Dworkin, *Law's Empire* at 325-54.

Indeed, the foundation for Dworkin's "one right answer" thesis --- the claim that there is always a uniquely correct resolution of even the hardest cases --- is provided by the supposition of the idealized Judge Hercules, endowed with maximally rational faculties. If one were to ask why it is we can be assured that there is a best justification of a judicial decision possible, the reply would be "because one may postulate an idealized judge who, upon being confronted with the case, *would be* able to construct the single right resolution for it."[10]

The "One Right Answer" Thesis

As has been seen, integrity rejects both classical natural law theory and legal positivism. As a substitute for these doctrines, Dworkin embraces a species of normative procedural rationality. There are three reflections of this commitment to procedural rationality in the integrity model. The first is found in Dworkin's allegiance to the basic tenets of Rawl's political philosophy. As is well known, in the idealized "original position" moral agents select principles such as justice and fairness according to a counterfactual bargaining process engaged in behind a "veil of ignorance" which masks their particular position in society. The reasonableness of the resultant acceptability of the moral principles of justice and fairness is a product of an idealized process involving rational decisionmaking. The second manifestation appears on the level of philosophical argumentation with critics of Dworkin's own theory of law. Thus, Dworkin challenges his opponents to meet his arguments with better arguments at the same level of specificity with which he has framed them, rather than spewing out the kind of overgeneralized diatribes that he associates with the critical legal studies camp. The following passage is illustrative:

> The only skepticism worth anything is skepticism of the internal kind, and this must be earned by arguments of the same contested character as the arguments it opposes, not claimed in advance by some pretense at hard-hitting empirical metaphysics.[11]

---

[10]. This basis for the one-right-answer thesis is challenged by J.L. Mackie. Briefly, Mackie supposes that a second mythical judge, Rhadamanthus, might formulate an alternative answer to the one Hercules constructs. See, J.L. Mackie, "The Third Theory of Law," 7 *Philosophy and Public Affairs* (Fall 1977).

[11]. R. Dworkin, *Law's Empire*, *supra*, at 86.

Dworkin demands that his critics match their arguments to the substance of his allegations. The plea here is similar to the type of argumentation demanded in the practice of law, such as the rules of civil procedure which require answers to complaints to fairly match the substance of the claims filed.

The third association with procedural rationality in the integrity model is to be found in its depiction of the nature of judicial reasoning employed in support of specific constructive interpretations of law. This type of reasoning strives to justify existing rules in terms of principles presupposed by the legal system as a whole. Unlike the deductive ideal of Cartesian rationalism, this method of judicial reasoning does not ultimately yield proofs of absolute certainty.

In connection with this genre of argumentation Dworkin claims that there is "one right answer" even in the hardest, most controversial cases. The point of constructive interpretation, Dworkin holds, is to make the law the "best it can be." The one-right-answer thesis, therefore, is wedded to the idea of reaching *the* best interpretation rather than, say, the notion that there might just be a number of "better" interpretations of rights available.

With the help of this paradigm of judicial rationality, Dworkin hopes to avoid the metaphysical implausibility of the "strongbox" theory of natural law on the one hand, and the ethically undesirable discretionism and conventionalism of legal positivism on the other. The strongbox theory, traceable to Augustine and Aquinas, conceives of legal truths as "locked away" in heaven and discoverable by mortals only by the "light of natural reason." Dworkin find this aspect of natural law theory particularly implausible. However, another feature of natural law theory, enshrined in Augustine's dictum that "an unjust law is not law at all," is implicitly adopted throughout Dworkin's writings. Dworkin clearly maintains there is a strong connection between law and morality. Since one cannot inquire into what the law is without also inquiring into morality (as has been seen, constructive legal interpretation employs general moral principles to make sense out of the rules it must apply in particular cases), there is a link between legal reasoning and moral reasoning.

For the legal positivists such a connection is routinely denied. Dworkin's sustained attack on positivism indicates an opposition to the so-called "separability thesis." That thesis is an outgrowth of positivism's view of law as a science of empirical propositions. Positivism aims to investigate the factual conditions under which a law is said to be valid. Such factual conditions are distinguished from matters of value which, to a number of thinkers (*e.g.*, C.L. Stevenson, A.J. Ayer, J-P. Sartre) express attitudes or feelings. Hence propositions of value are seen as subjective or arbitrary. This raises special problems for any jurisprudence which maintains a close interdependence between law and morality. For instance, the question arises whether, if ethical and evaluative propositions are subjective and arbitrary, then will not propositions of law be so as well? Such concerns motivate positivists to segregate questions about the "existence of law" from questions concerning a law's "merit or demerit."

But, as was seen in Chapter Two, positivism runs into its own special problems as a theory for adjudicating rights. One is the problem of judicial discretion. A second problem is dubbed the "semantic sting." For Dworkin, the mistake in the semantic sting is in supposing that the meaning of a proposition such as "x is valid law" is exhausted by factual conditions.[12] More specifically, for Hart, the meaning of "x is valid law" is reducible to an accounting of primary and secondary rules. These rules are linked to the conventional behavior of officials in the legal system. For this reason, Dworkin terms the view that all rights must be explicitly traceable to empirical texts (statutes, case precedents, the Constitution) "conventionalism." Dworkin sees this law-as-plain fact doctrine of conventionalism as misguided. Conventionalism simply cannot account for disagreement of the deep theoretical sort found in hard cases.

In hard cases disagreement centers around the meaning of a law, requiring that a creative attitude be taken by the adjudicator. Interpretation in hard cases typically demands that a judge come up with a conception of a law not thought of by its author, or which is not clearly covered by existing conventional doctrine or judicial practices. Conventionalism's obsession with consistency in the interests of ensuring predictability and fairness eventually leads to a crisis. The conventions to be consulted for the final answer are themselves unclear or contradictory. A justification for selecting one account of practices over another is therefore called for. The ends of the legal practices themselves must be considered.

Dworkin's solution posits a principled approach to judicial decisionmaking. In deciding a hard case, a judge first finds a "fit" with existing empirical sources of law. But in addition, he or she must justify an interpretation of the litigant's rights that will be grounded in principles of democratic political morality, such as justice, fairness, and due process. This entails asking whether the decision comports with the particular conceptions of justice, fairness, and due process that are presupposed by the system of rules as a whole. But as has been pointed

---

[12]. *See* the application of this concept to D'Amato's account of international human rights in Chapter 2, *supra*.

out, Dworkin rejects the substantive (*i.e.* divinely-based natural law) conception of justice as well as the "cynical" conception supplied by the positivists and realists.

Accordingly, Dworkin opts for Rawl's orientation towards justice and fairness. This conception is "procedural" rather than "substantive" in the sense that the root principle of maximum equal liberty in political matters (which ensures fair equality of opportunity and demands that inequalities work out to everyone's advantage) is the product of an idealized *process or procedure* of choice for rational agents situated behind the imaginary "veil of ignorance."

The Audience for Justifying Theories

The integrity model suggests that Hercules is the sole audience (an "audience of one") before which the acceptability of the justifying theories he constructs is ultimately assessed. Although Dworkin does not explicitly address this point, it seems to be a fair enough inference given that Dworkin attributes Hercules with attributes that would make him a maximally rational agent with regard to the theoretical material whose acceptability is in question. To the extent that questions arise concerning the "appeal" of a given theoretical justification of law to the prevailing "community morality," Dworkin clearly charges Hercules with the task of temperature-taking of that audience. However, the effect of this methodology of justification is to impose a double layer of counterfactuality with regard to audience justification. The first layer of counterfactuality consists in Hercules interpretation of how an ideal community (the "true" community) *would* react to a proposed theoretical justification (*i.e.*, by accepting or rejecting it). The second layer of counterfactuality consists in the interpretation of some concerned third party (say, a real judge) of how the ideal judge Hercules *would* in turn interpret the community's interpretation.

Obviously, such an already complicated model becomes even more complicated if one considers the possibility of divergent interpretations occurring within either of these two layers. Thus, if the make-up of the community is such that interpretations of how that community would react to a proposed theoretical justification are controversial, then a justifying theory is *pro tanto* less determinate. Such is the case when there is a significant amount of value diversity present within the community. Similarly, if one assumes that more than one ideally rational juridic interpreter can be postulated then, once again, the relative determinacy of the theoretical justification is jeopardized.

Interpretive Convergence

That the possibility of relativism associated with the diversity of positions taken with respect to a justifying theory need not absolutely undermine the validity of such a theory is seen by the corresponding possibility of convergence (or overlapping) of attitudes of acceptance toward a given theory. What is important to observe is that the possibilities of either divergence or convergence within the different levels of interpretation should not be ignored in an effort to impose simplicity on the matter. The principal danger of ignoring such varieties of possibilities is that of taking exaggerated skeptical or non-skeptical (as the case may be) stances on the validity *vel non* of human rights norms *as an entire class*. Thus, the existence of high levels of convergence with respect to a justifying theory for a given human right --- for instance, the right not to be tortured --- means that relativist-based skepticism of that right is so much the weaker. The reverse will of course be true in instances of low levels of convergence --- as in the case of the (sometimes) purported human right to a paid vacation.

Institutional Manifestations of Convergence

As Dworkin frames it, the integrity model bears the stamp of a number of institutional characteristics of the special kind of adjudication he includes within its scope. The high degrees of convergence which integrity must assume to exist in order to support the demands of the "one right answer" thesis is reflected institutionally in the way domestic legislation is passed (majority vote) and domestic adjudication is undertaken (ultimate juridic authority vested in one Supreme Court which issues its rulings as a majority, or sometimes as a plurality).

At the present time, however, although such institutional manifestations of convergence for human rights cases may be identified in the Torture Victim Protection Act, currently pending before Congress, the United States Supreme Court has not yet ruled on international human rights cases as interpreted by domestic federal courts. Therefore, there remains the possibility of conflicts remaining within the circuit courts of appeal, subject however to the possibility of a grant of certiorari to resolve any such conflicts, as is customary.

Conclusion

Although positivism and realism were rejected in favor of integrity in this study as frameworks for human rights adjudication, this does not mean that all aspects of those two models are invalid. Indeed, the integrity model incorporates some of the central tenets of both positivism and realism. That is, integrity shares positivism's recognition of those legal rights which are reflected in well-settled law texts as applied in clear cases. Moreover, integrity shares realism's insight that interpretations of rights are in fact influenced in a significant way by the moral controversies prevailing in the community.

At the same time, however, it was seen that several of the key tenets of integrity --- those pertaining to the peculiar sense of interpretation deployed in rights adjudication and to the role of the community in such adjudication --- required modification to permit integrity to withstand the special problems raised by its application to human rights law. The problems were: (i) Integrity's artistic/literary conception of interpretation did not adequately account for the sometimes distorted and inaccurate perspective of the author (a situation not present in the case of artistic or literary interpretation) and the complex and multileveled process by which the interpreter seeks to rectify that limitation. The psychoanalytic conception was needed to more accurately capture this dimension since it explains the epistemic limitations of the author better than the artistic/literary model. (ii) The integrity conception of the community as comprised of citizens only was seen to be underinclusive in the sense that it could not account for the legal obligations recognized as owing to aliens pursuant to the human rights decisions studied in Chapter Five.

A serious shortcoming of the positivist model was that it assumed that the task of the adjudicator was limited to applying the law. As such, it is not necessary for the adjudicator to inquire whether the law as presented in, *e.g.*, statutes, is formally valid in interpreting it in the context of a particular case. The statute is rather simply followed according to its directives. For the positivist, the existence of a statute which has been enacted according to the appropriate procedures is sufficient to establish the legitimacy of a judicial decision.

The integrity model acknowledges that adjudication may raise questions concerning the legitimacy of law in situations in which alternative well-reasoned interpretations can be provided. Thus, integrity suggests that a hard case may reflect a special sort of "legitimacy crisis" (in Habermas' sense) in which the interpreter must *mediate* between the (positivist's) system of law (the legal order construed as a formal system of valid norms) and the (realist's) "life world" (*Lebenswelt*). The hard cases posed by human rights interpretations highlight an exaggerated form of such a juridical crisis. This is so because the formal criteria of legality for the sources of human rights law are themselves in question. At the same time, the existence of an audience consensus concerning the legitimacy of those rights is called into doubt due to the presence of cultural and ethical diversity in the world. To the extent that justifying theories are constructed which will offer reasonable resolutions for these prevailing tensions, they will at least meet the task of offering the sort of regional justification that may be expected of them in virtue of their institutional relationship to domestic tribunals. Assuming that their proposed interpretations are indeed reasonable, the hope for the future of international human rights is that their theoretical integrity will be exportable to enlighten other regionally- or internationally-instituted tribunals as well.

The interpretive context for human rights which this study was predicated on illustrates that the legitimacy of legal norms is ultimately parasitic upon the acceptability of justifying theories. Such acceptability, in turn, is dependent on counterfactual suppositions concerning a variety of discreet yet sometimes intersecting audiences whose consensus is sought. The integrity model (with appropriate modifications) was best able to account for the necessary mediation between the systemic and Lebenswelt-related aspects of human rights adjudication by lessening the strictures imposed by the traditional positivist and realist approaches. Specifically, the positivist search for the legality of textual sources tout court was rejected in favor of the more nuanced conception of integrity, which allows key issues surrounding the legality of rights to be treated as controversial interpretive concepts. Moreover, the realist preoccupation with what it takes to be a necessary interpretive impasse posed by global value-diversity was put into balance by the deployment of particular (scope-restricted) ideal (counterfactual) audiences. The resultant possibilities of interpretive convergence of such audiences functions as a regulative device for the range of acceptability of justifying theories for human rights norms.

CONVENTION ON THE PREVENTION AND PUNISHMENT OF THE CRIME OF GENOCIDE. (Entered into force, January 12, 1961.)

Article I. The Contracting Parties confirm that genocide, whether committed in time of peace or in time of war, is a crime under international law which they undertake to prevent and to punish.

Article II. In the present Convention, genocide means any of the following acts committed with intent to destroy, in whole or in part, a national, ethnical, racial or religious group, as such:

(a) Killing members of the group;

(b) Causing serious bodily or mental harm to members of the group;

(c) Deliberately inflicting on the group conditions of life calculated to bring about its physical destruction in whole or in part;

(d) Imposing measures intended to prevent births within the group;

(e) Forcibly transferring children of the group to another group.

Article III. The following acts shall be punishable:

(a) Genocide;

(b) Conspiracy to commit genocide;

(c) Direct and public incitement to commit genocide;

(d) Attempt to commit genocide;

(e) Complicity in genocide.

Article IV. Persons committing genocide or any of the other acts enumerated in Article III shall be punished, whether they are constitutionally responsible rulers, public officials or private individuals.

Article V. The Contracting Parties undertake to enact, in accordance with their respective Constitutions, the necessary legislation to give effect to the provisions of the present Convention and, in particular, to provide effective penalties for persons guilty of genocide or of any of the other acts enumerated in Article III.

Article VI. Persons charged with genocide or any of the other acts enumerated in Article III shall be tried by a competent tribunal of the State in the territory of which the act was committed, or by such international penal tribunal as may have jurisdiction with respect to those Contracting Parties which shall have accepted its jurisdiction.

Article VII. Genocide and the other acts enumerated in Article III shall not be considered as political crimes for the purpose of extradition.

The Contracting Parties pledge themselves in such cases to grant extradition in accordance with their laws and treaties in force.

Article VIII. Any Contracting Party may call upon the competent organs of the United Nations to take such action under the Charter of the United Nations as they consider appropriate for the prevention and suppression of acts of genocide or any of the other acts enumerated in Article III.

Article IX. Disputes between the Contracting Parties relating to the interpretation, application or fulfillment of the present Convention, including those relating to the responsibility of a State for genocide or for any of the other acts enumerated in Article III, shall be submitted to the International Court cf Justice at the request of any of the parties to the dispute.

UNIVERSAL DECLARATION OF HUMAN RIGHTS. (December 10, 1948.)

PREAMBLE

Whereas recognition of the inherent dignity and of the equal and inalienable rights of all members of the human family is the foundation of freedom, justice and peace in the world,

Whereas disregard and contempt for human rights have resulted in barbarous acts which have outraged the conscience of mankind, and the advent of a world in which human beings shall enjoy freedom of speech and belief and freedom from fear and want has been proclaimed as the highest aspiration of the common people,

Whereas it is essential, if man is not to be compelled to have recourse, as a last resort, to rebellion against tyranny and oppression, that human rights should be protected by the rule of law,

Whereas it is essential to promote the development of friendly relations between nations,

Whereas the peoples of the United Nations have in the Charter reaffirmed their faith in fundamental human rights, in the dignity and worth of the human person and in the equal rights of men and women and have determined to promote social progress and better standards of life in larger freedom,

Whereas Member States have pledged themselves to achieve, in cooperation with the United Nations, the promotion of universal respect for and observance of human rights and fundamental freedoms,

Whereas a common understanding of these rights and freedoms is of the greatest importance for the full realization of this pledge,

Now, therefore,

The General Assembly

Proclaims this Universal Declaration of Human Rights as a common standard of achievement for all peoples and all nations, to the end that every individual and every organ of society, keeping this Declaration constantly in mind, shall strive by teaching and education to promote respect for these rights and freedoms and by progressive measures, national and international, to secure their universal and effective recognition and observance, both among the peoples of Member States themselves and among the peoples of territories under their jurisdiction.

Article 1. All human beings are born free and equal in dignity and rights. They are endowed with reason and conscience and should act towards one another in a spirit of brotherhood.

Article 2. Everyone is entitled to all the rights and freedoms set forth in this Declaration, without distinction of any kind, such as race, color, sex, language, religion, political or other opinion, national or social origin, property, birth or other status.

Furthermore, no distinction shall be made on the basis of the political, jurisdictional or international status of the country or territory to which a person belongs, whether it be independent, trust, non-self-governing or under any other limitation of sovereignty.

Article 3. Everyone has the right to life, liberty and the security of person.

Article 4. No one shall be held in slavery or servitude; slavery and the slave trade shall be prohibited in all their forms.

Article 5. No one shall be subjected to torture or to cruel, inhuman or degrading treatment or punishment.

Article 6. Everyone has the right to recognition everywhere as a person before the law.

Article 7. All are equal before the law and are entitled without any discrimination to equal protection of the law. All are entitled to equal protection against any discrimination in violation of this Declaration and against any incitement to such discrimination.

Article 8. Everyone has the right to an effective remedy by the competent national tribunals for acts violating the fundamental rights granted him by the constitution or by law.

Article 9. No one shall be subjected to arbitrary arrest, detention or exile.

Article 10. Everyone is entitled in full equality to a fair and public hearing by an independent and impartial tribunal, in the determination of his rights and obligations and of any criminal charge against him.

Article 11. (1) Everyone charged with a penal offence has the right to be presumed innocent until proved guilty according to law in a public trial at which he has had all the guarantees necessary for his defence.

(2) No one shall be held guilty of any penal offence on account of any act or omission which did not constitute a penal offence, under national or international law, at the time when it was committed. Nor shall a heavier penalty be imposed than the one that was applicable at the time the penal offence was committed.

Article 12. No one shall be subjected to arbitrary interference with his privacy, family, home or correspondence, nor to attacks upon his honour and reputation. Everyone has the right to the protection of the law against such interference or attacks.

Article 13. (1) Everyone has the right to freedom of movement and residence within the borders of each State.

(2) Everyone has the right to leave any country, including his own, and to return to his country.

Article 14. (1) Everyone has the right to seek and to enjoy in other countries asylum from persecution.

(2) This right may not be invoked in the case of prosecutions genuinely arising from nonpolitical crimes or from acts contrary to the purposes and principles of the United Nations.

Article 15. (1) Everyone has the right to a nationality.

(2) No one shall be arbitrarily deprived of his nationality nor denied the

right to change his nationality.

Article 16. (1) Men and women of full age, without any limitation due to race, nationality or religion, have the right to marry and to found a family. They are entitled to equal rights as to marriage, during marriage and at its dissolution.

(2) Marriage shall be entered into only with the free and full consent of the intending spouses.

(3) The family is the natural and fundamental group unit of society and is entitled to protection by society and the State.

Article 17. (1) Everyone has the right to own property alone as well as in association with others.

(2) No one shall be arbitrarily deprived of his property.

Article 18. Everyone has the right to freedom of thought, conscience and religion; this right includes freedom to change his religion or belief, and freedom, either alone or in community with others and in public or private, to manifest his religion or belief in teaching, practice, worship and observance.

Article 19. Everyone has the right to freedom of opinion and expression; this right includes freedom to hold opinions without interference and to seek, receive and impart information and ideas through any media and regardless of frontiers.

Article 20. (1) Everyone has the right to freedom of peaceful assembly and association. (2) No one may be compelled to belong to an association.

Article 21. (1) Everyone has the right to take part in the government of his country, directly or through freely chosen representatives.

(2) Everyone has the right of equal access to public service in his country.

(3) The will of the people shall be the basis of the authority of government; this will shall be expressed in periodic and genuine elections which shall be by universal and equal suffrage and shall be held by secret vote or by equivalent free voting procedures.

Article 22. Everyone, as a member of society, has the right to social security and is entitled to realization, through national effort and international cooperation and in accordance with the organization and resources of each State, of the economic, social and cultural rights indispensable for his dignity and the free development of his personality.

Article 23. (1) Everyone has the right to work, to free choice of employment, to just and favourable conditions of work and to protection against unemployment.

(2) Everyone, without any discrimination; has the right to equal pay for equal work.

(3) Everyone who works has the right to just and favourable remuneration ensuring for himself and his family an existence worthy of human dignity, and supplemented, if necessary, by other means of social protection.

(4) Everyone has the right to form and to join trade unions for the protection of his interests.

Article 24. Everyone has the right to rest and leisure, including reasonable limitation of working hours and periodic holidays with pay.

Article 25. (1) Everyone has the right to a standard of living adequate for the health and well-being of himself and of his family, including food, clothing, housing and medical care and necessary social services, and the right to security in the event of unemployment, sickness, disability, widowhood, old age or other lack of livelihood in circumstances beyond his control.

(2) Motherhood and childhood are entitled to special care and assistance. All children, whether born in or out of wedlock, shall enjoy the same social protection.

Article 26. (1) Everyone has the right to education. Education shall be free, at least in the elementary and fundamental stages. Elementary education shall be compulsory. Technical and professional education shall be made generally available and higher education shall be equally accessible to all on the basis of merit.

(2) Education shall be directed to the full development of the human personality and to the strengthening of respect for human rights and fundamental freedoms. It shall promote understanding, tolerance and friendship among all nations, racial or religious groups, and shall further the activities of the United Nations for the maintenance of peace.

(3) Parents have a prior right to choose the kind of education that shall be given to their children.

Article 27. (1) Everyone has the right freely to participate in the cultural life of the community, to enjoy the arts and to share in scientific advancement and its benefits.

(2) Everyone has the right to the protection of the moral and material interests resulting from any scientific, literary or artistic production of which he is the author.

Article 28. Everyone is entitled to a social and international order in which the rights and freedoms set forth in this Declaration can be fully realized.

Article 29. (1) Everyone has duties to the community in which alone the free and full development of his personality is possible.

(2) In the exercise of his rights and freedoms, everyone shall be subject only to such limitations as are determined by law solely for the purpose of securing due recognition and respect for the rights and freedoms of others and of meeting the just requirements of morality, public order and the general welfare in a democratic society.

(3) These rights and freedoms may in no case be exercised contrary to the purposes and principles of the United Nations.

Article 30. Nothing in this Declaration may be interpreted as implying for any State, group or person any right to engage in any activity or to perform any act aimed at the destruction of any of the rights and freedoms set forth herein.

INTERNATIONAL CONVENTION ON THE SUPPRESSION AND PUNISHMENT OF THE CRIME OF "APARTHEID." (Entered into force, July 18, 1976.)

Article I. (1) The States Parties to the present Convention declare that apartheid is a crime against humanity and that inhuman acts resulting from the policies and practices of apartheid and similar policies and practices of racial segregation and discrimination, as defined in article II of the Convention, are crimes violating the principles of international law, in particular the purposes and principles of the Charter of the United Nations, and constituting a serious threat to international peace and security.

(2) The States Parties to the present Convention declare criminal those organizations, institutions and individuals committing the crime of apartheid.

Article II. For the purpose of the present Convention, the term "the crime of apartheid" which shall include similar policies and practices of racial segregation and discrimination as practised in southern Africa, shall apply to the following inhuman acts committed for the purpose of establishing and maintaining domination by one racial group of persons over any other racial group of persons and systematically oppressing them:

(a) Denial to a member or members of a racial group or groups of the right to life and liberty of person:

(i) By murder of members of a racial group or groups;

(ii) By the infliction upon the members of a racial group or groups of serious bodily or mental harm by the infringement of their freedom or dignity, or by subjecting them to torture or to cruel, inhuman or degrading treatment or punishment;

(iii) By arbitrary arrest and illegal imprisonment of the members of a racial group or groups;

(b) Deliberate imposition on a racial group or groups of living conditions calculated to cause its or their physical destruction in whole or in part;

(c) Any legislative measures and other measures calculated to prevent a racial group or groups from participation in the political, social, economic and cultural life of the country and the deliberate creation of conditions preventing the full development of such a group or groups, in particular by denying to members of a racial group or groups basic human rights and freedoms, including the right to work, the right to form recognized trade unions, the right to education, the right to leave and to return to their country, the right to freedom of opinion and expression, and the right to freedom of peaceful assembly and association;

(d) Any measures, including legislative measures, designed to divide the population along racial lines by the creation of separate reserves and ghettos for the members of a racial group or groups, the prohibition of mixed marriages among members of various racial groups, the expropriation of landed property belonging to a racial group or groups or to members thereof;

(e) Exploitation of the labour of the members of a racial group or groups, in particular by submitting them to forced labour;

(f) Persecution of organizations and persons, by depriving them of fundamental rights and freedoms, because they oppose apartheid.

Article III. International criminal responsibility shall apply, irrespective of the motive involved, to individuals, members of organizations and institutions and representatives of the State, whether residing in the territory of the State in which the acts are perpetrated or in some other State, whenever they:

(a) Commit, participate in, directly incite or conspire in the commission of the acts mentioned in Article II of the present Convention,

(b) Directly abet, encourage or cooperate in the commission of the crime of apartheid.

Article IV. The States Parties to the present Convention undertake:

(a) To adopt any legislative or other measure necessary to suppress as well as to prevent any encouragement of the crime of apartheid and similar segregationist policies or their manifestations and to punish persons guilty of that crime;

(b) To adopt legislative, judicial and administrative measures to prosecute, bring to trial and punish in accordance with their jurisdiction persons responsible for, or accused of, the acts defined in article II of the present Convention, whether or not such persons reside in the territory of the State in which the acts are committed or are nationals of that State or of some other State or are stateless persons.

Article V. Persons charged with the acts enumerated in article II of the present Convention may be tried by a competent tribunal of any State Party to the Convention which may acquire jurisdiction with respect to those State Parties which shall have accepted its jurisdiction.

Article VI. The States Parties to the present Convention undertake to accept and carry out in accordance with the Charter of the United Nations the decisions taken by the Security Council aimed at the prevention, suppression and punishment of the crime of apartheid, and to cooperate in the implementation of decisions adopted by other competent organs of the United Nations with a view to achieving the purposes of the Convention.

Article VII. (1) The States Parties to the present Convention undertake to submit periodic reports to the group established under article IX on the legislative, judicial, administrative or other measures that they have adopted and that give effect to the provisions of the Convention.

(2) Copies of the reports shall be transmitted through the Secretary-General of the United Nations to the Special Committee on Apartheid.

Article VIII. Any State Party to the present Convention may call upon any competent organ of the United Nations to take such action under the Charter of the United Nations as it considers appropriate for the prevention and suppression of the crime of apartheid.

Article IX. (1) The Chairman of the Commission on Human Rights shall appoint a group consisting of three members of the Commission on Human Rights, who are also representatives of States Parties to the present Convention, to consider reports submitted by States Parties in accordance with article VII.

(2) If, among the members of the Commission on Human Rights, there are no representatives of States Parties to the present Convention or if there are fewer than three such representatives, the Secretary-General of the United Nations shall, after consulting all States Parties to the Convention, designate a representative of the State Party or representatives of the States Parties which are not members of the Commission on Human Rights to take part in the work of the group established in accordance with paragraph I of this article, until such time as representatives of the States Parties to the Convention are elected to the Commission on Human Rights.

(3) The group may meet for a period of not more than five days, either before the opening or after the closing of the session of the Commission on Human Rights, to consider the reports submitted in accordance with article VII.

Article X. (1) The States Parties to the present Convention empower the Commission on Human Rights:

(a) To request United Nations organs, when transmitting copies of petitions under article 15 of the international Convention on the Elimination of All Forms of Racial Discrimination, to draw its attention to complaints concerning acts which are enumerated in article II of the present Convention,

(b) To prepare, on the basis of reports from competent organs of the United Nations and periodic reports from States Parties to the present Convention, a list of individuals, organizations, institutions and representatives of States which are alleged to be responsible for the crimes enumerated in article II of the Convention, as well as those against whom legal proceedings have been undertaken by States Parties to the Convention;

(c) To request information for the competent United Nations organs concerning measures taken by the authorities responsible for the administration of Trust and Non-Self Governing Territories, and all other Territories to which General Assembly resolution 1514 (XV) of 14 December 1960 applies, with regard to such individuals alleged to be responsible for crimes under article II of the Convention who are believed to be under their territorial and administrative jurisdiction.

(2) Pending the achievement of the objectives of the Declaration on the Granting of Independence to Colonial Countries and Peoples, contained in General Assembly resolution 1514 (XV), the provisions of the present Convention shall in no way limit the right of petition granted to those peoples by other international instruments or by the United Nations and its specialized agencies.

Article XI. (1) Acts enumerated in article II of the present Convention shall not be considered political crimes for the purpose of extradition.

(2) The States Parties to the present Convention undertake in such cases to grant extradition with their legislation and with the treaties in force.

CONVENTION ON THE ELIMINATION OF ALL FORMS OF DISCRIMINATION AGAINST WOMEN. (Adopted by the U.N. General Assembly, December 18, 1979.)

Part I

Article 1. For the purposes of the present Convention, the term "discrimination against women" shall mean and distinction; exclusion or restriction made on the basis of sex which has the effect or purpose of impairing or nullifying the recognition, enjoyment or exercise by women, irrespective of their marital status, on a basis of equality of men and women, of human rights and fundamental freedoms in the political, economic, social, cultural, civil or any other field.

Article 3. States Parties shall take in all fields, in particular in the political, social, economic and cultural fields, all appropriate measures, including legislation, to ensure the full development and advancement of women, for the purpose of guaranteeing them the exercise and enjoyment of human rights and fundamental freedoms on a basis of equality with men.

Article 4. (1) Adoption by States Parties of temporary special measures aimed at accelerating de facto equality between men and women shall not be considered discrimination as defined in this Convention, but shall in no way entail, as a consequence, the maintenance of unequal or separate standards these measures shall be discontinued when the objectives of equality of opportunity and treatment have been achieved.

(2) Adoption by States Parties of special measures, including those measures contained in the present Convention, aimed at protecting maternity, shall not be considered discriminatory.

Article 5. States Parties shall take all appropriate measures:

(a) To modify the social and cultural patterns of conduct of men and women, with a view to achieving the elimination of prejudices and customary and all other practices which are based on the idea of the inferiority or the superiority of either of the sexes or on stereotyped roles for men and women.

(b) To ensure that family education includes a proper understanding of maternity as a social function and the recognition of the common responsibility of men and women in the upbringing and development of their children.

Article 6. States Parties shall take all appropriate measures, including legislation, to suppress all forms of traffic in women and exploitation of prostitution of women.

Part II

Article 7. States Parties shall take all appropriate measures to eliminate discrimination against women in the political and public life of the country and, in particular, shall ensure, on equal terms with men, the right:

(a) To vote in all elections and public referenda and to be eligible for election to all publicly elected bodies,

(b) To participate in the formulation of government policy and the implementation thereof and to hold public office and perform all public functions at all levels of government,

(c) To participate in non-governmental organizations and associations concerned with the public and political life of the country.

Article 8. States Parties shall take all appropriate measures to ensure to women on equal terms with men and, without any discrimination, the opportunity to represent their Governments at the international level and to participate in the work of international organizations.

Article 9. (1) States Parties shall grant women equal rights with men to acquire, change or retain their nationality. They shall ensure in particular that neither marriage to an alien nor change of nationality by the husband during marriage shall automatically change the nationality of the wife, render her stateless or force upon her the nationality of the husband.

(2) States Parties shall grant women equal rights with men with respect to the nationality of their children.

Part III

Article 10. State Parties shall take all appropriate measures to eliminate discrimination against women in order to ensure to them equal rights with men in the field of education and in particular to ensure, on a basis of equality of men and women:

(a) The same conditions for career and vocational guidance, for access to studies and for the achievement of diplomas in educational establishments of all categories in rural as well as in urban areas; this equality shall be ensured in preschool, general, technical, professional and higher technical education, as well as in all types of vocational training;

(b) Access to the same curricula, the same examinations, teaching staff with qualifications of the same standard and school premises and equipment of the same quality;

(c) The elimination of any stereotyped concept of the roles of men and women at all levels and in all forms of education by encouraging coeducation and other types of education which will help to achieve this aim and, in particular, by the revision of textbooks and school programmes and the adaptation of teaching methods;

(d) The same opportunities to benefit from scholarships and other study grants;

(e) The same opportunities for access to programmes of continuing education, including adult and functional literacy programmes, particularly those aimed at reducing, at the earliest possible time, any gap in education existing between men and women;

(f) The reduction of female student drop-out rates and the organization of programmes for girls and women who have left school prematurely;

(g) The same opportunities to participate actively in sports and physical education;

(h) Access to specific educational information to help to ensure the health and well-being of families, including information and advice on family planning.

Article 11. (1) States Parties shall take all appropriate measures to eliminate discrimination against women in the field of employment in order to ensure, on a basis of equality of men and women, the same rights, in particular:

(a) The right to work as an inalienable right of all human beings;

(b) The right to the same employment opportunities, including the application of the same criteria for selection in matters of employment,

(c) The right to free choice of profession and employment, the right to promotion, job security and all benefits and conditions of service and the right to receive vocational training and retraining, including apprenticeships, advanced vocational training and recurrent training;

(d) The right to equal remuneration, including benefits, and to equal treatment in respect of work of equal value, as well as equality of treatment in the evaluation of the quality of work;

(e) The right to social security, particularly in cases of retirement, unemployment, sickness, invalidity and old age and other incapacity to work, as well as the right to paid leave,

(f) The right to protection of health and to safety in working conditions, including the safeguarding of the function of reproduction.

(2) In order to prevent discrimination against women on the grounds of marriage or maternity and to ensure their effective right to work, States Parties shall take appropriate measures:

(a) To prohibit, subject to the imposition of sanctions. dismissal on the grounds of pregnancy or of maternity leave and discrimination in dismissals on the basis of marital status;

(b) To introduce maternity leave with pay or with comparable social benefits without loss of former employment, seniority or social allowances;

(c) To encourage the provision of the necessary supporting social services to enable parents to combine family obligations with work responsibilities and participation in public life, in particular through promoting the establishment and development of a network of child-care facilities;

(d) To provide special protection to women during pregnancy in types of work proved to be harmful to them.

(3) Protective legislation relating to matters covered in this article shall be reviewed 'periodically in the light of scientific and technological knowledge and shall be revised, repealed or extended as necessary.

Article 12. (1) States Parties shall take all appropriate measures to eliminate discrimination against women in the field of health care in order to ensure, on a basis of equality of men and women, access to health care services, including those related to family planning.

(2) Notwithstanding the provisions of paragraph 1 above, States Parties shall ensure to women appropriate services in connexion with pregnancy, confinement and the post-natal period, granting free services where necessary, as well as adequate nutrition during pregnancy and lactation.

Article 13. States Parties shall take all appropriate measures to eliminate discrimination against women in other areas of economic and social life in order to ensure, on a basis of equality of men and women, the same rights, in particular:

(a) The right to family benefits;

(b) The right to bank loans, mortgages and other forms of financial credit;

(c) The right to participate in recreational activities, sports and in all aspects of cultural life.

Article 14. (1) States Parties shall take into account the particular problems faced by rural women and the significant roles which they play in the economic survival of their families, including their work in the non-monetized sectors of the economy, and shall take all appropriate measures to ensure the application of the provisions of this Convention to women in rural areas.

(2) States Parties shall take all appropriate measures to eliminate discrimination against women in rural areas in order to ensure, on a basis of equality of men and women, that they participate in and benefit from rural development and, in particular, shall ensure to such women the right:

(a) To participate in the elaboration and implementation of development planning at all levels;

(b) To have access to adequate health care facilities, including information, counselling and services in family planning;

(c) To benefit directly from social security programmes;

(d) To obtain all types of training and education, formal and non-formal, including that relating to functional literacy, as well as the benefit of all community and extension services, inter alia, in order to increase their technical proficiency;

(e) To organize self-help groups and cooperatives in order to obtain equal access to economic opportunities through employment or self-employment;

(f) To participate in all community activities;

(g) To have access to agricultural credit and loans, marketing facilities, appropriate technology and equal treatment in land and agrarian reform as well as in land resettlement schemes;

(h) To enjoy adequate living conditions, particularly in relation to housing, sanitation, electricity and water supply, transport and communications.

Article 15. (1) States Parties shall accord to women equality with men before the law.

(2) States Parties shall accord to women, in civil matters, a legal capacity identical to that of men and the same opportunities to exercise that capacity. They shall in particular give women equal rights to conclude contracts and to administer property and treat them equally in all stages of procedure in courts and tribunals.

(3) States Parties agree that all contract and all other private instruments of any kind with a legal effect which is directed at restricting the legal capacity of women shall be deemed null and void.

(4) States Parties shall accord to men and women the same rights with regard to the law relating to the movement of persons and the freedom to choose their residence and domicile.

Article 16. (1) States Parties shall take all appropriate measures to eliminate discrimination against women in all matters relating to marriage and family relations and in particular shall ensure, on a basis of equality of men and women:

(a) The same right to enter into marriage;

(b) The same right freely to choose a spouse and to enter into marriage only with their free and full consent;

(c) The same rights and responsibilities during marriage and at its dissolution;

(d) The same rights and responsibilities as parents, irrespective of their marital status, in matters relating to their children. In all cases the interests of the children shall be paramount;

(e) The same rights to decide freely and responsibly on the number and spacing of their children and to have access to the information, education and means to enable them to exercise these rights;

(f) The same rights and responsibilities with regard to guardianship, wardship, trusteeship and adoption of children, or similar institutions where these concepts exist in national legislation. In all cases the interest of the children shall be paramount;

(g) The same personal rights as husband and wife, including the right to choose a family name, a profession and an occupation,

(h) The same rights for both spouses in respect of the ownership, acquisition, management, administration, enjoyment and disposition of property, whether free of charge or for a valuable consideration.

(2) The betrothal and the marriage of a child shall have no legal effect and all necessary action including legislation, shall be taken to specify a minimum age for marriage and to make the registration of marriages in an official registry compulsory.

EUROPEAN SOCIAL CHARTER. (Entered into force, February 26, 1965.)

PART I

The Contracting Parties accept as the aim of their policy, to be pursued by all appropriate means, both national and international in character, the attainment of conditions in which the following rights and principles may be effectively realized:

(1) Everyone shall have the opportunity to earn his living in an occupation freely entered upon.
(2) All workers have the right to just conditions of work.
(3) All workers have the right to safe and healthy working conditions.
(4) All workers have the right to a fair remuneration sufficient for a decent standard of living for themselves and their families.
(5) All workers and employers have the right to freedom of association in national or international organizations for the protection of their economic and social interests.
(6) All workers and employers have the right to bargain collectively.
(7) Children and young persons have the right to a special protection against the physical and moral hazards to which they are exposed.
(8) Employed women, in case of maternity, and other employed women as appropriate, have the right to a special protection in their work.
(9) Everyone has the right to appropriate facilities for vocational guidance with a view to helping him choose an occupation suited to his personal aptitude and interests.
(10) Everyone has the right to appropriate facilities for vocational training.
(11) Everyone has the right to benefit from any measures enabling him to enjoy the highest possible standard of health attainable.
(12) All workers and their dependents have the right to social security.
(13) Anyone without adequate resources has the right to social and medical assistance.
(14) Everyone has the right to benefit from social welfare services.
(15) Disabled persons have the right to vocational training, rehabilitation and resettlement, whatever the origin and nature of their disability.

(16) The family as a fundamental unit of society has the right to appropriate social, legal and economic protection to ensure its full development.
(17) Mothers and children, irrespective of marital status and family relations, have the right to appropriate social and economic protection.
(18) The nationals of any one of the Contracting Parties have the right to engage in any gainful occupation in the territory of any one of the others on a footing of equality with the nationals of the latter, subject to restrictions based on cogent economic or social reasons.
(19) Migrant workers who are nationals of a Contracting Party and their families have the right to protection and assistance in the territory of any other Contracting Party.

PART II

The Contracting Parties undertake, as provided for in Part III, to consider themselves bound by the obligations laid down in the following Articles and paragraphs.

Article 1. The Right to Work

With a view to ensuring the effective exercise of the right to work, the Contracting Parties undertake:

(1) to accept as one of their primary aims and responsibilities the achievement and maintenance of as high and stable a level of employment as possible, with a view to the attainment of full employment;
(2) to protect effectively the right of the worker to earn his living in an occupation freely entered upon;
(3) to establish or maintain free employment services for all workers;
(4) to provide or promote appropriate vocational guidance. training and rehabilitation.

Article 2. The Right to Just Conditions of Work

With a view to ensuring the effective exercise of the right to just conditions of work, the Contracting Parties undertake:

(1) to provide for reasonable daily and weekly working hours, the working week to be progressively reduced to the extent that the increase of productivity and other relevant factors permit;
(2) to provide for public holidays with pay;
(3) to provide for a minimum of two weeks annual holiday with pay;
(4) to provide for additional paid holidays or reduced working hours for workers engaged in dangerous or unhealthy occupations as prescribed;
(5) to ensure a weekly rest period which shall, as far as possible, coincide with the day recognized by tradition or custom in the country or region concerned as a day of rest.

Article 3. The Right to Safe and Healthy Working Conditions

With a view to ensuring the effective exercise of the right to safe and healthy working conditions, the Contracting Parties undertake:

(1) to issue safety and health regulations;
(2) to provide for the enforcement of such regulations by measures of supervision;
(3) to consult, as appropriate, employers' and workers' organizations on measures intended to improve in mistrial safety and health.

Article 4. The Right to a Fair Remuneration

With a view to ensuring the effective exercise of the right to a fair remuneration, the Contracting Parties undertake:

(1) to recognize the right of workers to a remuneration such as will give them and their families a decent standard of living;
(2) to recognize the right of workers to an increased rate of remuneration for overtime work, subject to exceptions in particular cases;
(3) to recognize the right of men and women workers to equal pay for work of equal value,
(4) to recognize the right of all workers to a reasonable period of notice for termination of employment,
(5) to permit deductions from wages only under conditions and to the extent prescribed by national laws or regulations or fixed by collective agreements or arbitration awards.

The exercise of these rights shall be achieved by freely concluded collective agreements, by statutory wage-fixing machinery, or by other means appropriate to national conditions.

Article 5. The Right to Organize

With a view to ensuring or promoting the freedom of workers and employers to form local, national or international organizations for the protection of their economic and social interests and to join those organizations, the Contracting Parties undertake that national law shall not be such as to impair. nor shall it be so applied as to impair, this freedom. The extent to which the guarantees provided for in this Article shall apply to the police shall be determined by national laws or regulations. The principle governing the application to the members of the armed forces of these guarantees and the extent to which they shall apply to persons in this category shall equally be determined by national laws or regulations.

Article 6. The Right to Bargain Collectively

With a view to ensuring the effective exercise of the right to bargain collectively, the contracting Parties undertake:

(1) to promote joint consultation between workers and employers;
(2) to promote, where necessary and appropriate, machinery for voluntary negotiations between employers or employers' organizations and workers' organizations, with a view to the regulation of terms and conditions of employment by means of collective agreements;
(3) to promote the establishment and use of appropriate machinery for conciliation and voluntary arbitration for the settlement of labour disputes;

and recognize:

(4) the right of workers and employers to collective action in cases of conflicts of interest, including the right to strike, subject to obligations that might arise out of collective agreements previously entered into.

Article 7. The Right of Children and Young Persons to Protection

With a view to ensuring the effective exercise of the right of children and young persons to protection, the Contracting Parties undertake:

(1) to provide that the maximum age of admission to employment shall be 15 years, subject to exceptions for children employed in prescribed light work without harm to their health, morals or education;
(2) to provide that a higher minimum age of admission to employment shall be fixed with respect to prescribed occupations regarded as dangerous or unhealthy;
(3) to provide that persons who are still subject to compulsory education shall not be employed in such work as would deprive them of the full benefit of their education;
(4) to provide that the working hours of persons under 16 years of age shall be limited in accordance with the needs of their development. and particularly with their need for vocational training;
(5) to recognize the right of young workers and apprentices to a fair wage or other appropriate allowances,
(6) to provide that the time spent by young persons in vocational training during the normal working hours with the consent of the employer shall be treated as forming part of the working day;
(7) to provide that employed persons of under 18 years of age shall be entitled to not less than three weeks' annual holiday with pay,
(8) to provide that persons under 18 years of age shall not be employed in night work with the exception of certain occupations provided for by national laws or regulations;
(9) to provide that persons under 18 years of age employed in occupations prescribed by national laws or regulations shall be subject to regular medical control;
(10) to ensure special protection against physical and moral dangers to which children and young persons are exposed, and particularly against those resulting directly or indirectly from their work.

Article 8. The Right of Employed Women to Protection

With a view to ensuring the effective exercise of the right of employed women to protection, the Contracting Parties undertake:

(1) to provide either by paid leave, by adequate social security benefits or by benefits from public funds for women to take leave before and after childbirth up to a total of at least 12 weeks;
(2) to consider it as unlawful for an employer to give a woman notice of dismissal during her absence on maternity leave or to give her notice of dismissal at such a time that the notice would expire during such absence;
(3) to provide that mothers who are nursing their infants shall be entitled to sufficient time off for this purpose;
(4) (a) to regulate the employment of women workers on night work in industrial employment;
(b) to prohibit the employment of women workers in underground mining, and, as appropriate, on all other work which is unsuitable for them by reason of its dangerous, unhealthy, or arduous nature.

Article 9. The Right to Vocational Guidance

With a view to ensuring the effective exercise of the right to vocational guidance, the Contracting Parties undertake to provide or promote, as necessary, a service which will assist all persons, including the handicapped, to solve problems related to occupational choice and progress, with due regard to the individual's characteristics and their relation to occupational opportunity: this assistance should be available free of charge, both to young persons, including school children, and to adults.

Article 10. The Right to Vocational Training

With a view to ensuring the effective exercise of the right to vocational training, the Contracting Parties undertake:

(1) to provide or promote, as necessary, the technical and vocational training of all persons, including the handicapped, in consultation with employers' and workers' organizations, and to grant facilities for access to higher technical and university education, based solely on individual aptitude,
(2) to provide or promote a system of apprenticeship and other systematic arrangements for training young boys and girls in their various employments;
(3) to provide or promote, as necessary:
    (a) adequate and readily available training facilities for adult workers;
    (b) special facilities for the retraining of adult workers needed as a result of technological development or new trends in employment;

(4) to encourage the full utilization of the facilities provided by appropriate measures such as:

    (a) reducing or abolishing any fees or charges;
    (b) granting financial assistance in appropriate cases;
    (c) including in the normal working hours times spent on supplementary training taken by the worker, at the request of this employer, during employment;
    (d) ensuring, through adequate supervision, in consultation with the employers' and workers' organizations, the efficiency of apprenticeship and other training arrangements for young workers, and the adequate protection of young workers generally.

Article 11. The Right to Protection of Health

With a view to ensuring the effective exercise of the right to protection of health, the Contracting Parties undertake, either directly or in cooperation with public or private organizations, to take appropriate measures designed inter alia:

(1) to remove as far as possible the cases of ill-health;
(2) to provide advisory and educational facilities for the promotion of health and the encouragement of individual responsibility in matters of health;
(3) to prevent as far as possible epidemic, endemic and other diseases.

Article 12. The Right to Social Security

With a view to ensuring the effective exercise of the right to social security, the Contracting Parties undertake:

(1) to establish or maintain a system of social security;
(2) to maintain the social security system at a satisfactory level at least equal to that required for ratification of international Labour Convention (No. 102) Concerning Minimum Standards of Social Security;
(3) to endeavour to raise progressively the system of social security to a higher level;
(4) to take steps, by the conclusion of appropriate bilateral and multilateral agreements, or by other means, and subject to the conditions laid down in such agreements, in order to ensure:
    (a) equal treatment with their own nationals of the nationals of other Contracting Parties in respect of social security rights, including the retention of benefits an*sing out of social security legislation, whatever movements the persons protected may undertake between the territories of the Contracting Parties;
    (b) the granting, maintenance and resumption of social security rights by such means as the accumulation of insurance or employment periods completed under the legislation of each of the Contracting Parties.

Article 13. The Right to Social and Medical Assistance

With a view to ensuring the effective exercise of the fight to social and medical assistance, the Contracting Parties undertake:

(1) to ensure that any person who is without adequate resources and who is unable to secure such resources either by his own efforts or from other sources, in particular by benefits under a social security scheme, be granted adequate assistance, and, in case of sickness, the care necessitated by his condition;
(2) to ensure that persons receiving such assistance shall not, for that reason, suffer from a diminution of their political or social rights;
(3) to provide that everyone may receive by appropriate public or private services such advice and personal help as may be required to prevent, to remove, or to alleviate personal or family want;
(4) to apply the provisions referred to in paragraphs 1, 2 and 3 of this Article on an equal footing with their nationals to nationals of other Contracting

Parties lawfully within their territories, in accordance with their obligations under the European Convention on Social and Medical Assistance, signed at Paris on 11th December 1953.

Article 14. The Right to Benefit from Social Welfare Services

With a view to ensuring the effective exercise of the right to benefit from social welfare services, the Contracting Parties undertake:

(1) to promote or provide services which, by using methods of social work, would contribute to the welfare and development of both individuals and groups in the community, and to their adjustment to the social environment;
(2) to encourage the participation of individuals and voluntary or other organizations in the establishment and maintenance of such services.

Article 15. The Right of Physically or Mentally Disabled Persons to Vocational Training, Rehabilitation and Social Resettlement

With a view to ensuring the effective exercise of the right of the physically or mentally disabled to vocational training, rehabilitation and resettlement, the Contracting Parties undertake:

(1) to take adequate measures for the provision of training facilities, including, where necessary, specialized institutions, public or private;
(2) to take adequate measures for the placing of disabled persons in employment, such as specialized placing services, facilities for sheltered employment and measures to encourage employers to admit disabled persons to employment.

Article 16. The Right of the Family to Social, Legal and Economic Protection

With a view to ensuring the necessary conditions for the full development of the family, which is a fundamental unit of society, the Contracting Parties undertake to promote the economic, legal and social protection of family life by such means as social and family benefits, fiscal arrangements, provision of family housing, benefits for the newly married, and other appropriate means.

Article 17. The Right of Mothers and Children to Social and Economic Protection

With a view to ensuring the effective exercise of the right of mothers and children to social and economic protection, the Contracting Parties will take all appropriate and necessary measures to that end, including the establishment or maintenance of appropriate institutions or services.

Article 18. The Right to Engage in a Gainful Occupation in the

Territory of Other Contracting Parties

With a view to ensuring the effective exercise of the right to engage in a gainful occupation in the territory of any other Contracting Party, the Contracting Parties undertake:

(1) to apply existing regulations in a spirit of liberality;
(2) to simplify existing formalities and to reduce or abolish chancery dues and other charges payable by foreign workers or their employers;
(3) to liberalize, individually or collectively, regulations governing the employment of foreign workers; and recognize:
(4) the right of their nationals to leave the country to engage in a gainful occupation in the territories of the other Contracting Parties.

Article 19. The Right of Migrant Workers and their Families to Protection and Assistance

With a view to ensuring the effective exercise of the right of migrant workers and their families to protection and assistance in the territory of any other Contracting Party, the Contracting Parties undertake:

(1) to maintain or to satisfy themselves that there are maintained adequate and free services to assist such workers, particularly in obtaining accurate information, and to take all appropriate steps, so far as national laws and regulations permit, against misleading propaganda relating to emigration and immigration;
(2) to adopt appropriate measures within their own jurisdiction to facilitate the departure, journey and reception of such workers and their families, and to provide, within their own jurisdiction, appropriate services for health, medical attention and good hygienic conditions during the journey;
(3) to promote cooperation, as appropriate, between social services, public and private, in emigration and immigration countries;
(4) to secure for such workers lawfully within their territories, insofar as such matters are regulated by law or regulations or are subject to the control of administrative authorities, treatment not less favourable than that of their own nationals in respect of the following matters:
    (a) remuneration and other employment and working conditions;
    (b) membership of trade unions and enjoyment of the benefits of collective bargaining;
    (c) accommodation;
(5) to secure for such workers lawfully within their territories treatment not less favourable than that of their own nationals with regard to employment taxes, dues or contributions payable in respect of employed persons;
(6) to facilitate as far as possible the reunion of the family of a foreign worker permitted to establish himself in the territory;

(7) to secure for such workers lawfully within their territories treatment not less favourable than that of their own nationals in respect of legal proceedings relating to matters referred to in this Article;

(8) to secure that such workers lawfully residing within their territories are not expelled unless they endanger national security or offend against public interest or morality;

(9) to permit, within legal limits, the transfer of such parts of the earnings and savings of such workers as they may desire;

(10) to extend the protection and assistance provided for in this Article to self-employed migrants insofar as such measures apply.

PART III

Article 20. Undertakings

1. Each of the Contracting Parties undertakes:
    - (a) to consider Part I of this Charter as a declaration of the aims which it will pursue by all appropriate means, as stated in the introductory paragraph of that Part;
    - (b) to consider itself bound by at least five of the following Articles of Part 11 of this Charter: Articles 1, 5, 6, 12, 13, 16 and 19;
    - (c) in addition to the Articles selected by it in accordance with the preceding subparagraph, to consider itself bound by such a number of Articles or numbered paragraphs of Part II of the Charter as it may select, provided that the total number of Articles or numbered paragraphs by which it is bound is not less than 10 Articles or 45 numbered paragraphs.

2. The Articles or paragraphs selected in accordance with sub-paragraphs (b) and (c) of paragraph I of this Article shall be notified to the Secretary-General of the Council of Europe at the time when the instrument of ratification or approval of the Contracting Party concerned is deposited.

3. Any Contracting Party may, at a later date, declare by notification to the Secretary General that it considers itself bound by any Articles or any numbered paragraphs of Part II of the Charter which it has not already accepted under the terms of paragraph I of this Article. Such undertakings subsequently given shall be deemed to be an integral part of the ratification or approval, and shall have the same effect as from the thirtieth day after the date of the notification.

4. The Secretary-General shall communicate to all the signatory Governments and to the Director-General of the international Labour Office any notification which he shall have received pursuant to this Part of the Charter.

5. Each Contracting Party shall maintain a system of labour inspection appropriate to national conditions.

PART IV

Article 21. Reports concerning Accepted Provisions

The Contracting Parties shall send to the Secretary-General of the Council of Europe a report at two-yearly intervals, in a form to be determined by the Committee of Ministers, concerning the application of such provisions of Part 11 of the Charter as they have accepted.

Article 22. Reports concerning Provisions which are not accepted.

The Contracting Parties shall send to the Secretary-General, at appropriate intervals as requested by the Committee of Ministers, reports relating to the provisions of Part II of the Charter which they did not accept at the time of their ratification or approval or in a subsequent notification. The Committee of Ministers shall determine from time to time in respect of which provisions such reports shall be requested and the form of the reports to be provided.

Article 23. Communication of Copies

1. Each Contracting Party shall communicate copies of its reports referred to in Articles 21 and 22 to such of its national organizations as are members of the international organizations of employers and trade unions to be invited under Article 27, paragraph 2, to be represented at meetings of the Sub-committee of the Governmental Social Committee.
2. The Contracting Parties shall forward to the Secretary-General any comments on the said reports received from these national organizations, if so requested by them.

Article 24. Examination of the Reports

The reports sent to the Secretary-General in accordance with Articles 21 and 22 shall be examined by a Committee of Experts, who shall have also before them any comments forwarded to the Secretary-General in accordance with paragraph 2 of Article 23.

Article 25. Committee of Experts

1. The Committee of Experts shall consist of not more than seven members appointed by the Committee of Ministers from a list of independent experts of the highest integrity and of recognized competence in international social questions, nominated by the Contracting Parties.
2. The members of the Committee shall be appointed for a period of six years. They may be reappointed. However, of the members first appointed, the terms of office of two members shall expire at the end of four years.

3. The members whose terms of office are to expire at the end of the initial period of four years shall be chosen by lot by the Committee of Ministers immediately after the first appointment has been made.
4. A member of the Committee of Experts appointed to replace a member whose term of office has not expired shall hold office for the remainder of his predecessor's term.

Article 26. Participation of the International Labour Organization

The International Labour Organization shall be invited to nominate a representative to participate in a consultative capacity in the deliberations of the Committee of Experts.

Article 27. Sub-Committee of the Governmental Social Committee

1. The reports of the Contracting Parties and the conclusions of the Committee of Experts shall be submitted for examination to a Sub-committee of the Governmental Social Committee of the Council of Europe.
2. The Sub-committee shall be composed of one representative of each of the Contracting Parties. It shall invite no more than two international organizations of employers and no more than two international trade union organizations as it may designate to be represented as observers in a consultative capacity at its meetings. Moreover, it may consult no more than two representatives of international non-governmental organizations having consultative status with the Council of Europe, in respect of questions with which the organizations are particularly qualified to deal, such as social welfare, and the economic and social protection of the family.
3. The Sub-committee shall present to the Committee of Ministers a report containing its conclusions and append the report of the Committee of Experts.

Article 28. Consultative Assembly

The Secretary-General of the Council of Europe shall transmit to the Consultative Assembly the conclusions of the Committee of Experts. The Consultative Assembly shall communicate its views on these Conclusions to the Committee of Ministers.

Article 29. Committee of Ministers

By a majority of two-thirds of the members entitled to sit on the Committee, the Committee of Ministers may, on the basis of the report of the Sub-committee, and after consultation with the Consultative Assembly, make to each Contracting Party any necessary recommendations.

PART V

Article 30. Derogations in time of War or Public Emergency

1. In time of war or other public emergency threatening the life of the nation any Contracting Party may take measures derogating from its obligations under this Charter to the extent strictly required by the exigencies of the situation, provided that such measures are not inconsistent with its other obligations under international law.
2. Any Contracting Party which has availed itself of this right of derogation shall, within a reasonable lapse of time, keep the Secretary-General of the Council of Europe fully informed of the measures taken and of the reasons therefore. It shall likewise inform the Secretary-General when such measures have ceased to operate and the provisions of the Charter which it has accepted are again being fully executed.
3. The Secretary-General shall in turn inform other Contracting Parties and the Director General of the international Labour Office of all communications received in accordance with paragraph 2 of this Article.

Article 31. Restrictions

1. The rights and principles set forth in Part I when effectively realized, and their effective exercise as provided for in Part II, shall not be subject to any restrictions or limitations not specified in those Parts, except such as are prescribed by law and are necessary in a democratic society for the protection of the rights and freedoms of others or for the protection of public interest, national security, public health, or morals.
2. The restrictions permitted under this Charter to the rights and obligations set forth herein shall not be applied for any purpose other than that for which they have been prescribed.

Article 32. Relations between the Charter and Domestic Law or International Agreements

The provisions of this Charter shall not prejudice the provisions of domestic law or of any bilateral or multilateral treaties, conventions or agreements which are already in force, or may come into force, under which more favourable treatment would be accorded to the persons protected.

Article 33. Implementation by Collective Agreements

1. In member States where the provisions of paragraphs 1, 2, 3, 4 and 5 of Article 2, paragraphs 4, 6 and 7 of Article 7 and paragraphs 1, 2, 3, and 4 of Article 10 of Part II of this Charter are matters normally left to agreements between employers or employers' organizations and workers' organizations, or are normally carried out otherwise than by law, the undertakings of those paragraphs may be given and compliance with them shall be treated as effective if their provisions are applied through such

agreements or other means to the great majority of the workers concerned.
2. In member States where these provisions are normally the subject of legislation, the undertakings concerned may likewise be given, and compliance with them shall be regarded as effective if the provisions are applied by law to the great majority of the workers concerned.

Article 38. Appendix

The Appendix to this Charter shall form an integral part of it.

APPENDIX TO THE SOCIAL CHARTER
Scope of the Social Charter in Terms of Persons Protected

1. Without prejudice to Article 12, paragraph 4 and Article 13, paragraph 4, the persons covered by Articles 1 to 17 include foreigners only insofar as they are nationals of other Contracting Parties lawfully resident or working regularly within the territory of the Contracting Party concerned, subject to the understanding that these Articles are to be interpreted in the light of the provisions of Articles 18 and 19.

This interpretation would not prejudice the extension of similar facilities to other persons by any of the Contracting Parties.

2. Each Contracting Party will grant to refugees as defined in the Convention treating to the Status of Refugees, signed at Geneva on 28th July, 1951, and lawfully staying in its territory, treatment as favourable as possible, and in any case not less favourable than under the obligations accepted by the Contracting Party under the said Convention and under any other existing international instruments applicable to those refugees.

PART I AND PART II

Paragraph 18 and Article 18, Paragraph 1. It is understood that these provisions are not concerned with the question of entry into the territories of the Contracting Parties and do not prejudice the provisions of the European Convention on Establishment, signed at Paris on 13th December, 1955.

PART II

Article 1, Paragraph 2. This provision shall not be interpreted as prohibiting or authorizing any union security clause or practice.
Article 4, Paragraph 4. This provision shall be so understood as not to prohibit immediate dismissal for any serious offence.
Article 4, Paragraph 5. It is understood that a Contracting Party may give the undertaking required in this paragraph if the'great majority of workers are not permitted to suffer deductions from wages either by law or through

collective agreements or arbitration awards, the exceptions being those persons not so covered.

Article 6, Paragraph 4. It is understood that each Contracting Party may, insofar as it is concerned, regulate the exercise of the right to strike by law, provided that any further restriction than this might place on the right can be justified under the terms of Article 31.

Article 7, Paragraph 8. It is understood that a Contracting Party may give the undertaking required in this paragraph if it fulfills the spirit of the undertaking by providing by law that the great majority of persons under 18 years of age shall not be employed in night work.

Article 12, Paragraph 4. The words "and subject to the conditions laid down in such agreements" in the introduction to this paragraph are taken to imply inter alia that with regard to benefits which are available independently of any insurance contribution a Contracting Party may require the completion of a prescribed period of residence before granting such benefits to nationals of other Contracting Parties.

Article 13, Paragraph 4. Governments not Parties to the European Convention on Social and Medical Assistance may ratify the Social Charter in respect of this paragraph provided that they grant to nationals of other Contracting Parties a treatment which is in conformity with the provisions of the said Convention.

Article 19, Paragraph 6. For the purpose of this provision, the term "family of a foreign worker" is understood to mean at least his wife and dependent children under the age of 21 years.

PART III

It is understood that the Charter contains legal obligations of an international character, the application of which is submitted solely to the supervision provided for in Part IV thereof.

Article 20, Paragraph 1. It is understood that the "numbered paragraphs" may include Articles consisting of only one paragraph.

PART V

Article 30. The term "in time of war or other public emergency" shall be so understood is to cover also the threat of war.

PROTOCOL (NO. IV) TO THE EUROPEAN CONVENTION FOR THE PROTECTION OF HUMAN RIGHTS AND FUNDAMENTAL FREEDOMS. (Entered into force, May 2, 1968.)

Article 1. No one shall be deprived of his liberty merely on the ground of inability to fulfil a contractual obligation.

Article 2. (1) Everyone lawfully within the territory of a State shall, within that territory, have the right to liberty of movement and freedom to choose his residence.

(2) Everyone shall be free to leave any country, including his own.

(3) No restrictions shall be placed on the exercise of these rights other than such as are in accordance with law and are necessary in a democratic society in the interests of national security or public safety for the maintenance of "ordure public," for the prevention of crime, for the protection of the rights and freedoms of others.

(4) The rights set forth in paragraph I may also be subject, in particular areas, to restrictions imposed in accordance with law and justified by the public interest in a democratic society.

Article 3. (1) No one shall be expelled, by means either of an individual or of a collective measure, from the territory of the State of which he is a national.

(2) No one shall be deprived of the right to enter the territory of the State of which he is a national.

Article 4. Collective expulsion of aliens is prohibited.

INTERNATIONAL CONVENTION ON THE ELIMINATION OF ALL FORMS OF RACIAL DISCRIMINATION. (Entered into force, January 4, 1969.)

PART I

Article 1. (1) In this Convention, the term "racial discrimination" shall mean any distinction, exclusion, restriction or preference based on race, colour, descent, or national or ethnic origin which has the purpose or effect of nullifying or impairing the recognition, enjoyment or exercise, on an equal footing, of human rights and fundamental freedoms in the political, economic, social, cultural or any other field of public life.

(2) This Convention shall not apply to distinctions, exclusions, restrictions or preferences made by a State Party to this Convention between citizens and noncitizens.

(3) Nothing in this Convention may be interpreted as affecting in any way the legal provisions of States Parties concerning nationality, citizenship or naturalization, provided that such provisions do not discriminate against any particular nationality.

(4) Special measures taken for the sole purpose of securing adequate advancement of certain racial or ethnic groups or individuals requiring such protection as may be necessary in order to ensure such groups or individuals equal enjoyment or exercise of human

rights and fundamental freedoms shall not be deemed racial discrimination, provided, however, that such measures do not, as a consequence, lead to the maintenance of separate rights for different racial groups and that they shall not be continued after the objectives for which they were taken have been achieved.

Article 2. (1) States Parties condemn racial discrimination and undertake to pursue by all appropriate means and without delay a policy of eliminating racial discrimination in all its forms and promoting understanding among all races, and, to this end:

(a) Each State Party undertakes to engage in no act or practice of racial discrimination against persons, groups of persons or institutions and to ensure that all public authorities and public institutions, national and local, shall act in conformity with this obligation;

(b) Each State Party undertakes not to sponsor, defend or support racial discrimination by any persons or organizations;

(c) Each State Party shall take effective measures to review governmental, national and local policies, and to amend, rescind or nullify any laws and regulations which have the effect of creating or perpetuating racial discrimination wherever it exists;

(d) Each State Party shall prohibit and bring to an end, by all appropriate means, including legislation as required by circumstances, racial discrimination by any persons, group or organization;

(e) Each State Party undertakes to encourage, where appropriate, integrationist multiracial organizations and movements and other means of eliminating barriers between races, and to discourage anything which tends to strengthen racial division.

(2) States Parties shall, when the circumstances so warrant, take, in the social, economic, cultural and other fields, special and concrete measures to ensure the adequate development and protection of certain racial groups or individuals belonging to them, for the purpose of guaranteeing them the full and equal enjoyment of human rights and fundamental freedoms. These measures shall in no case entail as a consequence the maintenance of unequal or separate rights for different racial groups after the objectives for which they were taken have been achieved.

Article 3. States Parties particularly condemn racial segregation and apartheid and undertake to prevent, prohibit and eradicate all practices of this nature in territories under their jurisdiction.

Article 4. States Parties condemn all propaganda and all organizations which are based on ideas or theories of superiority of one race or group of persons of one colour or ethnic origin, or which attempt to justify or promote racial hatred and discrimination in any form, and undertake to adopt immediate and positive measures designed to eradicate all incitement to, or acts of, such discrimination and, to this end, with due regard to the principles embodied in the Universal Declaration of Human Rights and the rights expressly set forth in article 5 of this Convention, inter alia:

(a) Shall declare an offence punishable by law all dissemination of ideas based on racial superiority or hatred, incitement to racial discrimination, as well as all acts of violence or incitement to such acts against any race or group of persons of another colour or ethnic origin, and also the provision of any assistance to racist activities, including the financing thereof;

(b) Shall declare illegal and prohibit organizations, and also organized and all other propaganda activities, which promote and incite racial discrimination, and shall recognize participation in such organizations or activities as an offence punishable by law;

(c) Shall not permit public authorities or public institutions, national or local, to promote or incite racial discrimination.

Article 5. In compliance with the fundamental obligations laid down in article 2 of this Convention, States Parties undertake to prohibit and to eliminate racial discrimination in all its forms and to guarantee the right of everyone, without distinction as to race, colour, or national or ethnic origin, to equality before the law, notably in the enjoyment of the following rights:

(a) The right to equal treatment before the tribunals and all other organs administering justice;

(b) The right to security of person and protection by the State against violence or bodily harm, whether inflicted by government officials or by any individual, group or institution;

(c) Political rights, in particular the rights to participate in elections - to vote and to stand for election - on the basis of universal and equal suffrage, to take part in the Government as well as in the conduct of public affairs at any level and to have equal access to public service;

(d) Other civil rights, in particular:

(i) The right to freedom of movement and residence within the border of the State;

(ii) The right to leave any country, including one's own, and to return to one's own country;

(iii) The right to nationality;

(iv) The right to marriage and choice of spouse;

(v) The fight to own property alone as well as in association with others;

	(vi)	The right to inherit;
	(vii)	The right to freedom of thought, conscience and religion,
	(viii)	The fight to freedom of opinion and expression;
	(ix)	The right to freedom of peaceful assembly and association;
(e)		Economic, social and cultural rights, in particular:
	(i)	The rights to work, to free choice of employment, to just and favourable conditions of work, to protection against unemployment, to equal pay for equal work, to just and favourable remuneration;
	(ii)	The right to form and join trade unions;
	(iii)	The right to housing;
	(iv)	The right to public health, medical care, social security and social services;
	(v)	The right to education and training;
	(vi)	The right to equal participation in cultural activities;
(f)		The right of access to any place or service intended for use by the general public, such as transport, hotels, restaurants, cafes, theatres and parks.

Article 6. States Parties shall assure to everyone within their Jurisdiction effective protection and remedies, through the competent national tribunals and other State institutions, against any acts of racial discrimination which violate his human rights and fundamental freedoms contrary to this Convention, as well as the right to seek from such tribunals just and adequate reparation or satisfaction for any damage suffered as a result of such discrimination.

Article 7. States Parties undertake to adopt immediate and effective measures, particularly in the fields of teaching, education, culture and information, with a view to combating prejudices which lead to racial discrimination and to promoting understanding, tolerance and friendship among nations and racial or ethical groups, as well as to propagating the purposes and principles of the Charter of the United Nations, the Universal Declaration of Human Rights, the United Nations Declaration on the Elimination of All Forms of Racial Discrimination, and this Convention.

PART II

Article 8. (1) There shall be established a Committee on the Elimination of Racial Discrimination (hereinafter referred to as the Committee) consisting of eighteen experts of high moral standing and acknowledged impartiality elected by States Parties from among their nationals, who shall serve in their personal capacity, consideration being given to equitable geographical distribution and to the representation of the different forms of civilization as well as of the principal legal systems.

(2) The members of the Committee shall be elected by secret ballot from a list of persons nominated by the States Parties. Each State Party may nominate one person from among its own nationals.

Article 9. (1) States Parties undertake to submit to the Secretary-General of the United Nations, for consideration by the Committee, a report on the legislative, judicial, administrative or other measures which they have adopted and which give effect to the provisions of this Convention: (a) within one year after the entry into force of the Convention for the State concerned; and (b) thereafter every two years and whenever the Committee so requests. The Committee may request further information from the States Parties.

(2) The Committee shall report annually, through the Secretary-General, to the General Assembly of the United Nations on its activities and may make suggestions and general recommendations based on the examination of the reports and information received from the States Parties. Such suggestions and general recommendations shall be recorded to the General Assembly together with comments, if any, from States Parties.

Article 11. (1) If a State Party considers that another State Party is not giving effect to the provisions of this Convention, it may bring the matter to the attention of the Committee. The Committee shall then transmit the communication to the State Party concerned. Within three months, the receiving State shall submit to the Committee written explanations or statements clarifying the matter and the remedy, if any, that may have been taken by that State.

(2) If the matter is not adjusted to the satisfaction of both parties, either by bilateral negotiations or by any other procedure open to them, within six months after the receipt by the receiving State of the initial communication, either State shall have the right to refer the matter again to the Committee by notifying the Committee and also the other State.

(3) The Committee shall deal with a matter referred to it in accordance with paragraph 2 of this article after it has ascertained that all available domestic remedies have been invoked and exhausted in the case, in conformity with the generally recognized principles of international law. This shall not be the rule where the application of the remedies is unreasonably prolonged.

(4) In any matter referred to it, the Committee may call upon the States Parties concerned to supply any other relevant information.

(5) When any matter arising out of this article is being considered by the Committee, the States Parties concerned shall be entitled to send

a representative to take part in the proceedings of the Committee, without voting rights, while the matter is under consideration.

Article 12. (1) (a) After the Committee has obtained and collated all the information it deems necessary, the Chairman shall appoint an ad hoc Conciliation Commission (hereinafter referred to as the Commission) comprising five persons who may or may not be members of the Committee. The members of the Commission shall be appointed with the unanimous consent of the parties to the dispute, and its good offices shall be made available to the States concerned with a view to an amicable solution of the matter on the basis of respect for this Convention.

    (b)   If the States parties to the dispute fail to reach agreement within three months on all or part of the composition of the Commission, the members of the Commission not agreed upon by the States parties to the dispute shall be elected by secret ballot by a two-thirds majority vote of the Committee from among its own members.

(2) The members of the Commission shall serve in their personal capacity. They shall not be nationals of the States parties to the dispute or of a State not Party to this Convention.

Article 13. (1) When the Commission has fully considered the matter, it shall prepare and submit to the Chairman of the Committee a report embodying its findings on all questions of fact relevant to the issue between the parties and containing such recommendations as it may think proper for the amicable solution of the dispute.

Article 14. (1) A State Party may at any time declare that it recognizes the competence of the Committee to receive and consider communications from individuals or groups of individuals within its jurisdiction claiming to be victims of a violation by that State Party of any of the rights set forth in this Convention. No communication shall be received by the Committee if it concerns a State Party which has not made such a declaration.

(2) Any State Party which makes a declaration as provided for in paragraph I of this article may establish or indicate a body within its national legal order which shall be competent to receive and consider petitions from individuals and groups of individuals within its jurisdiction who claim to be victims of a violation of any of the rights set forth in this Convention and who have exhausted other available local remedies.

(5) In the event of failure to obtain satisfaction from the body established or indicated in accordance with paragraph 2 of this article, the petitioner shall have the right to communicate
the matter to the Committee within six months.

(6) (a) The Committee shall confidentially bring any communication referred to it to the attention of the State Party alleged to be violating any provision of this Convention, but the identity of the individual or groups of individuals concerned shall not be revealed without his or their express consent. The Committee shall not receive anonymous communications.

(b) Within three months, the receiving State shall submit to the Committee written explanations or statements clarifying the matter and the remedy, if any, that may have been taken by that State.

(7) (a) The Committee shall consider communications in the light of all information made available to it by the State Party concerned and by the petitioner. The Committee shall not consider any communication from a petitioner unless it has ascertained that the petitioner has exhausted all available domestic remedies. However, this shall not be the rule where the application of the remedies is unreasonably prolonged.

(b) The Committee shall forward its suggestions and recommendations, if any, to the State Party concerned and to the petitioner.

(8) The Committee shall include in its annual report a summary of such communications and, where appropriate, a summary of the explanations and statements of the States Parties concerned and of its own suggestions and recommendations.